NINE
LIVES

Area covered by Sikorsky
rescue helicopters [210 miles]

DAVID COURTNEY

NINE LIVES

MERCIER PRESS
WHAT YOU NEED TO READ

MERCIER PRESS
Cork
www. mercierpress. ie

Trade enquiries to CMD Distribution 55A Spruce Avenue, Stillorgan
Industrial Park, Blackrock, County Dublin

ISBN: 978 1 85635 602 2
10 9 8 7 6 5 4 3 2

A CIP record for this title is available from the British Library

To Lynda, for saving me

 Mercier Press receives financial assistance from
the Arts Council/An Chomhairle Ealaíon

Printed and bound in the EU

CONTENTS

PREFACE

A close observation of the world's busiest mountain rescue service. (The author describes helicopter rescues she experienced first hand, during a three month period, spent with Police/ Gendarme Helicopter Rescue crews in the French Alps.)

> The highlight of my day at the helipad was a long conversation with Benoit Cousineau, who was just back from his holidays. He had been absent throughout the intensely dramatic period that we had been through here. I tell him about the strange summer that I had experienced – my doubts and vicarious suffering. He understands and offers an analysis. As a former 'blue helmet' (United Nations) doctor in Lebanon and Yugoslavia, he believes that the rescuers' encounters with death and suffering are equivalent to the psychological traumas of war. But this isn't recognised, and the medical check ups they perform in Chambery or Annecy, are performed by doctors who have no idea of the mountains. As they're unlikely to be understood, the rescuers don't try to explain. They can't really discuss it with each other, or burden their families. And so they're on their own to survive the ordeal.

Extract from *Mountain Rescue Chamonix – Mont Blanc*

Anne Sauvy

PROLOGUE

All ships, all ships, all ships. This is Valentia Coast Guard Radio. Here is the weather forecast, issued at 1800 hours, by Met Éireann. A strengthening westerly airflow over Ireland, will veer north-westerly as a weak cold front moves southwards across the country, this evening and tonight. Wind westerly gale force 6 to gale force 8 this evening, occasionally reaching gale force 9. Weather: widespread drizzle, rain and mist initially, followed by thundery showers. Visibility for all coastal areas: moderate, locally poor. Warning of a heavy swell.

We listened as we flew. In silence. The shuddering of the helicopter and the spattering of the rain confirmed better than the report we were listening to that it was only going to get worse. One hundred and eighty miles west of Kerry. Eleven o'clock at night. February 1998. We were the crew of the Shannon coast guard rescue helicopter, callsign *Rescue 115*. We were making our way out to a Spanish fishing trawler, the *Invention*, to evacuate a crewman who had multiple injuries having fallen below deck. In heavy rain and low cloud, a strong sou' westerly wind and heavy Atlantic swell awaited us.

With ten miles to go, we contacted the vessel on Channel 16. We gave the captain instructions to turn onto a westerly course. An interpreter from the Spanish embassy in Dublin had already been phone-patched through on marine radio, giving him instructions and finding out details of the casualty for us. An RAF Nimrod from Kinloss in Scotland flew above us at 15,000 feet, waited and listened as the vessel replied: 'Rescue helicopter. *Hola*. Hello. This fishing vessel *Invention* on Channel 16. Course 265 degrees. We make 6 knots. We ready.'

With five miles to go we could see the trawler on our radar. We descended to 200 feet clearing the cloud. We saw the ocean for the first time since leaving Shannon. Each of us lost momentarily in private thoughts as we saw the power and fury of the ocean below us. Noel Donnelly was winchman that night. Surely he would be apprehensive going out on the winch on a night like this?

The sea was white, angry, boiling. The wind was whipping the tops off the wave crests. The swell lived up to the forecast. It was raining. At two miles to go, we peered out to see where the trawler was. The radar showed it straight ahead, but still it was out of sight. The windscreen wipers smeared the rain left and right but the trawler lurked just outside the searchlight's beam. It was overcast and pitch black.

I knew we would soon see it. I moved the intercom micro-phone away from my mouth. I repeatedly inhaled deeply and exhaled forcefully. I did not want the others to hear my heavy breathing, either to laugh at it or worse, be unnerved by mistak-ing it for fear. This was my final preparation. Like an athlete preparing himself for one last big effort, one last jump into the long jump pit, or a rugby player setting himself for the last scrum of a match. Oxygenating myself and preparing for the struggle and effort that lay ahead.

I loved and hated this moment. Arm wrestling with the ele-ments, we descended and slowed down as we approached the position where the trawler should be. Through the rain I saw the dark shape come into view, wallowing on a wall of water. As the helicopter slowed at a height of 80 feet above the ocean, each of us took in the spectacle. The autopilot took us forward at its pre-programmed hover height, my hands covering the controls in case we got out of synch with the swell. I began to coax the helicopter closer and closer, until the rotor blades were within twenty feet of the back of the deck. We watched the deck's movements.

The trawler's efforts to move in a straight line were made more difficult by the swell hitting it broadside. It was like a wounded beast, as its tail slewed sideways across the crests. It slowed, rose up the next swell and suddenly dropped, sending a huge wave crashing over itself, disappearing momentarily from view.

As it fell, the back of the ship slowly raised itself out of the sea, the dripping propeller churning the air, searching for water. We could almost hear it groan. The aerials on the wheelhouse scythed this way and that, wickedly whipping at the rain.

The erratic movement slowed and stopped. The trawler lay across the swell like an exhausted wounded animal, panting and getting its breath back. This period of relative calm was short-lived but we watched, hoping to see a pattern. Knowing that a man's life depended on us finding some order in this chaos.

I thought to myself, 'How in God's name are we going to do this!'

1

DRAGONFLY

Every road has two directions.

Anon.

If you fold a map of Ireland north–south and then east–west, my home town is close to where the two folds intersect: Tullamore in the middle of Ireland, half of it flat fertile farmland, the other half peat bog. I had an idyllic childhood there. I was born in Cork, but left as an infant because of my father's work. The town is sports mad and my friends and I were sports mad too. We grew up trying everything, gaining some success along the way. Sport kept us out of trouble. At least for a while.

We rarely ventured as far as Dublin or back to Cork. That came later with athletics success. We played Gaelic football and rugby all around the midlands: from Longford to Roscrea, from Birr to Mullingar. We went to the Christian Brothers school. Northern Ireland was in the midst of 'The Troubles'. I was oblivious to religious differences, despite being one of only two Church of Ireland kids in the entire school. In Northern Ireland, being in a Catholic school would not have been possible. In the Republic, in Tullamore, I was just another kid. How lucky I was.

What a school. And what a class. A mixture of Christian Brothers and lay staff teaching us with humour and patience. Nudging the bookish towards college and the less academic towards anything that would get them jobs. Buying our school books from Brother Eoin Rossiter, the school vegetable gardener, who only traded in the Irish language and whose currency was vegetables:

'*... agus cóip leabhair uimhir a cúig, peann luaidhe agus compass, le do thoil* (... and can I have a number five copy, a pencil and a compass please).'

'Right so. *Níl airgead agam. Tabharfaidh me cabáiste agus roinnt onions duit do'd mháthair* (I have no change. I'll give you a cabbage and a few onions instead for your mother).'

As children we played and fought, did our homework and grew up together oblivious to the hard economic times when our older siblings had to emigrate to get jobs, to the pain their absence brought to families like ours all around town, all around Ireland. The money being sent home from England or France, America or Australia.

And what was I going to be when I grew up? What could anyone be? Tough times and emigration loomed for us all. The building sites of London called. But I could not hear their call yet. My childish ears heard childish things, and I was happy.

My father had been in the Second World War. Because he had worn a British uniform, he kept quiet about it. Ireland is more enlightened now, and we honour those who fought and died for the allied cause. He had been in the royal air force as a radio operator. He had been trained on Manchester bombers, forerunners of the more famous Lancasters, until ear problems grounded him, pushing him into the army instead. He was reluctant to talk about those years though. I sensed a pain of some sort: he was scarred by it. In later life he would describe those years as 'such a waste'.

I think the germ of flying was planted then. I made model aeroplanes, painted them and hung them from my ceiling just like any other boy. But I could ask my dad about those aeroplanes. He told me how noisy a Spitfire was when it took off, how smelly the inside of a bomber was. He even had black and white photos of them, taken as they flew above him on his way to the crossing of the Rhine, and during the liberation of Paris.

We lived near the bog which was drained by trenches that seemed to stretch for miles. I remember one day walking with our dog, Laddie, a terrier mongrel. The banks of turf glistened in the sun, pools of water beside them. Laddie searched and ran after scents. I explored each path, each gap and narrow way between the pools and the turf banks. I knew where the soft ground was and where it was dry, where you could get through and where it was impassable. At one of the turf banks, I stopped and waited. After a while I caught sight of a dragonfly as its wings caught the sunlight and flashed. It hovered motionless and silent. It was as big as my hand. I moved towards it, slowly, patiently, a pace at a time. I got to within a yard of it and decided that was close enough. Slowly I changed from standing to sitting. The dragonfly stayed in its position.

Watching it hover, I saw a pattern emerge. It was moving around the turf bank and the pool almost methodically. It was fantastic to see the ease of its flight and the total control it had over where it wanted to be in space and time. Its wings sparkled and shone in our amphitheatre. Beautiful and big too: the biggest insect I had ever seen.

By then I was lying on my back hoping that it would drift over me. And so it did. I shielded my eyes from the sun and watched it about four feet over my head, flitting this way and that. My dog came back, stood beside me and barked impatiently. That was the end of the show: the dragonfly was gone. As we walked away I heard a noise in the sky. It was an aeroplane of some sort getting closer. I could see it in the distance. It was coming straight towards me.

The noise it made was different though. As it came closer it seemed to have two noises. And then I realised it was a helicopter. One noise was the engine drone and the other was the beat of the blades. The blades made the louder noise when the helicopter was far away but when it flew over me the noise of the engine was more noticeable. It was silver, the same as the dragonfly's wings. It was an air corps Alouette 3, although I didn't know it at the time. I watched it come from the east, go right through my little world, and speed away to places unknown to me. The bog, which had seemed so big, had suddenly shrunk.

In the autumn of 1979 Pope John Paul II visited Ireland. A special time in history for us all, whether Catholic or not. Over a million people in the Phoenix Park for that famous mass at that famous cross. I and my classmates, teachers and friends in the throng. The excitement. The train from Tullamore. The crowds. The stampede from Heuston Station to the park. Finding our way. And waiting. Then the arrival of the man himself, in an Aer Lingus Jumbo Jet, flying over the crowd flanked by the diminutive air corps Fouga Magister fighter jets, shining silver in the clear skies above us. A million faces turned skywards. The conversations falling quiet. Silence. And then a cheer. The Holy Father himself no doubt looking down at us. The silky smoothness of their flight above us.

Someone announced over the public address that they would go to the airport and then come to us by helicopter. It would not be long. We waited again. Bernadette Greevy sang. And then the beat of helicopters blades announcing him. The excitement when he arrived. The pope blessed us all and made aviation sacred in my young mind.

My brother and sisters filled my childish ears with the music of the Beatles. Their songs providing a subliminal soundtrack to my climbing and exploring:

> Blackbird singing in the dead of night,
> Take these broken wings and learn to fly,
> All your life, you were only waiting for this moment to arise.

We used to go the Slieve Bloom Mountains for walks. Only hills really, a modest 1,500 feet height. But they were a car journey away and to young lads from flat midland towns, mountains they certainly were. Through The Cut, down to the wooded valleys of Glenafelly, Glenbarrow and Baunreagh. The dim light underneath the canopy of green, alive with the echoes of our footsteps on the dry branches underfoot. The birds calling to each other. Hoping to see deer. Another wilderness to explore. Sometimes Terry Adams, our neighbour's dad and an avid birdwatcher, used to take us. He drove his car along, changing gears and steering with one arm because he had lost the other in an accident. It never held him back though. He was a magical person: one of the best golfers in the country, one or two armed, a solicitor of some standing. A quiet and wise man. We went up into the hills and lay on a river bank in the grass, Terry beside me with binoculars, and his sons Rory and Fergus.

'Shh', he whispered, when we fidgeted. 'Look on the other side there, near that bridge on that branch'.

We strained to see.

'Where daddy?' said Rory.

Terry put his finger to his lips again and pointed. Across from us was a kingfisher. It sat on a branch and every few minutes it would dive into the stream and come up with a small fish. After a few successful catches it flew away. It was bright blue with an orange breast; quite different from any bird I had ever seen before. I lay in the grass as Terry whispered all he knew about it: where the nest probably was, how long it was there, how many eggs it would have, whether it was male or female.

Terry died at a young age from cancer. His death was my first experience of mourning. My first experience of missing someone, grieving for someone, not related to me. In life with only one arm, and on the brink of death, he had never shown an ounce of self pity.

Bonny Kennedy was another person who tirelessly shared her love of nature with children. She was an artist, the wife of one of the town's prominent solicitors. To children, he was tall, officious with a deep booming voice. She was small, almost birdlike, chattering gaily, rosy-cheeked and cheerful, like the robins she loved and described to us. Cycling around town on her little bicycle, with its wicker basket and a scarf around her neck, she brought bird song and colour, bog thistle and barn owls to our classrooms. We laughed at her at first but forgot to make fun when the classroom came alive with our imitations of wood pigeons, chaffinches, crows and thrushes. She stood at the top of the class, dwarfed by the huge blackboard with Irish verbs and conjugations listed neatly on it.

Our house was at the end of a lane leading to that bog. I began to explore it more and more. When I became interested in fitness and athletics, I ran over and back across that bogland, mapping every ditch and stream and cutting. Some of the bog was worked. The cutting, footing and stacking done in fair weather; the turf burned in winter. But most of it could not be worked as it was too wet. And in that wilderness, which seemed immense to my young eyes, were pheasant, foxes, grouse, deer, hares, badgers, dragonflies and God only knows what else. And bees. And bee hives kept by Trevor Rainsberry, our neighbour.

I would see him going to the fields beside the bog in his tractor with his bee-keeping paraphernalia. I began going with him every now and again. At first I watched from a distance as he would suit up, light his smoker and open the hive, gently talking to the bees and to me as he inspected the honeycombs. Gradually he brought me closer and showed me how to do it myself.

One summer I even went on a bee-keeping course with him to Gormanston College, north of Dublin, a huge old boarding school, with a cinder running track and beautiful grounds. Used by all sorts of groups during summer months for courses and meetings. Right beside it was the air corps' second air base of the same name. Wearing my white protective suit, with a smoker in my gloved hand, I peered up into the sky through a netted veil as the small green aeroplanes flew over us, little knowing, that it would not be that long before I would be flying them myself.

Trevor talked about the bog, its flowers and which ones the bees favoured, what season they thrived in. He talked about the bees, their habits, their migration, and their skill in gathering nectar. The more time I spent in his company, the more I realised that his knowledge was limitless: from astronomy to classical music, from the world around him to the world beyond the horizon.

We used to go on holiday to Roundstone in Connemara each summer staying in a caravan or a cottage owned by friends. We fished for mackerel and pollock from the rocks, and picked mushrooms in the morning or drove to Clifden, Letterfrack or Renvyle, admiring the view and buying fishing tackle and scones. We explored the coast and wondered what was on the islands just out of reach offshore and played darts in O'Dowd's while my parents had a few drinks.

One day an Alouette 3 flew over us, glinting in the sunlight, silvery and bright heading west to the Aran Islands. It was
one of those warm summers, made more tranquil by memory.
I stopped fishing to watch the helicopter appear from the east,
passing the mountain of Erris Beg, Gorteen and Dog's Bay.
Standing on an outcrop of rock at Murvey, I watched it go west
towards the islands until it was just a dot fading into the heat
haze. My father too had stopped. When it was gone, he turned
to look at me as he would do from time to time to make sure I
had not fallen in. He smiled and shouted to me, 'That'll be you
one day.'

The helicopter was on its way to Inis Mór, the largest of the
Aran Islands. It had on board a bomb disposal team, EOD (ex-
plosive ordnance disposal), going to make safe a Second World
War mine that had washed up on the beach. I found that out
fifteen years later flying the same helicopter and with the same
EOD officer in Donegal. My father had been right.

2

THE ARMY CALLS

If you chase two hares at the same time, you will catch neither of them.

Proverb

1980. The Leaving Certificate exams. Our futures being shaped by whatever we could drag out of the swirling mass of information and ideas in our heads, and how much we could commit to paper within the given time. The exam inspectors patrolled the rows of desks. The sunshine beat down outside. Sitting upright when I paused or was unable to write, I envied the men outside who trimmed the bushes and painted the buildings.

Half the summer was spent doing those exams. Once they were over I left school but could not get a summer job. I was broke. In beautiful summer weather, I spent my time cycling to the open-air swimming pool on Church Road, buying freshly baked buns in O'Shea's bakery in the Tanyard, if I had the money on the way back, or cycling along the miles of tow paths east and west on the Grand Canal.

We waited fearfully for our Leaving Certificate results and then suddenly we all went in different directions: to work, to college, to Dublin or places further afield. No one told us that we were crossing a line but our groups, gangs, athletics squads, rugby teams were all splintered.

I completed interviews for the defence forces' cadets but had to wait. In the meantime I was accepted into UCD and started science. Not knowing where it was going to lead, I wandered around the campus feeling lost and lonely, admiring the pretty girls but painfully shy. I took refuge in the companionship the athletics' track offered. As the evenings darkened and as the temperatures dropped, I could be found throwing the javelin at one end of the infield while at the other end was Seán Egan, Ireland's Olympic hammer thrower, just retired from the army.

We would meet each other in the centre field, passing on coaching tips. The length of the infield no barrier to conversation or technical criticism. 'That one was a bit high, Dave. Hit it a bit lower' or 'Your run up was very good, but your crossover was awkward. Slow down and only speed up on the crossover, OK?'

And so a very small friendship grew between a diminutive javelin thrower of modest achievement and a giant Olympic hammer thrower. It was, and is, something I love about sport. Your performance is respected, no matter what the sport, regardless of your size. But I would say that. One day I told him I was leaving. It was a goodbye.

'Where are you going?' he asked, surprised.

'I'm joining the army,' I said.

'Oh Jaysus, not the army! Sure I'm after leaving the army! Sure aren't you grand here.'

He had decided to leave to concentrate on the hammer, something army time did not allow. He laughed and wished me the best of luck. I told him of my dream of flying. He wondered aloud whether I would leave after a while to follow the same dream as him. I wondered too privately. I continued to throw the javelin after that but peaked a few years later. I suppose that was the point when I chose to fly above everything else.

The letter had come in the post with a harp on the brown envelope. I read it in disbelief:

> With regard to your application to become an Officer Cadet in the Defence Forces, the Minister of Defence is pleased to ...

I was getting my chance. I was on my way.

The seventeenth of November 1980. My dad was working. I don't recall a sombre moment between us before I left the house. He gave me no pithy advice. He went to work. I joined the army.

My mother drove me to the Curragh training camp. We had to be there by eleven in the morning. We left Tullamore and made our way through Killeigh, Mountmellick, Emo and then Kildare before we turned off for the Curragh Camp. Her black Morris Minor with squeaky windscreen wipers taking me away from my childhood. Such a short distance and yet it seemed to be a different planet. Driving between huge notices warning us that we were entering military property. Red brick buildings, white-washed kerb stones, armoured cars and troop carriers and soldiers in various uniforms, walking and marching.

It passed in a blur. She was gone, having briefly met the senior staff officers and military college commandant, the future chief of staff, Lt Colonel Noel Bergin. With me sitting quietly beside her, he explained that what lay ahead would be tough but fair, that her son would be expected to conform to the rule of discipline, that he would be allowed home as a privilege. She cheerfully replied and chatted to them as if it all was fine and dandy. It was not fine and dandy to me.

My cadetship began immediately. Our cadetship, that is, for we were a class. The fifty-seventh cadet class. Those who had previously been in the FCA, or reserve defence forces, had an idea of what lay ahead. If you had been to boarding-school, you would have been forewarned. If you were from a town that had an army barracks you would have had a clue. But most of us were clueless and in for a shock. I was one of those.

We were marched around in our suits, our only suits, the same ones we had worn to our interviews months before. NCOs barked at us as we collected equipment, uniforms and finally, our rifles. We were each issued a personal weapon; a high velocity self-loading rifle, or SLR, called an FN. It went everywhere we went. Over the coming weeks, we learned to strip it down and put it together again with our eyes closed. That is what they did to us too; they stripped us down and re-assembled us, army style.

There were forty-three in the class from all over Ireland. Tall and short, academic and athletic, good guys and bad guys. Some team players, some selfish and of course all sorts of personalities. Forty male and three female. The staff of the cadet school worked through a curriculum, changing us from civilian to soldier, and then from soldier to non-commissioned officer, NCO, and finally to commissioned officer. The curriculum was academic and practical, physical and psychological. It went from politics to the constitution, setting up roadblocks to understanding the legalities of firing our weapons and supporting the gardaí. It was vast.

We were constantly exhausted, physically and mentally. Five mile runs. One day in tracksuits. The next day in boots and combats. Singing 'Lady Madonna' in my head: 'Friday night arrives without a suitcase/Sunday morning creeping like a nun/Monday's child has learned to tie his bootlace/See how they run'.

When we were finished with our lectures, our marching drill, our tactical exercises and our constant parades, we polished brass, cleaned toilets, ironed uniforms, studied battles of the

Second World War and Vietnam, crawling into our beds after midnight. Each week our roles changed. Polishing floors until they shone like mirrors; white-washing kerb stones. We were pitched against each other. One week we had responsibility. The next we performed menial tasks. Cadets who would not pull their weight doing the menial tasks, would get a threat of non co-operation when they were in charge the following week. I remember one classmate, who was a charmer and a great guy but notoriously lazy, pleading with us to clean mirrors and floors before a commanding officer's inspection.

We refused. He knew his fate was in our hands but we would not budge. None of us. Just before the inspection team arrived we burst into action and did all the cleaning that needed to be done. We all passed the inspection. So did he. Afterwards we all laughed about it, but we had learned something. Acting with each other, for each other.

We arrived home at Christmas, battered and bruised licking our wounds. Each Christmas in Tullamore, a rugby match was played between the first team and a team made up of 'exiles', home from abroad. I was now an exile and played in the match on St Stephen's Day. The two teams laid into each other with no quarter given. The Tullamore team pummelled the exiles, who were disorganised, unfit, hung over and needed reminding that they were not big shots, just because they worked all year in London or Sydney or New York. Or the Curragh. It was great to be home.

The New Year came and we were back in the saddle very quickly. The landmarks of the cadetship started to pass by. There was a senior class ahead of us who tutored, bullied and perse- cuted us when the officers and NCOs had finished with us. In the spring, they were commissioned as officers. For weeks after- wards, they returned at night and sneaked into the corridors where we polished, studied and slept, to wish us luck, apologise for being bastards and encouraged us. Their encouragement and their success spurred us on.

With them out of the way, we were treated better by the staff. We had passed the six month mark. The next big element of our training was to go on three week tactical exercises to the Glen of Imaal. Everything was geared for those three weeks. We trained on a range of weapons and we studied classical defence and attack scenarios as conducted by sections of ten men, platoons numbering thirty and companies numbering a hundred. With the benefit of map-reading exercises, mountain-running and orienteering, we were ready.

For three weeks we alternated between living in the main camp or in trenches we dug, or in makeshift camps in midge-infested forests. We established perimeters and sentries and guard duties; attacked or were attacked at all hours of the day and night. Pyrotechnics and machine gun fire woke us amid shouting, roaring and confusion, soaking wet, not having slept for a couple of nights.

A pattern became established. They drove us into the ground. When we made stupid tactical decisions and mistakes, we were ridiculed for it. Then we would make up for it and made perfect attacks and ambushes on the staff, 'killing' them or taking them prisoner. Learning and getting the message. Afterwards, marching back to the main camp, Coolmooney. In an orderly fashion, we signed in our ordnance to security, tidied up, gave medical attention to those who needed it, real or simulated, and collapsed. We showered and they gave us the afternoon off. And then a few hours later, one of us would be called: 'Cadet McGeehin: you will lead a patrol to the following grid reference at 2200 hrs …' And so it started again.

Every one of the forty-three of us at some time or another

was singled out for attention during that time in the Glen. Whatever your weakness was, it would be preyed on mercilessly. Those who needed time to make a plan were harried and hurried and overworked. Those who were less fit were given enormously long patrols and long hours. The selfish were put in the spotlight and given menial tasks to do. The bullshitters were found out.

Pleasures were so simple: a ten-minute stop without being shouted at, a three hour lie in the sun, queuing for stew and lumpy mashed potato instead of trying to cook rations out of a pack. And sometimes I could see that the Glen was beautiful. The sun rising, as I stood in a trench, our platoon having rebuffed several attacks during the night, the others sleeping under shelter in their sodden sleeping bags. A mist forming on the slope around me, a heron gliding along the stream and choosing a place to stand, one legged, watching for movement, just as I was. Grey sky, slowly giving way to weak colour, heat returning.

When we pressed pause on our war, the birds sang, the river gurgled, the tall grass rustled in the wind. One afternoon, I lay flat on my back looking up at the clouds watching them trace a lazy pattern across the sky. The same sky and the same noises, the same peace as my bog at home. I closed my eyes and slept. I daydreamed of the bog, the buzzing of bees, the flash of my silver dragonfly. The rhythm of its wings became a beat, a beat that I could hear. I leaped up. There was a beat all right! A helicopter was coming in to land. Its approach had startled others, who rose and watched it. An Alouette 3.

I had forgotten why I was putting up with all this warfare. I had forgotten about flying. I was just getting through each day. The arrival of the Alouette saddened me and cheered me up, at the same time. Would I ever get to fly? It landed and the crew took off their helmets and chatted to some of our staff. Standing beside the helicopter, hands in pockets, nonchalant and unhurried. A slower pace than ours.

We were told to be ready for aerial reconnaissance of Knickeen Ford, for yet another all night assault. Divided into groups of four, we listened to the safety brief from the crewman: how to get in, how to get out, don't try to talk to the pilot, he's too busy. To wait for the signal to get in and to get out. Where to go after you get out and what the radio procedures were.

My head fuzzy from the short sleep, my mind trying to remember what he had just said, I got in and we were off. All the junk in my mind evaporated as soon as the wheels left the ground. The pilot pitched us over aggressively, and we flew across the camp roof tops gaining speed. He pulled us up into the sky and we headed for the hills. I watched the pilot and the crewman talk to each other. They turned to each other and their lips moved. They smiled and I think I could hear laughter. They were on intercom and we were not. We approached the exercise area and tried to make an aerial assessment but it was too fast and we were disorientated. At least I was. There was Cemetery Hill, and Knickeen Ford, and the cluster of houses at Knockanarrigan. Stranahely Wood and the maze of trails and fire breaks that we were trying to memorise.

I also imagined I saw Roundstone, flying over Murvey watching my dad reel in a good-sized pollock. I smiled. I waved to him saying: 'You were right dad. Here I am!!' I watched the pilot's every move and learned nothing. But I was at last inside a helicopter.

On our last day, we marched back to the Curragh. It was the same distance as a marathon, twenty-six miles. No problem, it was a march not a race. But we carried all our gear, all our weapons, including GPMGs and the mortars, base plates included, radios the size of a heavy rucksack (the radio operator would wear his rucksack on his back, his radio on his chest and shoulder his FN rifle), helmets with no padding. The weather was hot and sunny: a hellish end to a hellish three weeks.

We all got through. We all survived. It is the same with every class. I would not have made it without my classmates' help. We carried gear for each other, shouted warnings when supervisors were nearby, kept each other food, rations or sandwiches when we were late off patrols, stopped each other from setting off booby traps, nudged each other awake at lectures on courtesy and etiquette. Our individual personalities were focused on reaching the following April and our commissioning day. One day one of our senior class was killed. In disbelief we heard that Eddie Barry had died on a training flight in Baldonnel. Eddie. Our own senior class. A young officer with his life ahead of him. Eddie, the handsome Limerick man, great rugby player, great craic, and full of life. Our first encounter with death in service. We knew that flying training had its risks, but never expected one of our own peers to be taken so young. Those that knew him personally and who were from Limerick, went to his funeral. In later years, we played an annual rugby match in his memory. With his Garry-owen club-playing brothers, Nicky and Ian, playing too. Nicky went on to play for Ireland at international level, making it to the premier tier. In the stands in Landsdowne Road, we stood and roared him on. Eddie's prospective fellow pilots, cheering raucously, as if it was Eddie himself. Our cadetship continued. The army pausing to lay Eddie to rest, his shadow hanging over us for months and years to come. But the show had to go on.

Summer eventually came and passed in a blur. When we returned, the road to commissioning was mapped out before us. A new class of cadets would arrive just before Christmas. We would become the senior class and our privileges would improve. We would return to the Glen of Imaal around that time too. The emphasis would be on leadership rather than hardship, on aid to the civil power and counter-terrorism, rather than conventional warfare.

All our energies were focused on that target: physical training, lectures on the legal aspects of our roles and responsibilities, on how other forces worked, such as the garda and the United Nations. From the following April, we would be young officers leading armed men, potentially on United Nations peace-keeping duties in the trouble spots around the globe, as well as supporting our own gardaí in the ongoing battle against terrorists and subversives. It was not a game. And because it was not a game, the staff shouted at us less, reasoned with us more, and probed us for answers.

'What would you do, cadet? He has no papers, he speaks no English and he wants to drive through your checkpoint?' 'What would you do cadet? The car is driving at one of your platoon: do you give the order to open fire?'

Like the FN rifles we carried still, shouldered, greased and ready to fire, we were being re-assembled and made ready.

The final run into commissioning was a rush to cover the rest of the huge syllabus and how the different arms of the defence forces worked. It served two purposes: giving us insights into each corps, each area of expertise, and helping us decide which path to follow. From communications in the signal corps, to basic bomb disposal in the ordnance corps, driving Scorpion tanks in the cavalry corps and eventually visiting Baldonnel and the air corps.

Our day at the air corps was sunny. I have photos to prove it. There were eight of us who wanted to be pilots, who were gambling almost two years of our lives to get the opportunity to fly. We walked around smiling in hope. We were getting closer with each passing day. We met some of the flying instructors at the basic flying training school (BFTS). We met our own senior cadets, young officers now, in the middle of their own flight training. We stood uneasily as they lounged in the sun waiting for their flight time to come around. They smoked. They laughed. They told us about the flying training. We fidgeted.

The rest of the class who had no interest in becoming pilots goaded and teased us but the eight of us returned a week later for interview. We explained as best we could why we wanted to fly, answered their technical questions as best we could, and tried to demonstrate enthusiasm. I knew some of the eight of us had flying experience. I had none. Taking flying lessons had been beyond me in Tullamore, but on a weekend's leave earlier that year, I did a course in hang-gliding in Wicklow, so I told them about that. Then they took us flying in the SIAI Marchetti tandem-seater, fully aerobatic. It was fantastic. And then I felt sick. Uh oh. Was I really cut out for this? Time would tell.

It is pot luck whether you get the corps you want or what the army wants. There is a formal evening two weeks before the commissioning when the class has a meal with the military college and cadet school senior officers. After the speeches, the cadets are told where they are going. Reading from the class list, in alphabetical order, our futures are revealed.

'Cadet Courtney …' (Drum roll in my mind. Some smart arse says, 'Infantry Corps', lots of laughter) '… general list, air corps Baldonnel. Congratulations'.

I received a round of applause, as each of us did, and a small brown envelope with an air corps shoulder badge. No letter. Nothing else. It was my golden ticket for Willy Wonka's Chocolate Factory.

The eight cadets who wanted the air corps were all selected. Most of the rest of the class got what they wanted too. Suddenly the Curragh was a great place. I forgot the icy winter mornings, smoke from turf fires drifting across us in the dark as we stood on parade. I wiped clean my memories of the hardships and difficulties.

We marched now with purpose and great intent. We cleaned and polished our Wilkinson Swords for the commissioning ceremony and for the mass. We walked around the cadet school less nervously, sometimes being stopped by staff and congratulated, where being stopped by a college officer previously could have meant a weekend's pass denied or extra work details. Just as they had picked us off, one by one, persecuting us and making our lives hell, once more they picked us off methodically, this time telling us that we were a great class and wishing us well. Tommy Doyle, Tom Ahearne, Ed Moran, Tony O'Sullivan, Maureen McEnery and Peter Murphy arrived at our rooms, politely knocking for a change and shaking hands: 'Good luck lads. In case I don't see ye.' Frank O'Leary, Paddy Moran, Liam Clancy, Jim Sreenan and of course Lt Col Noel Bergin himself all wishing us the best as did the non-commissioned officers, Val Goss, Declan Meade, Martin Hickey, Dav McHenry, Joe O'Brien, Austin Clarke. Our tormentors, the college heavies who made us do extra push ups, told us to run up and down the hill at Donnelly's Hollow again, hissed threats in our ears as the turf smoke wafted around us in the dark, were now making fun of it all.

'You're not commissioned yet, cadet. I'm watching you, cadet, for the next week. After that I'll call you sir.'

Their example in leadership was more instructive than the many hours of lectures.

The commissioning day arrived. No one fluffed their lines. The mass was beautiful. The guard of honour marched up the middle of the church. Two lines splitting left and right before the altar. Suppressed gasps from those relatives, like mine, who had never seen anything like this before. The shining swords held in front. The barely heard orders in Irish, as the officers turned as one, to face the altar, and wait. Then the blessing, the communion, the orders again, the swords stabbing first upwards, and then being lowered gracefully. Each sword held at exactly the same angle.

A ceremony in the garrison Church of Ireland too. The chief of staff attended. The senior college staff were there too. My chosen classmates. My parents. My brother back from London. My two sisters back from France. Greg Murray, my school principal and athletics' coach. We had communion. The prayers were short and sweet; Very Rev. John Patterson, later dean of Christ Church cathedral, gave us communion. A short service that those present would never forget.

In the gymnasium of the army school of physical culture, our families and loved ones took their places as we lined up silently inside. Eighteen months' preparation, months of drill practice and polishing of swords and leather. They held their breaths as the orders echoed around the hall. The stamp of our tipped shoes as we came to attention. The tension as our families held their breath. The whispered timing instructions: *'Aon, do, trí … aon …'*

First stopping at the eight tables at the head of the hall. The beat and rhythm of our shoes on the wooden floor. The taut faces of our fathers, struggling to control moist proud eyes. Mothers squeezing husbands' hands. Leaning forward at the same angle, placing our right hands on the bibles there. In unison. Up together with bibles in hand. We swore our oaths to Ireland: *'Minimse, Daithí Ó Cuirneain, go solómonta, go mbeinn dílis don Bhunreacht …'*

As I get older, and as I struggle to remember details, I look at the photos and I see that everyone is smiling.

3

—

BALDONNEL

Dreams do come true. Why else would nature
incite us to have them in the first place?

Anon.

April 1982. Commissioned and back home in Tullamore. The
New Road lined with cherry trees, in alternating pink and white
blossom, seemed to celebrate my return. The town was shaking
off the winter chill, emerging from the shadows and laughing
again.

We did a lot of laughing. My parents laughing at my stories
and recounting commissioning day. Me laughing at the close
calls, the almost-got-in-trouble anecdotes that all of us were
telling that week to our families all around Ireland. A happy
but relieved laughter as I was the youngest in the family and I
had a job.

The basic flying training school/BFTS is in Baldonnel, just
outside Dublin, but we began back at the Curragh, where we
returned the last bits and pieces of kit and cleared our rooms. It
was our first time to have a coffee in the officers' mess but I was
too nervous to relax and did not stay long. We were to report to
the adjutant of training wing by ten o'clock. We drove in convoy
in our newly acquired second-hand cars, stopping in a lay-by
to fix our ties and check each other's uniforms. Still paranoid
about appearances. It would pass.

The students on pilots' training courses have been either commissioned officers or cadets, depending on the system in vogue at the time. We were second lieutenants which meant we were treated very well, called 'sir', saluted and helped. It was a shock. It took us a while to get out of saluting anyone wearing a peaked cap, forgetting we wore one now ourselves.

We were given rooms and issued with flying helmets, suits and gloves, and all the flying paraphernalia: books and flying manuals, logbooks, slide rules and flying boots. As we learned to find our way around Baldonnel. There was a large ramp or apron facing south. The hangars faced onto it and aircraft would emerge each day and jostle for position. On one side was the helicopter area where Alouette 3s and Gazelles stood. Beside them were advanced trainers, the Fouga Magisters. Then came the basic trainers, the SIAI Marchettis. Pushed out on demand were Beech King Airs and the HS 125 ministerial transport and government jet.

Soon we would understand the hierarchy. Overseeing the whole lot, was the tower – air traffic control (ATC). Like a referee standing over us all, it admonished us on the ground and in the air. We learned very quickly to do what they said. A very sensible way to start our aviation careers.

Suddenly we were airborne. We learned the basic theory of flight and the mechanics of the systems for a few hours in the morning, and then went flying, each flight preceded by a formal pre-flight briefing, where the aim of the lesson was outlined. We started at the very best place, the start – learning the basics of controlling an aircraft. Our first significant hurdle would be our first solo.

The physics, chemistry and maths of my school days, patiently explained and explored by John Pareira and Ann Ryan in the Christian Brothers, gave me a foundation for the subjects ahead. Venn diagrams returned, and made more sense now, as we went through all the forces that affect flight: lift and gravity, thrust and drag. Weather and meteorology explained by Gerry McDonald from the met office in Baldonnel. Classroom lectures on icing and fog, the formation of fronts, and all the changes that went with their passing, explained when the weather itself was too bad outside.

As we flew, we could feel the forces in our hands, imagining the vector arrows changing size, as the aircraft transformed from a mass on the ground to a graceful soaring flying machine. It was June. We came in each morning and ran to the timetable to see who was paired with which instructor, who was doing what. The instructors would arrive. The tension mounted. All on first name terms because we were officers too. But not pilots, not yet.

Our instructors knocked us into shape, repeating their mantra 'Don't get low and don't get slow', until we got the message. Climbing to altitude, they demonstrated stalls and spins so that we could see the dangers of letting speed fall away. At that stage in a pilot's training, even though you know not to let your speed drop, you made mistakes. The criticism hurt, but it had to as the stakes were too high. Getting low or slow or worst, both, would surrender the aircraft to gravity. Some of the instructors, not much older than ourselves, had the huge responsibility of moulding us into the desired aerodynamic shape.

Into the Magic Roundabout. Circuits. The take-off and landing pattern, called a circuit is shaped like a racecourse or athletics track. We took the aircraft cold on the ramp, started it up, did the engine checks and pre-flight checks, taxied out having received the right ATC clearance, lined up on the runway, and took it into the air safely. Then we turned downwind while doing the correct checks, having taken up the undercarriage and flaps, adjusting the engine power settings. And finally set up for landing, gear down again, landing flaps and ATC permission to land. And repeat that over and over again to demonstrate consistency, safety, reliability. Then the emergencies were thrown in for good measure, engine failures at different stages in the circuit.

I was doing OK. I was enjoying it but getting tense as I clocked the hours up and coming nearer to the solo check ride. It was a make or break. Then I flew with a new instructor, Nick McHugh. After one or two circuits, he said 'Same again Dave: that's grand.' He tuned in one of the navigation radios to a local station and listened to pop music, only turning it down when we were doing the final checks before landing. He sang along to a song by Toto, 'Africa'. I can hear it now:

> I hear the drums echoing tonight,
> But she hears only whispers of some quiet conversation,
> She's coming in twelve thirty flight …
> Her moonlit wings reflect the stars that guide me towards salvation

The checks and actions became automatic, as he hummed putting me at ease. It was not that he was better than the others – they were all excellent – but he was better for me. Then came the pre-solo check ride. Recommended as ready, I flew with the chief instructor, Commandant Ken Byrne. He had flown with each of us before so that we could get a feel for each other when airborne. He was a man of few words, at least with us, but we were in awe of his silky flying skills, his quiet control and power in the air. My nerves threatened to mess it up but he reassured me and it went fine. I passed my pre-solo check. On Friday 13 August 1982, three of us went solo: Tony, Seán and myself. As I taxied away to line up, Ken and the other instructors made their way to the tower to watch and to talk us through a landing if we had an emergency or if we froze. They were probably more nervous than we were.

As I lifted off the ground, I let out a shout that no one could hear. I did my checks and looked beside me at the empty seat. I levelled out and looked at the view, briefly, turned onto finals and got ready. My landings were fine, not great, not bad but they were mine, all mine. I don't remember any deep insights during that short flight but there was a realisation that another hurdle had been crossed and apart from one or two shouts of delight, I think the feeling was a quiet and private one. And emotional.

It was emotional for some of the other lads too as not all of us were going to continue flying. Four of them returned to various army corps and pursued different careers. It came as a big disappointment to one or two who were as keen on flying as we were. Our delight was tempered with disappointment for them. Whenever I have met pilots who are jaded and negative about their working lives, I think of those who knocked the first fence and know that I am lucky. There but for the Grace of God go I.

We each had our lives back having been all but imprisoned in the Curragh. The flying programme was Monday to Friday, although we had loads of ground studies and the odd security duty to perform. For the first time since we had left school, we had a lot of weekends off. I returned to Tullamore Rugby Club one evening a week and played at the weekends, fitting it in with my studies. I had the best of both worlds. Rugby was my umbilical chord to Tullamore. That season our team, the club seconds, won the Midland League. And I had a job.

Going solo was the building block upon which everything else was constructed. The flying course, or wings course, had an allowance of some 200 flying hours. At the end of the course, we would be sent to different squadrons and onto other aircraft and fly whatever roles those squadrons performed. So we had to be delivered, fit to fly in all the weathers that Ireland experiences.

Flying solely by the aircraft's instruments, was prominent in the programme. I would get strapped into the aircraft, put on a hood that blocked out the outside world and navigated cross country making the different types of instrument approaches: VOR, ILS, NDB, SRA. Boring and mind-numbing when you are nineteen years old and want to do aerobatics and chase clouds.

But they knew this, so in between the instrument flights we would do exactly that: loops and rolls, wing-overs and spins, roll-off-tops and barrel rolls. Over the Bog of Allen, just west of Baldonnel, was our playground between the turf-cutting machines below, and the clouds above. Part of our mid-course assessment was to make up, and fly, an aerobatic display. Then navigation: maps, charts and theory, with flying navigation exercises after that. Marking straight lines across Ireland on our maps and trying to follow them. Checking our progress with halfway points and prominent features. Learning how easy it is to convince yourself you are where you should be, when in fact the wind has blown you off course.

The pilots and engineers, who worked in the squadrons and ate meals at other tables near us, gradually welcomed us into their company. We attended the ground course lectures, grappling with the frequency spectrum or the earth's rotation and its bearing on time zones. Our friendships grew studying together in the evenings, helping each other. If bad weather was forecast for the next day, we would sometimes head off to the bright lights, and postpone the study. This was thirsty work. Lift, thrust and drag, power, attitude and trim; trying to get the information into our heads and then into our hands and feet.

We finished the basic course with formation flying, first

with instructors and then without. Six months previously, Seán, John, Tony and I, sat into the Marchettis for the first time, and wondered how we were ever going to do it. Now we were taking off, four of us, flying in formation in line astern and vic formation, finishing with a formation break over the airfield. We had come a long way, together.

The Advanced Flying Training School awaited us. This consisted of changing the sign on the door, and walking fifty yards further up the ramp to the Fouga Magisters. The course aimed quite simply to do the same exercises again, this time in a twin engine jet, and at max speed 400 knots at low level or mach 85 at altitude. Faster than my mother's Morris Minor.

In the Marchetti the pilot sits with the engine and propeller in front of him. In the Fouga, the pilot sat at the front with the engines behind. My first impression of jet flight was the quiet, the smoothness and the feeling at times that I myself was flying. It was beautiful.

The syllabus was repeated again for the jets, right up to formation flying. The Fouga only had enough fuel for a flight of just over an hour, so flights were short and sweet. We took off, our breathing into our oxygen masks amplified by the intercom, our voices and transmissions sounding more like Apollo astronauts than trainee pilots. We groaned into the intercom as the G forces made us strain and sweat, feeling the power in our finger tips, increasing or decreasing the G force and the pressure on our bodies, with a slight squeeze or release of the controls. The famous poem by John Gillespie Magee, Jr, an American Spitfire pilot in the Second World War, never so apt:

> Oh! I have slipped the surly bonds of earth,
> And danced the skies on laughter-silvered wings;
> Sunward I've climbed and joined the tumbling mirth,
> Of sun-split clouds and done a hundred things

You have not dreamed of – wheeled and soared and swung
High in the sunlit silence.
Hov'ring there I've chased the shouting wind along, and flung
My eager craft through footless halls of air ...
Up, up the long delirious blue, I've topped the wind-swept heights
   with easy grace
Where never Lark, or even Eagle flew – And while with silent lift-
   ing mind I've trod
The high untrespassed sanctity of space,
Put out my hand and touched the face of God.

In July 1983, the sixteenth young officers wings course received their silver wings. John, Seán, Tony and I, watched by our proud families and friends. Our instructors were on parade with us: Ken Byrne, Paddy Curley, John Flanagan, Dermot McCarthy, Nicky McHugh, Dave Gohery, Jack Killoch, Kevin Barry. We owed them a lot and still do.

The Army Number One Band played, 'Those Magnificent Men in their Flying Machines' and then Verdi's 'Nabucco'. The music brought all the pilots present, back to their own wings day and their own memories, joining past, present and future pilots to-gether as one for a moment. It brought tears to some, others felt the hair on their arms and necks rise, and some of us smiled beneath our peaked caps.

4
—
HUT 55

Friendship consists of forgetting what one gives,
and remembering what one receives.

Anon.

New pilots, no matter how well trained, are just that, new and
have to be integrated. In the air corps attitudes and policies
change with time; new aircraft are introduced; pilots retire, and
the show goes on. The corps, modest in size, provides aerial support of security around the country, maritime surveillance, helicopter air ambulance and rescue, government air transport, as
well as a myriad of other tasks. It's busy.

A turning point in a pilot's career is the decision to stay with
fixed wing aeroplanes or to covert to helicopters. The decisions
are not always made by pilots themselves but based on the needs
of the organisation, and their ability. The training schools themselves need instructors so that becomes another career path.

When we qualified, we were put through the humble Cessna
172 squadron. We operated out of a grass airstrip in Gormanston, carrying out a wide range of tasks at the behest of the
army and various government departments. As time went on,
we gained experience of command and then were assigned to
other squadrons as vacancies arose. We arrived in Gormanston,
shiny, new and raring to go. Beside the grass airstrip was a row
of old Second World War huts, prominently numbered. In one
of these was housed our operations' room and our new com-

manding officer's office. Our new home was Hut 55, the 'potting shed' for new pilots like us.

1983. Summer. The smell of the grass being cut on the airfield. The sound of the Cessnas starting up, taking off and heading north, south and west, on various tasks. We waited our turn to do a few hours flying to convert onto the aircraft. Our new commanding officer, Commandant Liam Mulligan, awaited us. He was worth the entry fee.

In Hut 55 there was an intercom linking each of the rooms and offices. Using a 'squawk box', Liam could bellow at us and get us to do one or other important task: get ready for a flight that had just come in, do a ground run on one of the aircraft or just make him a cup of tea. The sound of the squawk and his bellow would make us jump at first but after a while, knowing he could not see or hear us until we pressed the button on our own squawk box, we would just groan and say, 'What now?!'

We were all aged about twenty. Liam was forty or so. A big, fit man with a moustache, not quite a handlebar but almost. He could be polite or gruff, yet warm and welcoming, bawdy and full of life. Sometimes laughing until he cried at the jokes and stories we would bring back from the pubs in Drogheda. He was adored by many of his subordinates, engineers, pilots and administration staff alike. His leadership was a great cloak of protection and advice to young pilots like us.

Our flying duties took us all over the country. We flew by day in visual conditions. We were gradually accumulating flying time and experience, each additional hundred hours a cause for celebration. We were away from supervision, away from training. Free as a bird, literally. Collecting observers and radio operators all over Ireland, providing communications links and a watchful eye over army patrols countrywide. Without mobile phones and with patchy radio communication, our presence was highly valued. Movements of large amounts of cash as well as explosives and high-profile prisoners were potential targets for subversive attack. The Northern Ireland 'Troubles' rumbling under the surface countrywide.

Our roles apart from that? Anything and everything. From dropping army parachutists to counting seals on the west coast islands at low level, to flying government ministers when more glamorous aircraft were not available. I often got the opportunity to fly past our house en route to or returning from somewhere.

I flew over the landmarks of my childhood like the canal and the two church spires before recognising the brown scrubland and bog just beyond our house. Just enough time for one or two passes, my mother would come out and wave an apron up at me, shielding her eyes from the sun on bright days. Now and again my father would be at her side looking up. Our little house, with its vegetable garden and rockery, bees buzzing.

Gormanston had an atmosphere about it that was unique. Its official title, which rankled with the army, was 'Air Station Gormanston'. Its grass runways and dated huts evoked a bygone era. Now that we were able to live a little (or a lot!), we could take in our surroundings and appreciate what the air corps meant, the significance of its history.

The photographs hanging in the officers' mess were of Lysanders, Hawker Hurricanes and Spitfires. The officer pilots wearing jodhpurs and leather jackets and jaunty caps. Gormanston had an atmosphere that was evocative of wartime. Or maybe it was just that the boy who had dreamed of flying was now living that dream and instead of Duran Duran or Foreigner in my mind I could hear Vera Lynn, singing 'We'll meet again'. The wooden huts, the smell of the aviation fuel and the roar of the engines brought life to my imaginings of my father in the war and the stories he and my mother told me as I grew up. And who better than Liam Mulligan to play the part of squadron leader bawling us out for being late or untidy, chiding us for sloppy flying on check rides, buying us beer on Friday nights in the officers' mess.

After two years our quartet was broken asunder. John and Tony went on to become instructors in the school. While Seán and then I went to helicopters. We left Gormanston after one final night in the mess, repeating our initiation ritual, acrobatically hanging upside down, our legs draped over the wooden rafters for a farewell drink.

5

THE DEAD MAN'S CURVE

Better to ask twice than to lose your way once.

Anon.

Rudimentary knowledge was all I had when I arrived in Baldonnel to learn how to fly helicopters. They take off and land vertically without runways. Using winches they rescue people clinging by their finger tips to sinking ships or rocky precipices. That was all I knew.

Paul Deevy, Dave Sparrow and Dónal Cotter, Frank Russell, Pat Donnelly were the instructors of myself and Ciaran Parker. In December 1985 we arrived and started our conversion course. It took twice as long as usual because of training crews for the newly arrived Dauphin. The helicopter squadron, as it had formerly been known, had been re-designated and re-named as a new wing: Number 3 Support Wing.

We were issued with flying helmets again, having not worn them since our wings course. These helmets had throat mikes were used by the winch operators so that the sound of wind whooshing past would not deafen us on the intercom. ATC had to contend with us novice trainee helicopter pilots getting in the way of their traffic and transmitting garbage over the radio.

'Alpha 211, say again.'

'Alpha 211, confirm ready to cross active runway from the Fox's Covert?'

Our helicopter was the Aerospatiale (now Eurocopter)

Gazelle, a sleek powerful light and fast single engine machine. We came and went from the concrete ramp, learning to manoeuvre and make speed and power changes, gradually improving our skills. Once the helicopter was moving, learning how to turn, climb, descend, accelerate and decelerate were easier because of the stability that came with speed. Coming into land and slowing down until all speed was gone brought instability and the next and most critical flight phase: the hover.

Being able to hover is certainly a milestone in your career akin to going solo. The hover beautifully demonstrating Newton's laws of physics. On the ground the blades rotate at full speed, clockwise in the case of the Gazelle. *For every action there is an equal and opposite reaction.* Consequently, the helicopter tries to rotate underneath the blades in the opposite direction. This is prevented by the force of the weight of the helicopter on the ground.

Off the ground, the helicopter will try to rotate under the main rotor blades. The tail rotor counteracts this keeping the machine stable. The helicopter's twisting force is measured as torque. Applying rudder and making the helicopter turn against the tail rotor torque uses more power. Rudder in the opposite direction uses less.

Finally, the helicopter reacts to the increase in collective and tail rotor pitch by rolling slightly. This is counter-acted by the pilot applying opposite cyclic. This moves one main blade at a time, cyclically through the same control linkages. All of these actions and reactions, controls and responses, happen instantaneously.

We hovered over the grass between the taxi-ways and runways hidden from prying eyes. As we improved and became adept at landing and taking off without dragging the skids, we started to make landings on the concrete apron.

Dave Sparrow was with me one day as we approached the ramp after a training flight. Instead of taking over control, this time he remained silent. It was my turn to make my first apron landing. We approached the hover, I half glanced sideways to our HQ building and saw faces pressed against the windows. I got into a hover over the designated spot. I started to drift right. I corrected, but a bit too much. Within a foot or so of the ground, I tried to find that happy hover with zero movement. I over-compensated and kept moving left and right. The gallery watched. Dave waited encouraging me. 'Relax, you're almost there. You had this nailed for the last few days over the grass. Be positive.' I relaxed and touched on reasonably gently. Not perfectly but not bad either. I shut the engine down, applied the rotor brake and did the checks. Beads of sweat going down my face and my back, my armpits soaked. Dave said something very ordinary like 'That's grand', and we went into debrief. I was shaking like a leaf. I learned during my wings course, but even more during the helicopter course, that it takes a great pilot to instruct another and allow him to make mistakes while flying.

One day I found that I could hover.

The Dublin/Wicklow mountains became our playground as we explored and learned how to find the wind and fly approaches to land on ridges or summits or hover beside cliffs and in corrie bowls. The helicopter may not be confined to landing on a runway but it needs to approach and land as near as possible into wind.

In science and in meteorology, they say that the behaviour of air is akin to the behaviour of liquid. Air flows and mixes, warms and cools, dries and moistens, as it moves around planet earth. Still air and no wind over the mountains behaves like a large flat lake with very little gradient; still and predictable. As the air starts to move through the mountains, in Ireland normally as a result of the cycle of Atlantic weather systems that wash across us *ad infinitum*, it gets funnelled and its behaviour changes. Although we cannot see it, this air is moving faster, just like a river when it accelerates due to a steeper gradient or when it passes through a gorge. If the river encounters boulders, white water and rapids develop. The 'white water' made by turbulent air is invisible. Or is it?

Dave and Paul and Dónal showed us the tell tale signs of wind in the mountains. Smoke from house chimneys, wind vanes on lakes, how to watch the way the helicopter drifts over the ground. Clouds being formed over ridges and summits due to winds blowing moist air up from valley floors. Winds changing in strength and direction depending on the altitude and terrain. A benign westerly wind at altitude could be shaped by mountain ridges, funnelled by the valleys below and could become easterly and much stronger and more turbulent in a corrie bowl. Predicting where this turbulence would be, this 'dirty air'. Flying over ridges and potential landing zones, LZs, and saying to us, 'Make an approach and land there'. To see if we could recognise these invisible traps. We would methodically fly over and reconnoitre each time to judge whether we would be able to safely approach an LZ or abort an approach to an unsuitable LZ. Decisions we would have to make unsupervised very soon.

Always have an escape. Approach each summit and ridge and LZ with an option to fly away to safety. With our improvement came enjoyment. We would fly away from Baldonnel, heading south, for an hour and a half's mountain flying, and then find red deer close to where we intended to land, watching them, startled, turn and dart across the mountain side. Special moments. And plenty of them.

On the ground we were busy too. Sgt 'Billo' Booth gave us our technical training but much more than that, he introduced us to a subject that was to become popular in aviation years later; CRM, crew resource management. By this I mean that Billo brought us very much down to earth, reminding us that even though we were the officers, we were only part of a team that included engineers and winchcrew too. His gift was that he did it with humour and wit. He was brilliant at explaining how the controls worked, how the mixing units received the cyclic and collective control inputs, and translated them into pitch angle changes in the main blades. He made sense of the gear box and its complex sun and planet gearing and how it turned at 2,000 RPM, into a manageable 350 rotor RPM. He poked fun at us, mocked us, made us laugh and taught us everything we had to know, and more. By the end of the course, he had delivered a master class, not just in the engineering of a helicopter, but also in how helicopter crews operate.

While all this was going on, Dauphin training was reaching fever pitch. The Dauphin's arrival was impatiently anticipated. It would mark the beginning of a new era of night rescue, when we would not be dependant on RAF and royal navy helicopters. While this was going on, our course foundered and ground to a halt.

Eventually we got back in the air again. Having completed the Gazelle part of the course, the Alouette 3 was our 'new' aircraft. This was the workhorse of the air corps, twenty-three years in service already then. Flying the Alouette 3 was our introduction to flying with crewmen on all sorts of missions as well as winching and search & rescue (SAR). Billo Booth got us into the spirit of things in terms of working and flying with engineers and crewmen. Flying the Alouette 3 developed that even further.

In a single engine helicopter, you need to be vigilant in case that engine fails. If you are hovering, you need to be relatively close to the ground. If the engine fails, you flutter down to the ground, if you do the right thing that is. Landing without engine power, auto-rotating, was something we had done in the Gazelle from the hover and would be repeating in the Alouette from the cruise. If you were flying along at a cruise of 100 knots, an engine failure would lead you to an auto-rotation in which you would drop down to the ground decelerating initially to 60 knots.

Flying slowly and at a low altitude could be catastrophic. So when we were flying, our instructors would unexpectedly either say 'simulated engine failure' or lower the collective lever to the floor. We would then swoop into whatever terrain we could find for an emergency landing. This led to an instinctive continuous scan of the terrain as we flew along, noting potential emergency landing spots all the time or flying higher to have more time. If we could not fly higher because of cloud, we would try to fly into the wind or take a different route.

We learned to obey the doctrine of 'The Dead Man's Curve' also known as 'The Avoid Curve'. This is a graph of speed versus height on a simple X and Y graph. The 'Avoid' shaded part being the area that would most likely lead to fatal accident in the case of engine failure, characterised by low and slow flight. Other variables were the wind and its strength and direction, as well as the terrain.

Now that we knew how to hover and fly, we could adapt to the Alouette and all the roles it performed. Flying with a crewman now, who would be our eyes and ears as we came to the hover, in particular watching the tail rotor clearance, was new to us. Back to the mountains again, this time into ever smaller LZs, smaller forest breaks with barely enough room for the blades to clear. Double angle approaches and vertical descents, all with the crewman talking us through on intercom: 'Forward and down three, forward and down two, height good'; this meant, *keep going forward in the direction I was giving you, but STOP descending.*

'Forward one, Steady': this meant, *no more lateral movement.*

Pause. No instructions. This meant he was looking out to check clearance or he had an intercom failure. If he had an intercom failure, hopefully you would realise it, and not sit there in a hover, drifting closer to the tree tops while getting no further instructions. This was done regularly to check that we were in fact listening and would do the sensible thing and fly away.

This was called patter. The numbers were not measurements. Five did not mean five yards, metres or feet. The numbers chosen matched the personality of the crew. It was a rhythm. One crewman and another pilot might like short, sharp staccato patter. Other crewmen and pilots liked slower patter. The rhythm matched your pace to the LZ and would magically reach the number one, as you reached the intended hover position. Then fill-in-patter would be added. More information. Helping to build a picture in the pilot's mind of what was unseen below him.

This was a critical aspect of our flying. Patter helped build our mental models of what we could not see. It was both rigid and flexible at the same time. The senior SAR crewmen, who were involved in training pilots in this area, had differing views on how it should be done. But that was not a weakness. That was a strength that equipped us for the unknown, for the unpredictable, for different personalities, different weather and different pressures. The names that stick out are Ben Heron, Dick O'Sullivan, John Manning, Owen Sherry and Dick Lynch. To come through the formality of military college and wings course training, and then find an atmosphere that was so relaxed, fluid and informal was almost a shock.

They did not give us just rules but also advice and guidelines. I have very fond memories of Dick O'Sullivan guiding me in monosyllabic patter in later years to a vessel at night. We debriefed afterwards on a good sortie and he said, 'Ah Dave, I didn't need to give you much chat. We had it sorted in the run in. You knew it. I knew it. Everybody happy'. That telepathy took years to develop, but at that point we were laying down its foundation.

The Alouette 3's exploits were famous as were some of its crews. We were very conscious of following in their footsteps and trying to emulate them. People like Dónal Loughnane, Owen Sherry and Paddy O'Shea who had rescued climbers off Muckish Mountain in Donegal at night, landing with barely enough fuel, the Alouette not being a night capable aircraft. Other rescues in the Dublin Mountains, where the squadron were hailed as heroes. Rescues at sea at the limit of the aircraft's range by Hugh O'Donnell, Dave Sparrow, Paddy McGurk and many more.

While we grappled with the difficulties of navigating around the country in the worst weather and visibility that we could find, the rest of the unit was making the step up into night SAR. The sooner we could be trained, the sooner we could free up another two pilots for Dauphin training.

The Alouette was used for security duties along the border, based in Monaghan and Finner camp, Co. Donegal. The northern situation was volatile to say the least. Our roles were constant standby during daylight hours to bring armed troops, EOD teams and whatever else was needed to wherever it was needed. The border between Northern Ireland and the Republic being invisible from the air, meandering over fields, hills, bog and scrub, took a lot of practice and time to get used to.

Wherever roads crossed from one side to the other was a border crossing. Some were easy to spot, as they had customs posts, or British army or garda checkpoints. Some were blocked by concrete obstacles and trenches. Others were marked by Xs painted on the road. Our job was to know each and every one of them and their adjacent LZs, as well as the topography, power lines and anything else that could make life difficult for us. We had no roving map display and no GPS.

The Alouette had no auto-pilot. The friction on the collective control had to be tightened while you changed a radio frequency or held a map. It became quite a balancing act, particularly in detailed navigation in poor weather. In border areas where the difference between being north or south of the invisible line could be a ditch or stream, it was exacting. In much the same way as they had forced us to make simulated emergency landings in the Dublin mountains, our instructors chopped and changed our route as we flew to and from barely distinguishable border crossings. We stayed in army bases and barracks, living and flying with the army.

Our instructors were getting to the point where their input was minimal. They would brief us on what they wanted done and off we would go. The new aspect was flying with a crewman. They were generally engineers and their job was to ensure the tail rotor was clear, coming and going from LZs. Alouette flying built up our relationship with crewmen and our understanding of crew co-operation. As pilots we could fly but we were a whole lot better assisted and informed thanks to our crewmen. Border flying developed that enormously to the point where crewmen became our map holders, navigators and weather advisers, effectively our co-pilots. Two CRM years before the term was incorporated into pilot training.

We were almost there. The unit needed us and we were almost finished. We would not be put straight in SAR yet but we were trained in its fundamentals. Our crew grew to three:

winch operator and winchman. One operated the electric hoist and the other attached to that hoist to go down to the person in distress.

The hoist cable on the Alouette 3 was 100 feet long. It could be lengthened by adding straps, 20 feet each, onto the hoist hook, onto which the winchman hooks himself. First of all we would attempt to pick something up off the ground. A large multi-hooked grapple was attached to the hoist hook and we were ready. The 'thing' we were trying to pick up was called a 'drum'. It was a home-made box with wires and bits sticking out to snag the grapple hook. The circuit we had flown in the Marchetti was repeated again, this time at 200 feet instead of 1,000, and much tighter. The drum was a survivor, waving at us in the water. We had to turn and bank and descend aggressively, keep it in sight, fly over the drum and pick it up.

With the drum on the ground we called this exercise 'dry drums'. I remember flying the circuit, coming in on finals, seeing the drum all the time, watch it disappear below me as I came over it and then the fun began: 'Forward four, forward three, forward two, forward one; steady. Steady.'

Steady, meant that we were right over the target. I looked at my instruments and I had no help in holding my position. I looked out at a tree a hundred yards away. It seemed steady but when I looked to my right, I saw that I was starting to drift. I had no height references. The tree was too far away and I could only look at my power and attitude, which were not precise.

And so the patter would go on, and on. Ten minutes is a long time trying to pick up a dry drum. Ten minutes is a long time when you become frustrated and exhausted. In the debrief, the winch operator encouraged me by saying that if I could stay within one unit of the drum, the winchman would be able to swim to a survivor in the water. Like everything with flying, it gradually comes. Gradually that beautiful patter comes over my helmet intercom: 'Forward and down three, forward and down two, forward one, height good, steady, steady, grapple beside the drum, drum attached, winching the drum clear, drum approaching the cabin door, good hover. Clear up and around'. I had managed to 'rescue' a drum from the long grass.

Next was wet drums. Same exercise except at sea or in the Blessington lakes. First of all we were issued with immersion flying suits. These were like dry diving suits with pockets, a neck seal and wrist seals. They were either yellow or green and were standard issue to military aircrew around the world. We wore tracksuits or warm long johns or 'bunny suits' underneath to keep warm. The immersion suit kept out water but did not keep you warm. Getting in and out of them was a skill in itself, contorting ourselves to fit in snugly, then pull the neck seal over our heads, having chalked it first so it would not rip. Then pull the zip up and finally make sure the suit was airtight by bending at the knees, expelling air through the neck seal. A routine that became automatic over the coming years. The whole reason for the suit was to survive as long as possible in case we ditched.

At Dublin Bay we picked a position that was clear of boats and set to work. Hovering over the sea was the new environment, the new sensation for us. A pattern developed quickly. A frustrating pattern. I would fly the tight winching circuit, even though it was daytime, the instrument scan and timing were critical as the sea was featureless and monotonous. The winch operator would tell me when the target was at the correct position: 'Target at four o'clock'.

'Roger, turning finals,' I would reply.

I would turn finals, see the drum bobbing in the water, listen to the winch operator and line myself up on it, slowing gracefully to the hover. But I could not pick it up. I had nothing to use as a reference in any axis. I started to drift right. Then I would correct and start to sink. Starting to sweat and getting annoyed with myself, then the winch operator would say: 'You're very close all the time, but let's pull back and start again. Get a new line'.

I would obey his patter again, moving back until I could see the drum.

'In sight', I would reply, looking at the drum rising and falling on the minuscule waves. 'Running in', I would say, ready to have another go. This went on and on. Sometimes I could pick it up after a few minutes. Other times it took the entire flight. Now and again I could not get it at all and our winchman would attach to the cable and go down to get it, much to my embarrassment.

Wet drums was a humbling exercise that heightened a pilot's sense of hearing and appreciation of the winch operator and his patter. I used my eyes to scan inside and outside as usual, but sound was becoming even more important. In aviation they say that your mental model of where you are, your spatial awareness, is critical. I was beginning to understand that the mental model of a SAR helicopter pilot is formed not by him alone but by the entire crew.

Picking up wet drums out of the sea became a cause for celebration. It is great to line up on the target, ease forward, hear the winch operator say 'steady' and then 'winching the drum clear'. Ignoring the waves that go past your feet on the pedals, trying to fool you into thinking that you are moving forward when you are holding a good hover. Believing your ears and your winch operator and not your eyes. Quite a change from instrument flying.

Time for the business of SAR. No more drums, dry or wet.

We flew out to a small boat contracted for the purpose, and did deck winching on and off the aft deck, the fore deck and then the bridge. The small boat operated by Mick Purcell and his family, ringing us each morning to see if we wanted him. 'Hi. Mick Purcell, boatman here. How are we fixed?' Training over the years depended on Mick's modest boat setting out into Dublin Bay, each helicopter crew flying for an hour or so, Mick staying sometimes all day, changing course and speed on our instructions. A generation of SAR crews alighted onto his deck. He would hear us coming over Dún Laoghaire, hurriedly put away his flask of tea and ham sandwich; call us on Channel 16.

Few of us got to know him. That was the nature of our business. It would be repeated over our careers. People who were integral to our training, our operation and our success, overlooked and forgotten. Not intentionally but forgotten nonetheless. Much as we ourselves would be. One day, his own boat sank. Mick clung to his boat with his son, as it took water and sank below him. Our own Alouette 3 came to the rescue. It was his first time inside the helicopter.

Mick would chug along at ten knots and we would fly along behind, easing forward to drop our winchman on and then flying our circuit back to collect him again. With this type of winching I could see the deck right below my feet, very close, the Dublin Bay sea state very light. We would go through all the different types of deck winching scenarios. Left to right, right to left, downwind, drifting; whatever could happen, we would practice it. Sometimes able to see the deck, sometimes not. The winchman used hand signals to communicate with the winch operator above; the winch operator pattered me to position.

Thrown in for good measure was communication failure when the patter stopped. The winch operator could unplug his helmet lead by accident as he leaned out the cabin door or water from rain or sea spray could get in the system. The solution was hand signals. Once everything went quiet, the pilot was supposed to freeze wherever he was. This would give the winch operator time to winch the winchman clear. Like a referee giving a standing count to a dazed boxer, the hand thrusting forward into our peripheral view, first four fingers, then three, and so on. The winch operator indicating with the number of fingers held up, the number of units to go, the hand pointing out the direction. And when in position, a clenched fist meaning 'Steady'. The pilot having to turn slightly to see. Our co-operation stripped down to its barest essentials and still able to function.

Before finishing our course and being released into helicopter operations, we were to do engine off landings (EOLs), and then travel the entire west coast, navigating to all the island LZs and refuelling points. EOLs gave us practice at auto-rotating down to the ground without the engine running and therefore no safety net. We climbed to about 1,500 feet and then lowered the collective, simulating an engine failure and dropped like a stone. We turned into wind and lined up on the runway, the windmilling blades still providing directional control, and then shut the engine down as we passed 500 feet. The technique after that was to flare with nose up to slow down the rate of descent. Then pitch forward to level the aircraft and protect the tail and finally and most crucially, pull in the dormant collective. This had the effect of increasing the angle on the pitch blades, so they would act like a parachute and we would alight gracefully onto the runway. With the engine off, we only had one chance to get it right.

Once we had it figured out, we repeated it until we were consistent and then repeated it without the instructor. That was every bit as enjoyable as the first solo, five years previously. Exhilarating to start up the Artouste turbine engine, climb, and then turn the same engine off again. The whine of the engine fading as we dropped, the blades getting faster. Checking that acceleration with a nudge of collective to keep the rotor RPM at the same figure. And then the ground coming closer, rapidly. Doing what we had done before, pitch up, collective check, pitch forward and then pull the remaining collective: level attitude for landing. The wheels touching on gently and a shout into my helmet, audible to me and my crewman alone as the blades slowed.

After all the training and media coverage, the Dauphin helicopters finally arrived in Baldonnel in June 1986. Our course was still dragging along, low on the list of priorities as the new age dawned. I was very proud to be a part of the unit on that day. Operating unseen for much of the year, taking unbalanced criticism for the delay in the Dauphin's arrival, the unit basked for a day at least in the positive glow of media publicity. Two helicopters arrived, with their distinctive deeper drone and beat, coming to a hover to great applause on the ramp.

Speeches were made, photographs taken and then a reception was held in the officers' mess. One of the symbols chosen for the helicopters was the cross of St Brendan. Made famous by Tim Severin after he crossed the Atlantic a few years before in a boat made of hide like St Brendan's. We would take on the Atlantic with his cross as our lucky emblem. The music in the mess that day, provided by none other than Liam Óg O'Flynn playing excerpts from *The Brendan Voyage* by Shaun Davey. Growing up in Tullamore in the 1970s, Liam Óg O'Flynn was a hero of my youth. To find him in Baldonnel that day seemed appropriate. I was not even close to flying the Dauphin but his presence and the choice of St Brendan, and the way the pipes made the hairs stand up on the back of my neck, is unforgettable. We were stirred by the music as it evoked the ocean, the islands and the elements.

And so they called. The ocean, the west coast and the islands called. We went soon after that, along the west coast on navigation and familiarisation flights, visiting the islands, refuelling depots and lighthouses. Each place had its own personality; each LZ its own difficulties and challenges. The west coast helicopter refuelling depots comprised the regional and international airports dotted along the way: Waterford, Cork, Farranfore, Shannon, Galway, Sligo, Carrickfinn, as well as other sites at Castletownbere, Clifden and Blacksod in Mayo. We made our way to the south-west, visiting each of these airports and landing at the lighthouses on the coast and the offshore islands and rocks, some of them still manned at that time.

The Fastnet Rock south-west of Cape Clear, the Bull Rock west of Castletownbere, Skellig Michael off Portmagee in Kerry, An Tíaracht west of Dingle, the Black Rock off the Mullet peninsula, Mayo. Dangerous precipitous landing pads depending on the wind direction. Making me appreciate the skill of our civil counterparts, who fly to those places routinely to maintain the warning lights. Each of the three Aran Islands and their small landing strips, as well as Inishturk, Inisboffin and Clare Island off Mayo. Numerous islands off the Donegal coast: Aranmore, Gola, Inisboffin, Tory and Inistrahull.

I briefly met people who would become friends over the coming years. Dónal Holland in Castletownbere and Vincent Sweeney in Blacksod. Little did I know the seeds of friendship that were being sown when we visited. Dark stormy nights ahead, when they and their families, unhesitatingly and cheerfully, would refuel us before we headed west.

In March 1987, Ciaran Parker and I finished that conversion course. That trip along the west coast, was our swan song, a reward for our patience on a slow, dragged-out course, for tests passed and effort made.

The helicopter is a modern machine, a machine of the twentieth century. But its bloodline goes much further back in time, to Leonardo da Vinci in Renaissance times. Imagined and created on vellum, its flight nothing but a dream. Our taking the Alouette 3 to the coast, to the ocean, to the islands, to the bleak beauty of our indented and dangerous coastline, felt like taking it home, to where it was meant to be. At least it felt like home to me.

6

IN THE DRAGONFLY

Make happy those who are near, and those that are far will come.
Anon.

We were firmly positioned on the bottom rung of the operational ladder. Considered competent enough to venture out on short trips in good or reasonable weather, we strained at the leash to battle the elements and prove our worth. Gradually over the years, we rose through the grades, filtered like coffee in reverse, emerging with our own 'there I was' stories to entertain ourselves and others on Fridays in the Bremen Bar.

Winchcrew constantly being trained, we busied ourselves flying in and out of confined LZs and making mountain approaches in the Dublin and Wicklow Mountains. The senior crewmen sat behind us, watching and instructing the new winchcrews while we flew, little realising, until later on, that as pilots, we ourselves were being assessed for when we would crew together as four men SAR crews. They made mental notes of our flying ability, our recklessness or carefulness, our arrogance or our willingness to listen to our crews. The more we flew the more we were being shaped, and accepted or rejected.

At that time, an Alouette 3 was always on SAR duty in Baldonnel. It represented the top rung of the ladder, a stepping stone to Dauphin night SAR, which was just about to commence. We started to fly along the border based once more in Monaghan and Donegal. For a week at a time, I used to stay there and fly. I spent the next few years flying from the Cooley Mountains near Carlingford Lough all the way to Lough Swilly near Derry. In between those weeks spent away, I returned to Baldonnel and lived there and in Tullamore whenever I could. Donegal, then a few days off. Then air ambulance flights and VIP flights. Then Monaghan and a few days off. Then every time there was an EU summit or visit or political meeting, or when whenever security was upped, we would be flying with heavily armed anti-terrorist members of the ranger wing.

I grew up in Tullamore with friends who stayed friends for ever. John Dowling, Brendan Galvin, Brian Jaffray, Paul Hogan, John Slattery, and many more classmates and adversaries in sport and young love. Ghosts from my past I still meet at home in the 'Brewery Tap', at funerals or rugby internationals. The Adamses, Ray Farrell, the staff at the school who always welcomed me when I came in to say hello or talk to potential aviators. But I was drifting away from Tullamore. An inevitable drift for sure, brought about by flying, and also playing rugby in a Dublin club with new friends. But a sad drifting that I did not notice, caught in a current that was slow and gradual, like the ocean itself sweeping me onwards to God knows where.

Just as I had been fortunate with my friends at school, so I was again in Baldonnel and the army. My friends were fellow pilots. We flew the same missions, in the same changeable weather, in the same parts of Ireland. When we were off duty, we played rugby and drank cheap beer in the officers' mess, and expensive beer in Dublin. My wings course colleagues, John Hurley, Tony Owens and Seán Murphy, were now firm friends. We went to each other's weddings and the funerals of each others' loved ones. No words. Silent firm handshakes. Those that had qualified before us and after us, now merged into one group: Pearse MacCrann, Jim Lynott, Shane McKeown, Mick McNulty, Barry McLoughlin, Neil O'Mahony, Jim Kirwan and Andy Whelan, not just pilots but the engineers, army officers, professionals and administrators, Frank Tone, Maurice McCarthy, Gerry Williams and Paul Farrell. A big boisterous group, where laughter alternated with argument. Rivalries and in-fighting were put away as we sang 'Amhrán na bhFiann' with moist eyes in Landsdowne Road each spring, or Croke Park each summer.

Apart from one or two very good players, we were average to good rugby players. The defence forces rugby championship had not been won by an air corps team for twenty-one years. In 1987 we won it and again in 1988. (It has not been won since.) I still meet former players from that team. Flying memories are pushed out of the way quickly, like furniture in a dusty attic in a search for the family photograph album, as we talk again about those victories.

I was flying around the country, working with the army and seeing Ireland in all weathers. In the most unlikely of places, the army could surprise you – bridge night in Collins Barracks, Cork, a dining-in night with music in Renmore, Galway. Music and culture were just under the surface. An officer in Donegal, Noel O'Grady, took us to traditional music nights in the winter. Margaret McGinley, musician, music teacher and composer, sometimes there, her music brought to life by Noel and others as we listened in reverential silence.

The geography books that we had pored over for years with Seamas O'Dea in the school in Tullamore, came to life below me. The basket of eggs, the drumlins, stretching from Clew Bay across Monaghan, to the Mourne Mountains. He had asked us to look up from the fields and bogs around our town, and imagine the hanging valleys and corrie lakes, that glaciers had left in their wake. As I flew, I saw them. Just as he had patiently explained. Killary Harbour, our only fiord. The corrie lakes in the Dublin Mountains, in Kerry and in the Twelve Bens.

There are many places in the world so beautiful that locals and visitors alike, call them 'God's own place'. Donegal is one such place, from the Blue Stack Mountains, over to Slieve Snaght to Glenveagh National Park and the Poisoned Glen. There were times when I could fly undisturbed and silent, while I listened to music provided from my own mental store. Enya was popular at the time. How appropriate it was to listen to 'Orinoco Flow', as I flew over her own townland, her own people. No need for an ipod. I had a limitless store of music in my brain that I could play and change at a whim. Her modern interpretation of old Irish tunes giving way to slow airs and the drone of uileann pipes as I flew over long deserted famine villages or islands where communities once lived, gone now, their memories enshrined in picture calendars in Boston and Adelaide and Letterkenny.

Accompanying me on some of those flights, was the chaplain of the battalion, Rev. Alan Ward. We struck up an unlikely friendship. Up and down the beautiful county we flew, me dropping off troops or supplies, he visiting the sick or saying mass at the various outposts. We flew in comfortable silence, me pointing out this valley or that ruin, his conversation rambling from spirituality to politics. And always time for a joke and a smile. Alan was a spiritual leader to the soldiers wherever they worked. In Donegal or south Lebanon, his soft northern accent, his listening patient ear, reassured the traumatised, the injured and the bereaved. As we returned to Finner Camp, I would often fly along the coast to where the seals lay basking in the sun at Murvagh beach, and on to where the surfers paddled into waves at Tullan Strand. It is never quite as enjoyable when you watch a film alone. So it was with flying in Donegal with Alan.

Over the years, Alan was chaplain to several United Nations Irish battalions in the Lebanon. He and another chaplain, Rev. Des Campion, took it in turns be in Donegal or the Middle East. Des was a cheerful man whose company illuminated many the grey wet day. Like Alan, he loved the novelty of flying and also enjoyed the sparring that went on between army and air corps, officers and soldiers, pilots and engineers, taking sides mischievously and watching the sparks fly.

I would ring up our private met forecaster, Gerry McDonald in Baldonnel, getting the low down on the weather. Gerry taught us how to understand the complexities of weather, the charts, the tephigrams and the TAF codes, when we were training, but once we were qualified, his weather briefs were altogether more practical: 'Inishowen and Buncrana? Today? I don't think so.'

Mountcharles and the Blue Stack Mountains. Gola Island and the beaches of the Rosses. Tory Island in defiant isolation. Islanders dashing back and forth in stormy twilight as we delivered milk and food. The lighthouse beam relentlessly searching the Atlantic, and then turning back to dazzle us in the grassy, muddy field. A brown paper bag and a bottle of whiskey thrust onto my lap. A clap on the back. I held the controls, the blades still turning. A shouted 'Gurra My' (*Go raibh maith agat* in a Donegal accent). Rathlin O'Beirne Island and the sweep of the cliffs at Slieve League. Donegal Bay and the lighthouse at St John's Point. Passing Killybegs and the trawlers coming or going. Ben Bulben brooding to the south.

The border from Ballyshannon to Beleek towards Lough Erne and Enniskillen was close to the ocean and Donegal Bay. In war years, RAF Sunderland and Catalina aircraft were based nearby at Castle Archdale, taking off on the lakes, flying across that narrow strip of Irish territory, on their way to protect allied shipping, and Irish shipping, from u-boats, thanks to a secret

deal with de Valera. My father had said little about his war years
when I was growing up, but I unconsciously created my own
story for him, stitching together the snippets that he divulged.
He appeared in cameo roles in my mental home movies, perhaps
smoking a cigarette in the gloom, in the background at Castle
Archdale, as pilots started their engines, the Sunderlands pushing back from the moorings, their engines coughing and belch-
ing in the twilight. The distance in time, between his war and my
life at the time, closed while I daydreamed.

I had a chance encounter with war time flyers. A Second
World War bomber was discovered in the bogs to the east of
Buncrana, on the Inishowen peninsula. I took Paddy Boyle and
his EOD [explosive ordnance disposal] team there. The Boyle
name is itself a Donegal name, and Paddy and I loved to fly
there for the sheer joy of it.

Underneath the wreck was a bomb, still intact, potentially
lethal. Paddy and his team went to work. I could see him meeting the gardaí, shaking hands, talking, and then walking towards a tractor. I waited as he carried out his first inspection.

When he came back, I asked if I could have a look too. We
walked across to where the aircraft lay hidden. A sunny day,
Lough Swilly behind us as we walked towards where a farmer
stood beside his tractor. While armed soldiers from the Rock-
hill post ranged around, we peered down into a waterlogged
hole in the ground. I could see the gleam of one of the engines.
Perfect engines.

A team of excavators had painstakingly researched the crash
and located the site. While digging, they had found one of the
500 lb bombs still intact. He pointed to it, black and oily with
yellow markings, almost invisible in the peat. It took the team a
long time to make it safe. It was a very real danger, and perfectly
preserved. While they worked, we waited, standing in the sun-

light listening as the story of the aircraft was told. It turned out that it was either a Bristol Blenheim or an Armstrong Whitworth Whitley. The crew had baled out and survived while returning to Belfast Aldergrove airport from a bombing mission targeting German u-boats. The clear skies above us, criss-crossed by forgotten aircraft and forgotten men.

Further east, from Cavan or Monaghan or Dundalk – 'Oh stony grey soil of Monaghan …' wrote Patrick Kavanagh – the drumlins and the lakes making a mockery of my efforts to find the invisible line of the border. We took off from Monaghan Barracks just before sunrise, low cloud and fog banks nestled in the hundreds of small drumlin valleys, waking up the boarders in St McCartan's College. The spire of the cathedral, standing sentinel over the sleeping town. An early rendezvous with fifty troops, in a field God knows where.

With troops on board in groups of four or five, we swooped up over the trees and made our way to some checkpoint, different altitudes, different routes, banking and weaving and following telegraph wires and local features. Unceremonious landing, we dropped them off and they ran, half crouching to avoid the blades overhead, weapons, radios and bergens, camouflaged and red-eyed. Over and back we flew, as the sun rose around us. The early low light, shining off the lakes and streams and rivers and dewy grass, blinded us as we banked. Flicking our sun visors down we turned east; visors up when we turned west, arriving at the pick up or drop off point, at different speeds, over different trees, from different directions, just as we had read in 'Chickenhawk', the story of a Vietnam helicopter pilot, in case someone unfriendly was watching through a cross hair. The fuel would run low and then we would fly away to return later to repeat the whole thing in reverse. 'How many was that, Paddy?' 'Forty-eight.' 'I told you we would get them all in!!' 'I wasn't sure we'd clear those trees when we had the big fellas on!' 'Ah come on, Paddy. You of little faith.'

The crewmen were our engineers too. The pilot was the officer, and therefore in charge. Officially. But we were a team, a crew of three. The old-fashioned rank structure may have stood between us but many became friends: Paddy McGurk, Iggy Callaghan, Frank Coughlan, Paul Coppinger, Colm O'Connor, Nick McNulty, Marti McGovern, Paddy Myles, Dan Baylor, Des Tone, Padge Carroll, Josh O'Shea, Simon Kennedy, Billo Booth, countless others. Professionalism and cheerfulness. What a great combination.

A sunny Saturday in Baldonnel. Summer time and the living was easy. The Alouette 3 SAR crew were arriving for duty along with all the other crews from around the base: those on security guard for the day, as well as the cooks and cookhouse staff, medics and drivers and so on. The small army of men and women who routinely serve the state, each and every day, unseen but always there. Some of their tasks modest, some not so, all essential. At the Wing HQ, the kettle boiled continuously, spoons and cups providing the percussion for the constant chatter of the crews, some leaving for their weekend off, replaced by the incoming duty crews.

The duty SAR crew that day was myself as pilot, Paddy Mooney and Paul Ormsby as winchcrew, and Paddy McGurk and Frank Coughlan our duty engineers. I had finally arrived at the hallowed ground of SAR qualification. Even though our responsibility was to be on rescue call for all coastal and mountain areas, weekends like this were often quiet. Flying hours were rationed so that the eager would not fly too much and push the aircraft back into maintenance too soon. At least that Saturday we had an exercise planned with Dublin-Wicklow Mountain

Rescue. Something to look forward to instead of hoping for an accident somewhere.

Every opportunity to train brings benefits to an SAR crew. The weather is always different, the wind direction never the same, the personality of each crew member and their interpretation of unfolding events and situations different. Each time they train, a new layer of experience is added. Extreme conditions are the ultimate challenge of course, but fair weather exercises still offer the opportunity to build.

We took off from Baldonnel that Saturday and flew towards the Wicklow Gap, checking in on the way with Dublin Radio on Channel 10, and always listening on the distress frequency, Channel 16.

We made our way south to the rendezvous point. Getting lower and lower as we reached the barren boggy mountains, our shadow following us like a ghost, mirroring our passing. Contouring the hills and banking sharply over the forests near Glenbride. We landed and shut down, and as the blades came to a stop, they began to move towards us. As the duty crew, we were flying with our full SAR kit on board: medical gear, folding stretcher, dry-immersion suits, weights, hi-lines and so on. All cumbersome and all in the way of our training if we were to take any of these team members flying.

As well as that, we had to organise ourselves and make the most of our time, both for their benefit and ours. It was the first time for some of us to meet each other, so tact and diplomacy were nice qualities to have too; no point in arriving and bossing around civilian volunteers who were giving up their weekend for nothing. But at the same time, a little bit of direction and instruction was and is necessary, especially when explaining the dangers of a helicopter to new people. The tail rotor, invisible at full RPM, could cut you in two like a bacon-slicer. The rotor blades capable of decapitating you if the terrain is sloping and if you don't crouch as you come and go from the helicopter. And the noise; disorientating, confusing, making you feel you have to rush. A lot to explain. And then we planned to take them flying. A lot to do.

The teams introduced themselves, and then the show began. I introduced myself, Paddy and Paul. I stepped aside pretty quickly, and Paddy began to talk. For the next hour or so, everyone was rapt. Paddy came from the ranger wing. He was a witty, quietly spoken Meath man, and was modest about his physical toughness. He gave a master class in briefing new rescuers. He put everyone at ease without understating potential dangers. He asked for questions and answered each one patiently. He unloaded all the SAR gear, explaining each and every part on the way, until the aircraft was almost empty. The aircraft was now ready for flying and the gear lay neatly stacked beside one of the Mountain Rescue jeeps. Paul was like the conjuror's assistant, demonstrating each item of the kit as Paddy directed him.

I sat on a wall, watching and listening. With me was Kevin O'Herlihy, an observer from the Baldonnel met office, who had come along for the outing. The rescuers were broken into groups of four. Paddy made them get into and out of the helicopter in the correct way, stopping them when they did the wrong thing, pausing to show dangers, asking them what they would do if this or that happened, all in his easy laconic style. I was hearing things I had not heard before and marvelled at how comfortable Paddy made everyone feel. I could see Kevin smile as Paddy cast a spell over us all. An hour passed by quickly and then we got ready to fly.

Cups of tea from thermos flasks first, of course, and hasty cigarettes for the smokers. And more learning for me as Paddy answered more questions, this time more probing; 'Are you ever scared?' 'How bad does the weather get?' 'What's the hardest rescue you ever did?' 'Can you fly at night?'

We took them flying then, collecting them and dropping them off on the slopes of Tonalagee. The three of us did not need to be in the aircraft at the same time, so Paddy and Paul took turns waiting at the Wicklow Gap, keeping a listening watch to the distress channel. We shut down for the last time and loaded the SAR kit back into the helicopter. The team leaders, Derek Keegan and Joe O'Gorman, with great ceremony thanked us on their behalf to applause. We returned the compliment and made ready to leave. As the blades reached full RPM, my abiding memory is of Paddy with his back to me, about thirty feet in front of the helicopter, wearing his helmet, shaking the hands of about fifty rescuers before we left. They waited their turn to shake his hand like a papal procession. Each smiled and shouted an inaudible, mouthed thank you to him. Paddy had made a big impression. He turned and got into the helicopter and we departed.

When Paddy died in Tramore years later, in the Dauphin crash, this was a memory of him that etched itself into my mind. Paddy was typical of the winching crew that I came to depend upon. They were the first to meet the public, to talk to them, to welcome them and brief them. The first to administer first-aid and emergency medical care to the injured, the maimed, the dying. Their example, their generosity, their humour and laughter, their zest for life, their ability to always find something positive in any situation, was evangelical at times. Sometimes bawdy, always tough and honest, they faced challenges and personal danger with a glow. As a pilot, it is difficult to put a winchman onto a deck in rough seas. After you have done it, and when you hold the helicopter back slightly from the deck, you can see the winchman looking up at you. You watch the deck rolling, seeing him struggling to hold his footing as waves wash over the deck, seeing him look upwards, and giving a thumbs-up sign. And then being led away by one of the ship's crew, down into the bowels of the ship, to attend to an injured person.

In rugby, scoring tries is the glamour part but a big tackle can reverse the flow of a game. So it often was with a winchman and a SAR crew. Watching and waiting and then seeing the winch-man reappear on deck. Perhaps with a casualty on a stretcher, slipping and sliding, struggling with the other deck hands, telling us on the radio or with a thumbs-up that he was ready. The buzz of adrenaline that it gave us, gave me.

They way that Paddy faced challenges, the way winchcrew faced challenges, was with a glow that was almost holy. That glow illuminated my path for many years.

7

WHAT THE DRAGONFLY SAW

Commitment to the team – there is no in-between. You are either in or out.
Anon.

Because of its speed and ability to get in and out of small places, the Alouette 3 was ideal for air ambulance. If a call came in, a decision would be made to use the SAR aircraft or whatever was available. Training would stop and the stretcher, oxygen equipment and medical gear hastily fitted. We were called by the gardaí, ambulance controllers or hospital matrons, sent to any part of the country, sometimes taking people to specialist care, or to a hospital for emergency procedures, other times taking islanders ashore in rough seas; whatever was demanded.

The National Rehabilitation Hospital in Dún Laoghaire developed a special spinal stretcher for the Alouette 3. Over the years, the Alouette and its crew would dash over to Dún Laoghaire, collect a doctor, and make their way to accident scenes, stabilise the patient in the stretcher, take them rapidly back for specialist care. A simple stretcher, a modest helicopter but a potentially life-changing mission that could put people back on their feet walking again. My first insight into working with teams, outside of my own, was with medical teams working unheralded, helping us to live up to our motto: '*Go Mairidis Beo*; That Others May Live.'

One day I received a call to go to Inisboffin, off the Galway coast. Someone needed urgent medical care. An air ambulance mission or, island medevac for short, as we called them. Weather bad, seas rough, rain, as Eamonn Burns and I set off under a cloud layer that squeezed us lower and lower. At Galway we could see no clearance to the west, so we turned north and made our way along the Lough Corrib shoreline, hoping to get through to Killary Harbour and the sea. After Oughterard we turned north-west with the Maumturks on our left, hidden in the gloomy rain. The road was a good feature to follow, and Eamonn was poring over the map as the cloud got lower still, the road closer and closer. The dark sky started to brighten. The horizon ahead of us showed the road cresting with clearness behind. 'Thanks Eamonn', I would have said.

I started to accelerate as the visibility improved. A car coming towards us, flashed its lights as we eased over into Killary Harbour. It was clearer and we were greatly encouraged. Turning west and passing Renvyle, we could make out the distinctive shape of the island. The rest of the flight was easier. The sick person was a woman who needed an operation the next day, worried about being marooned in a storm. Under a brightening sky, we loaded up, said hello and goodbye and made ready. 'Will it take ye long to get to Galway?' 'Is that all?' 'She's a great machine altogether. She's been here before, but its been a while.' 'Which way did ye come?'

Tears of goodbye and good luck. A nurse holding the woman's hand, smiling down at her as we flew south. The improved weather allowed us to fly right over Ballyconneely and Roundstone, where I had spent so much time as a child. 'We'll be at the hospital in ten minutes', I shouted to the nurse and the woman in the stretcher, both nodding, relieved. The vagaries of Irish weather were gone from my mind now. We were going to complete our mission. Eamonn and I could enjoy flying with the finish line in sight. Success. A nice feeling.

Wouldn't it be great if every flight could be like that? They're not. I took a man home to die on another flight. It was not phrased like that but we knew. It was whispered to me before I left Baldonnel. 'His treatment is over now. He is too weak to travel back by road. He lives nearly seven hours from Dublin. You are taking him home. To be with his family'.

We picked him up in Phoenix Park from an ambulance. What could I say? I introduced myself, awkwardly, and showed him the route to his home. 'When we get closer, you can show me where it is exactly, and what way you would like to fly over the area. OK?'

He smiled weakly. The nurse asked him if he wanted to lie flat, or to have the stretcher raised so he could look out. He decided to sit. It was a beautiful day. The view from an Alouette 3 is fantastic on days like that, especially going to his part of the country, the plains of Kildare, the familiar Bog of Allen, the mountains to the west, then rugged coastline, inlets and islands. As we flew, I turned to him and called out the names of the towns, the villages. Now and again I turned and his eyes were closed, half smiling, the shadow of the turning blades flickering across his pale forehead. I looked out at Ireland through the eyes of a dying man.

And when we got him home, he pointed and smiled, as we flew over his village, his fields, before alighting at the nearby hospice. 'Will ye come in for tea lads? There's sandwiches made. Come on, come on'. Embarrassed by the offer of tea so soon, we shook his hand and wished him well. As he was brought inside, his family and his friends gathered around him welcoming him warmly. We took our cups of tea and plates of sandwiches outside sitting on a stone wall not wanting to intrude. Children came with more tea and buns. 'Mammy wants to know do ye want more tea!'

VIPs do not like to see their pilots straining over maps or flying low to read road signs and they like them to be neat, wearing caps and ties. The reassurance of neat pilots, cushioned seats, newspapers and coffee, go hand in hand with flying VIPs. And why not? At least that was our approach, slightly different to normal flying. When you were considered VIP flying standard, you had the job of flying government ministers to this or that meeting, army generals to parades and exercises – shiny flying boots, neat haircut (done the day before, when you were told you were 'caught' for a VIP flight), a crisp salute.

'Good morning sir. If you'd like to step this way. Our crewman, sir. This is Sgt McNulty. He will need to sit beside the door. Which seat would you like? The weather is fine. There are a few showers forecast. It should take us about an hour and a half'.

Their eyes would widen as they took in the cramped space they and their three colleagues were to occupy. As the blades started turning the Alouette 3 vibrated and shook. As Nicko got in, strapped in and connected to the intercom, they waited with bated breath. On the ground is not where the Alouette 3 is happiest. Once in the air, it was as if the helicopter sighed with relief and went on its way, vibrationless and smooth. The VIPs often sighed too.

The president himself as well as successive taoisigh and government ministers were frequent passengers. By the time I flew the Alouette 3, the Dauphin had just arrived and was the first choice. Nevertheless, our trustworthy helicopter, leaking rainwater a bit at the door seals, with few seats and lacking in comfort, obediently brought them where directed. On a very wet day in Castlebar airport, one government minister almost finished my career and his life. We landed in a downpour. As I was explaining to him, again, that I would shut down the rotors and the engine before he could get out, the minister dashed out of the helicopter. Before I could stop him, he ran towards the back of the helicopter, the part you never approach. Ever. The tail rotor was practically invisible. A veritable vegetable slicer, towards which my VIP was sprinting in the rain.

'Red!!' I shouted. Red O'Keane, my crewman, was already after him.

A lot went through my mind in those seconds: my career, his life. Should I pull max collective and lift vertically? Was there any point in shutting the engine and blades down? I looked over my right shoulder, waiting for him to emerge hoping that I would not feel a thud and see blood spray onto the perspex. Would the RPM drop if the tail rotor cut him neatly in two?

Red emerged arm around the minister's shoulder, laughing amicably in the rain. They shook hands. The minister went to his waiting car. Red came to me.

'Well?' I said.

'I rugby tackled him just before he got to the tail. He got a shock but I didn't knock him over: he's a big man. But he got the message.'

'And did you say anything?'

'No. I was going to but it's raining and he's in a hurry. But as we walked around the tail, I pointed the tail rotor to him. He understood then.'

'Red, I owe you big time. Well done and thanks very much.'

Red and I flew on numerous occasions over the coming years and it was not the only time he did me a favour. On one flight, the VIP was not in the helicopter but on the ground. On St Valentine's Day, we diverted from a patrol. As we approached a farmhouse, we saw a girl looking up at us. As we flew past and returned, she waved and more people came out of the house. Red opened the door and dropped a well wrapped box of choco- lates. Looking up was my girlfriend, my future wife, as her father retrieved the box, on which was written: 'And all because the lady loves Milk Tray.'

The roles and missions given to the Alouette 3 were many and varied, but SAR was arguably the number one. It was the role that captured the imagination of the public when helicopters first came into air corps service. It captured the imagination of the crews who performed that role as well. When time caught up on her in the late 1980s, with the arrival of the Dauphin, her SAR days drew to a close. The crews were busy training for Dauphin operations and all the challenges that came with night SAR.

However, in early 1989 the Alouette 3 found itself back in a daylight SAR role. This time without a winch, as all the winching crews were committed to the Dauphin. The cynics unkindly called this role 'Search & Wave', and said it was a waste of time because all we could do for someone in distress was to wave to them! Personally, I relished the flying. Fifty percent of SAR is Search I reckoned, and it was better to do that well and direct rescuers on the ground or at sea than do nothing at all.

Those who flew the Alouette 3 in this role were either waiting (hopefully!) for their turn to train on the Dauphin, or not going to continue in SAR. For example, engineers were no longer to operate as winchcrew, but stick to engineering. Winchcrews were to be totally dedicated to their craft. Alas, such was the wisdom of the time. However, some of the winch-qualified engineers continued to operate as crewmen on the new 'winchless' Alouette 3. Their experience was vast, a great asset. Along with them were winchcrew who were finishing in SAR. The result was a hybrid crew of pilots, bubbling with enthusiasm and experienced former winch operators who knew everything there was to know about the aircraft and about rescue. It was an under-rated and highly effective mix.

During a beautiful spell of early summer weather, a German walker went missing on Mount Brandon in Kerry. We were tasked with sending an aircraft down to search for him. For us as Dublin and Wicklow trained crews, the Kerry mountains held an extra appeal. They were altogether more dangerous, with more pronounced glaciated features, knife edges instead of grassy saddles, corrie bowls and lakes that could lure you in and suck away all your power. Even the names of the features were more threatening: the Devil's Ladder, the Eagle's Nest, the Black Valley, Howling Ridge. Dauphin SAR training was in full swing, so my partner was to be Sgt Jimmy Dunne. I was in the queue for Dauphin training while Jimmy was moving aside for the younger guns, having already given a lifetime to SAR.

We set off for the south-west in beautiful weather. We were to overnight in Ballymullen Barracks, Tralee and refuel out of barrels stored there and at the met office at Valentia and met station at Caherciveen. We had unlimited flying hours and were to do whatever the gardaí and the mountain rescue team wanted. We flew to an LZ in a large grassy field behind O'Connor's pub in Cloghane village on the east side of Mount Brandon. A large crowd was assembled there. Garda cars and blue flashing lights: helmeted, rope laden teams stood around as we touched down. Mount Brandon had grown in size as we had approached from Tralee, passing Castlegregory and Fermoyle on the way. The second highest mountain in Ireland, at 3,100 feet, it towered above us now that we were at its base. This was going to be interesting.

Over the next two days, the whole area was combed and searched by our combined teams. Kerry Mountain Rescue searched on the ground, making their way in and out of the various search areas, by walking in on foot or being dropped off by us where possible. When we were not dropping teams off or collecting them, we were searching the inaccessible and difficult areas from above. From north to south, from Sauce Creek, a horseshoe shaped indent where Brandon drops into the Atlantic in a 1,500 feet drop, to An Cnapán Mór, north of Dingle. We landed teams of searchers on Masatiompan, Brandon Mountain, Brandon Peak, Ballysitteragh, among the corrie bowls and their chain of lakes running from the Owenmore river valley up to Brandon itself. The terrain rising in terraces, ever more precipitous, beautiful but deadly for us with its unpredictable winds, flying in the shadow of Brandon itself.

All our training of mountain flying was put into effect. We prepared and briefed each and every team, breaking away from ridges when the power checks failed, hovering cautiously on the arrêtes with the terrain dropping off on both sides, and all in fantastic clear weather, the helicopter working hard all the time. Watching the power on the pitch gauge, waiting for each person to de-plane, I still admired the view of the Blaskets or the Three Sisters and Smerwick Harbour. Each sweep of the mountain revealed more and more beauty.

I flew with search dogs for the first time and marvelled at their calm as the helicopter landed, lying still in the grass, motionless, waiting for instructions. Their heads on their front paws, looking asleep, their alertness given away only by their unblinking eyes fixed on mine as I touched down. Given the signal to load up, they rose lazily to their feet and walked slowly to the helicopter. They did not get in until they got another signal and then they sat behind me. Jim closed the door and just before we lifted off, I looked round and found myself face to face with a very large German Shepherd. If it is possible for a dog to smile, he was smiling at me.

Those dogs and their handlers covered vast areas of land. Whenever we arranged to meet them on the mountain, no matter where, no matter when, the dog-handlers and their dogs would appear as we touched down or hovered over uneven ground. It was, quite literally, beautiful to behold.

We were driven relentlessly by the Kerry Team leader, Con Moriarty, and his cohort Mike O'Shea. He had a helicopter at his beck and call, and a helicopter crew who had not said 'no' yet, and by God was he going to make the most of it! We did almost everything he asked, limited only by having to go away at intervals to refuel. Otherwise we showed up very early each morning and stayed until just before last light. Con and Mike subsequently went on to achieve fame and notoriety as high altitude climbers around the world. What a way for a pilot to cut his teeth in mountain flying.

We returned to Baldonnel after exhaustive searching. We said our goodbyes to the many people we had met and searched with: the mountain rescue teams, gardaí, people from Cloghane who put up with the disruption and gave us limitless tea and sandwiches and the use of the telephone. Leaving Kerry, flying over the countryside, each lost silently in thought. Jim Dunne certainly had my respect. I wondered if I had his? He had been cautious of the lack of wind and the high temperature, and knew we would be stuck for power. He was wary of my exuberance. He held me in check. 'That ridge over there looks like a better bet, Dave'. He encouraged me. He helped me. He praised me now and then and scolded me just as often. He cautioned me with his deadpan humour. 'Give me a chance to slow down to a gallop, and I'll be right with you, sir.' (Jim had an automatic on the ground/off the ground 'sir' switch. He couldn't call me sir in the air and he couldn't call me Dave on the ground. Standard issue in SAR crews.)

Jimmy was on one of his last SAR missions but left an indelible mark on me. He taught me a lot, about flying, about winchcrew, about rescue. He was typical of the winchcrew I would encounter over the years: tough, modest, brave and witty and great company to boot.

The missing man was found on the third day by a shepherd and his dog. He had fallen beneath rocks, and suffered fatal injuries. It was a sad and tragic end to our search. For his family, there was closure, and the comfort of laying him to rest with dignity. For me, it gave a taste of what was to come in SAR: the struggle of man against the elements, learning to come to terms with disappointment as well as success.

8

PILATUS MOUNTAIN 1938

If you see no reason for giving thanks, the fault lies in yourself.

Anon.

Looking through family photographs, I found black and white snapshots of my parents. 'Where's that mum?' I asked, looking at a photograph of my father and another man standing on the icy slope of a mountain. 'I think that was in Switzerland. Before the war. Ask your father when he comes home.' The photos were in boxes, unnamed and undated. For some reason the one of my youthful father standing on a mountain with a pipe in his mouth intrigued me. I was home for the weekend from Baldonnel. I had arrived in, as usual, with a bag of washing and an appetite.

While a casserole bubbled in the oven, I sat by the fire and told them my news. They would tell me the local news: the births, deaths and engagements. I was eager to meet up with my schoolfriends, to go to The Brewery Tap and then the rugby club. When I saw the box of photographs, I hesitated, no longer in a rush to get out.

'Ah yes. That was when I was eighteen. It was 1938, just before the war started. Went to Switzerland. That mountain was near Lucerne. I think it was called Pilatus Mountain.'

'How high was it, dad? Did it take long to climb?'

He laughed. 'No, there was a railway to very near the top. We just walked across the snow and posed, pretending to be climbers. Then the war started and all hell broke out just after that.'

The war stole almost seven years of my parents' lives. They lost their entire peer group of friends. They survived with their lives, just about. But those lives were shattered completely. All they had known was wiped out. The man in the photograph, at eighteen years of age, looked at me, his son, nineteen years of age. Both with their lives in front of them. Both not knowing what lay ahead, but facing it with an optimistic smile.

He never talked about his war years except late at night after too much to drink and even then he would tell the anecdotes that were funny and ironic about the black market and cherry brandy, chocolate and cigarettes. The thin line between comedy and tragedy, when his tears of laughter would turn to tears of pain, at the memory of dead friends and comrades. Always he would finish, shaking his head ruefully, sniffing back those tears, and saying 'Those were such wasted years'. At parties when we lived in town, smiling defiantly and raising his glass to me and whoever was there, the Adamses, the Mac-Canns, Paddy Lloyd, he would say, 'Eat drink and be merry, for tomorrow we die!!'

The air corps meets and swaps ideas with other military air forces from time to time to share the latest techniques on training and operating, keeping up to date and fresh. Over the years, exchanges have regularly taken place with the RAF and royal navy. Search and rescue and in particular, night operations, have been high on the list of priorities for discussion. Exchanges with the French navy and US coast guard have also taken place, particularly as they use the Dauphin. In 1990, the Swiss air force extended an invitation to the air corps to send two pilots to fly the Alouette 3 in the high Alps. Because so many of our unit's senior pilots were no longer 'current' on the Alouette 3, being involved with the Dauphin, they had to go further down the list of pilots to pick two: Dermot Hickey and me. 'You jammy bastard', said more than one or two, as I got ready to go.

The two weeks were spent in Alpnach air force base near Lucerne. Our liaison pilot was Capt. Reudi van Flue. We also flew with Lt Col Charlie Bachman. Flying approaches in the Superpuma to knife-edged ridges, lifting timber with long lines and explaining so much of that aircraft and its operation. A thoroughly generous man with his knowledge and flying wisdom. We were indeed fortunate to have him and Reudi looking after us. Our flying programme was organised and run with typical Swiss precision, taking us over the basics of mountain flying, and building up to high altitude flying. It came as a pleasant surprise to us to see that the techniques and theory of helicopter flight in the mountains were the same for them as for us. The obvious difference being the much higher altitude. For the first few flights we simply got to know our hosts and demonstrated that we could fly as per their style and standard. All the while looking forward to getting into the higher Alps.

The Alouette 3 helicopters they used were coloured green, had different radios and slightly different modifications but apart from that it felt like flying one of our own machines. Gradually we reached the high Alps and the infamous mountains: the Matterhorn, Eiger, Breithorn, Jungfrau, Monta Rosa, Dufour Spitse. Carefully flying in the thin air, our shadows followed us across glaciers and arrêtes, instead of bays and bogs.

Our hosts were gracious, and we travelled all around Switzerland. We met other pilots, both military and civil. We visited REGA, a civilian helicopter rescue organisation that used the Alouette 3 too. It was a revelation to me to see that that SAR was shared between civilian and military operators. They worked together. They respected each other. I must have soaked that in at some level although I did not realise it at the time.

The following year we returned the compliment. Reudi and another pilot visited Ireland and by that stage, I flew both the Alouette 3 and the Dauphin. We were able to mix the flying and take them on many low level coastal navigation flights taking in the many jewels Ireland has to offer. We barely showed them the mountains for obvious reasons, but we showed them the wild west coast and they loved it.

I took many memories home from that exchange. We tried to incorporate into our operation at home in the air corps the things that were new to Dermot and me. For instance, they had a different way of demonstrating and avoiding vortex ring, a potentially fatal phenomenon, where a helicopter cannot stop dropping through its own downdraft, and tail rotor control failure exercises. Flying at altitude among those beautiful mountains, valleys and glaciers, was unforgettable.

But there was one mountain that I particularly enjoyed. It was about 7,000 feet high. Half the height of some of the mountains we landed on. It was beside Alpnach air base, so it was not a long distance in flying time. We landed on it during the first week. Before we left, I asked if we could include it one more time, on a training flight. Close to the top was a restaurant with panoramic views, linked to the valley floor by the world's longest cogwheel railway. The same one my father had travelled on fifty-two years before. It was Pilatus Mountain.

ST BRENDAN THE NAVIGATOR

A minute of success pays for years of failure.

Anon.

My Alouette 3 days were drawing to a close. I had completed training on the Dauphin in late 1990. In February 1991, I flew my first mission on it. That flight sticks in my mind. I had done numerous training flights, getting used to the different instrumentation, flying as part of a two pilot crew and returning to instrument flying. Dauphin flying also meant a return to night flying but that flight was for me the start of my new SAR career. It was an enjoyable flight made easy by the light workload and the company of my captain that day, Comdt Aidan Flanagan.

The mission was an island medevac once more from Inisboffin to Galway Regional Hospital. Aidan was a midland man like myself. As a commandant, he was a senior officer, a man I saluted on the ground and called sir but in the air he was Aidan: great company, a gifted and patient instructor and pilot. That day, he abbreviated the checks so that my 'newness' would not slow us down, he took control and we were off.

From Shannon, we climbed up and over the Burren into low cloud, the wet greyness leaving lines of moisture on our windscreens as we made for Slyne Head, an area that would become very familiar to me over the next decade. I tried to keep pace with the Dauphin as it slipped along at almost 180 MPH makin

ATC calls to Shannon, completing the flight log and perform-
ing the descent, approach and pre-transdown (transition down)
checks as required. I got the maps and charts ready and checked
our position against the radar return and the Nadir computer. It
was going to be a misty, foggy and very low level approach to the
island. I was busy.

All the while Aidan helped and explained, demonstrating
the radar and comparing its return with the admiralty chart
positioned between us. Once assured of our position over Galway Bay, clear of the Aran Islands and the coast, we descended
carefully until we could see the white tops of the sea 200 feet
below us, and enough visibility for us to keep moving forward.
Just about. All the while Aidan chatting to our winchcrew, Ben
Heron and Alan Gallagher, as if walking in the park.

The LZ on the island is a small concrete pad beside Murray's
Hotel. Just west of the harbour, on the south-west of the island,
we orientated the map so that the features of the island would
match the radar screen in front of us. With less than a mile
visibility, we got ready for landing, decelerating, watching the
red shape of the island grow on the screen in front of us. All
of this automated, programmed, monitored, smooth, controlled,
surreal. We were facing into the wind, the wind magically sensed
by the helicopter's air data system, fed into the auto-pilot and
displayed on our screens. We were magically lined up on the LZ
and then the island came into view. First grey and vague, then
darkening until we could clearly make out rocks, white water
and the hotel in front of us. A sudden sense of speed, as we had
visual references again.

Ben opened the door beside the winch and started to patter
us forward. As he did, his microphone picked up and amplified
the sound of the engines as they responded to the extra workload of slowing us to the hover. As we made our approach I

watched the engine parameters and power as I was trained to do. But I watched the shore too, as it got closer and then went under us. The sea giving way to rocks and then grass beneath my feet. I watched the onlookers come into view on the right hand side then disappear as we came high over them then appearing again, levitating like angels, rising upwards as we sank to the ground. In front of us we could see other people in the hotel pub looking out of the window raising their pint glasses to us in salute as they caught our eyes.

Aidan turned to me and Ben and laughed: 'Afraid we can't have a pint here today, lads. Some other time maybe!' We shut down and got out to meet the islanders. The casualty was in a nearby car. Ben went over to get him ready. Others mingled and introduced themselves. With no gardaí on the island, Aidan had to mix his friendliness with authority. He did it easily seeking out the local hierarchy with a smile, keeping others at a safe distance.

I had been to the island before by boat and in the Alouette helicopter. In good weather and bad. I had been in that very pub and looked out with a pint in my hand, walked it from east to west and back again. I had read about it in one of my parents' favourite books: *The way that I went*, by R.L. Praeger, a book taken from the shelf whenever a newspaper article or TV programme dealt with islands or the far flung wilderness of our Atlantic coastline. It was brought on holidays with us to Roundstone, Kenmare, Dunlewy and Inisboffin. This time low cloud and mist and fog had not hampered us. I liked this a lot.

We departed soon afterwards with our patient on board. The descent into Galway Bay, easier and faster, we landed at the hospital pad where a medical team and ambulance awaited us. The flight was effortless because Aidan had done all the work for me. He was an experienced captain, while I was still getting

used to the aircraft and the routine. As time went on, the workload shifted onto me and the other co-pilots as we were made
ready for command. A gradual process of propping us up and
helping us and then bit by bit withdrawing that assistance. In
a four man crew, the assistance was never actually taken away.
Part of the learning process was to be able to make decisions
based on the contribution of the crew. We were eager to be
promoted to command but also privately half afraid of the role
and the responsibility that went with it.

In those days Shannon Marine Rescue Control centre was
located in a nearby building. Mick Cotter and Eamonn Dillon,
among many others, built up a great rapport with the Dauphin
crews. But, apart from that mission out of Shannon, all of my
SAR duties after that were carried out in Finner Camp, Donegal. The Dauphin had started first in Baldonnel, then it had
moved to Shannon then to Donegal when civil SAR started in
Shannon. My flying duties were a rotation between SAR duty
for a week followed by a naval patrol with the *LE Eithne*, with
VIP and general flights after that. Having spent the previous
few years on the Alouette 3, I looked forward with relish to the
challenges that lay ahead: night operations, night navigation,
night winching. Following in the footsteps of St Brendan.

We all know the geography of the Atlantic coast. Heavily
indented, beautiful by day, its cliffs, bays, inlets and many islands
make for challenging navigation. Wherever a SAR mission takes
a crew, accurate coastal navigation is critical at all times. They
must be able to get to anywhere in any weather, in darkness. The
simple act of slowing down and making an approach to an island
is all the more dangerous with zero visual references and cliffs
and mountains whistling past unseen in the dark.

Winching someone on and off a deck at night is an altogether
different proposition than by day with no peripheral vision to

help the pilot, only the instruments and whatever can be picked up by the searchlight's beam. Everything is done slowly, methodically, carefully. Every last detail of the winching and hover is briefed thoroughly beforehand. That is what going to Finner in Donegal meant to me. I was a P2 or co-pilot and had a lot to learn, a lot to practise. It was like starting again. Again.

The Dauphin SAR crew consisted of eight people: four aircrew and four groundcrew. The aircrew consisted of two pilots: one the captain, one co-pilot. Two winchcrew and paramedics: one the winch operator, the other winchman. The groundcrew consisted of two engineers: one specialising in avionics, the other in engine and airframe; one communications and radio operator and finally the refueller driver. We were fed by our 28th Battalion hosts but operationally we were independent.

We had a routine varying from crew to crew. It was very fluid and relaxed generally. We all expected to fly a lot and train a lot but there was time for lie-ins in bed, card games and indoor soccer in the gym. We joked that SAR duty would be very pleasant if it were not for the callouts.

A plan would fall into place that incorporated as many SAR flying disciplines as possible. Also, some of the crew would vote for their preferences if they felt they needed specific exercises. Sometimes we went north to Aranmore Island to the RNLI lifeboat crew who used to meet us for training, year on year, one of the busiest lifeboat crews in Britain and Ireland. They quietly and modestly saved lives in the teeth of Atlantic weather out of the glare of publicity and praise. They stopped what they were doing to train with us whenever we wanted on the ring of a phone.

'That'll be grand. Sure we have two new crew, we can show them the ropes. Will ye lift them for us?'

Around the coast we went, rounding the western edge of

Donegal Bay, turning north, passing Glencolumcille as the radio came alive.

'Malin Head Radio, this is Aranmore Lifeboat. Launching for training exercise west of Owey Island, with the air corps helicopter. Seven souls on board. Over.'

'Aranmore lifeboat, good evening. Malin Radio reading you strength five. Delta Hotel 247 has checked in, passing Glen Head. Estimates your position at time four five. Have a good exercise. Out.'

Finding them between Aranmore and Rutland Island, heading north to Owey Island, where we would start to train. Looking west to darkness, to where u-boats had lurked in the Second World War, and looking south, to the lights of the island village of Leabgarrow slipping out of view as we followed the lifeboat. Then the lighthouse would emerge from the dark again, as we came north of the invisible cliffs cloaked in night. On clear nights, its light rotated above us sweeping the sky from south to north. The relentless beam never tiring, never blinking, reassuring us that we were safe and sound, warning us to take heed of the cliffs and the rocks she guarded. It was a pity that we never got to know those people who crewed the lifeboat: islanders, fishermen, migrant workers, the infamous diggers of tunnels like the Channel Tunnel, their upturned faces in the searchlights beam, smiling in the sea spray, holding signal flags aloft.

Another popular start to our week, particularly in the winter when the evenings were dark early, was to head to Blacksod Lighthouse in Mayo, the helicopter refuelling depot. That would give us low-level-coastal-navigation as well as a night transdown and on the way back rendezvous with the ferry contracted to us to carry out deck winching at night.

Weather checked, helicopter fuelled and ready, we would carry out the crew briefing where our plans for the flight would be ironed out: the cruising altitude, the exact coastal route to and from Blacksod and finally, the deck winching, normal and emergency brief. Suits on next. Warm thermal layers on first and then the dry immersion suit, the same principle as a dry diving suit only not as thick. Chalking the sleeves with the dry powder, so the seals would not rip, pulling the suits on and sealing the diagonal zips, hunkering down so that the trapped air would expel through the neck seal by opening the seal slightly with the fingers. Why? Because in the event of a ditching, the trapped air in the suit could trap you in the helicopter. Finally pulling on the Mae West life-jacket fitted with personal EPIRB distress beacon, mirror, light and whistle.

We walked to the helicopter and strapped in, in no great hurry, a training crew with work to do but relaxed. We started up and checked all our equipment. Then having started up, we moved off the concrete pad, out onto the small tarmac runway nearby. The runway had originally been built for Cessna aircraft, and I had come here many times before as a Cessna pilot. We took off over the sand dunes at dusk passing Tullan Strand, Rogie Rock and Bundoran, out into Donegal Bay, down to 200 feet above the sea. Auto-pilot engaged, radar on, we swept the coastline on our left, with our route displayed, superimposed on the headlands and islands on the way. Checking in on Channel 16: 'Malin Radio, this is Delta Hotel 245 on Channel 16. Ops normal en route to Blacksod from Finner on training exercise. Listening out.'

'Delta Hotel 245, this is Malin Radio: all copied, strength five. Have a nice flight. Out.'

We flew low level not for the fun of it but because the Dauphin had to avoid icing conditions. We trained constantly at low altitude, getting used to the perspective, to the poor view we had of the coast and the features. The long line of north Mayo was parallel to the left as we headed west. The radar picked up the shape of first Mullaghmore in Sligo, and then Inishmurray, a very low island, inhabited only by sheep, and the ghosts of an old monastic settlement. If the night was clear, we could see villages on the way, like Easky or Killala, or cars driving back and forth on the roads. As we neared the top of Mayo, the concentration increased.

Why? The car that has lost its way can stop and ask for directions. A train is always on a track. An aeroplane making its way to an airport follows navigational aids and instrument landing systems to reach its goal. A drifting boat or yacht can stop, drop anchor and double-check its position or wait for daylight. A rescue helicopter has no such luxury, at least not then. Global navigation could only be used as back up. We relied on our eyes, even at night, to identify the light flashes of lighthouses together with the on-board Doppler navigation system updated with our radar. Finally, we used NVGs, night vision goggles, to see into the darkness as we skirted islands and headlands. These NVGs were binoculars used by either the winch operator or the non-flying pilot. Though they could help us to see at night, even with only the faintest starlight, they were not able to see cloud or rain. Depth perception and judging distance and perspective with NVGs at the time was also suspect so we did not rely on them.

The navigation flight to Blacksod was for very good reason. Blacksod Lighthouse is at the very bottom, the most southerly tip, of the Mullet Peninsula. To probe further west into the Atlantic, we needed to refuel there. It was and is a critical place for a rescue helicopter. The coast itself is beautiful but it is dangerous. It has many islands and reefs, currents and eddies. For this reason, it has several lights and lighthouses guarding the route in and out, showing safe and unsafe passage on two rocks, Eagle to the north, and Black Rock to the south, each several hundred feet high, then Blacksod Light in the bay itself. All along the west coast of Mullet are many islands no longer inhabited except by geese once a year, more outposts of Irish life, long gone: Inish Glora, Iniskee south and north, Duvillaun Mór and Beg.

With no lights warning of their presence, we first passed the Stags of Broadhaven, two sea stacks over 300 feet high, just north of Benwee Head. They were north of the area, so we could fly north of them and well clear if we could not see them or we could fly between them and the cliffs a mile or so south of them. A mile is a long way by day but flying through that gap at night using NVGs and radar, it felt like we could reach out and touch rock on both sides.

Once clear of the Stags, we turned towards Blacksod choosing either to fly outside and west of the peninsula or along the eastern side and over the road leading to Belmullet town which was an uncomfortable thing to do except in good conditions. The terrain just seemed so close on either side. I preferred the western route. It was longer, but I could count off and identify the islands and confirm the flash of the lighthouses.

The prevailing wind is south-westerly in Ireland. For us, that wind, particularly when stormy, was very unhelpful, to say the least. In order to fly south along the peninsula, the helicopter had to face south-west to counter the winds blowing it east. Because of this, the helicopter's radar, which scanned a 120° arc ahead of the helicopter, would face not straight ahead where we wanted but off to the right to the west, useless to us (try cycling along an unlit road at night with your torch shining onto the ditch). The solution was practice, knowing the islands, knowing that when you turned east for Blacksod that the radar would show you what you needed to see. A little faith. Technique. The four man crew used every piece of on-board equipment, every ounce of their experience and wisdom, to slide like a slalom skier between the islands, climbing slightly in case you had drifted and were close to one island or another, knowing that the black shape to the south was Achill, its northern cliffs at Croaghan standing at 2,192 feet, the highest sea cliffs in Europe.

Like a person in a dark cave, leaving a string behind them to find their way back, except in reverse, we followed the waypoints that we had created for our route into the bay. Like stepping stones in the middle of the bay, they led us south, then south-east, then east, away from high ground. The distinctive shape of the Blacksod would appear on the radar. This repeated navigation drill, its method, its checks and its emphasis on crew teamwork, guided us not just into this bay in darkness but anywhere. Flying below the SSA (safe sector altitude), below the level of the nearest high ground, at night is an essential skill around the Irish Atlantic coast.

The lighthouse keeper, Vincent Sweeney, would talk to us on aero band and on channel 16: 'Delta Hotel 245, this is Blacksod. *Tá fáilte romhat*. Wind sou' westerly at twenty-four, good visibility with low cloud.'

The lights of the pad would be so bright, we could sometimes see them through cloud and fog. Very reassuring. We would fly past and position for a transdown, the auto system of taking us automatically from our cruise to a hover, over the harbour near the lighthouse pad, finally gliding over the eight-foot granite walls and landing.

As we were training, and in radio contact with Malin Head radio all the time, we could stop there for a while. Vincent would refuel the helicopter perhaps with his young sons, David or Simon, or daughter Erika. New members of the SAR crew would be introduced, as we went inside for a cup of tea and a cigarette. Dónal Scanlan was the captain on my first trip on Dauphin SAR, with Ben Heron as the winch operator. 'Hi

Vincent. Good to see you again. We have some new lads this week. This is Dave Courtney, our new P2 tonight.'

'Hi Vincent. I was here with Dave Sparrow and Ciaran Parker, a few years back, with the Alouette. And this is Neil McAdam, our winchman.'

'Howaya Vincent. I've flown past, but it's my first time to land here.'

A laugh from Vincent: 'It won't be your last.'

The inside of Blacksod lighthouse was cold and bare. Immersion suits hung on a rack used by the commissioner of Irish Lights maintenance teams. They regularly went out to the lighthouses in a commercial helicopter. We made for the room formerly used as a sitting-room when the lighthouse had been a family home. Life-jackets, cargo nets for equipment, an empty fire place, a sink, an electric kettle, a wooden table in the middle, a plastic carton of milk, a bag of sugar, spilled, some tea spoons and some mugs. All from the Sweeney house. An ashtray. A cold granite building, the room was heated by a two bar electric heater that Vincent put on for us. 'Are ye winching on the way back?' Vincent enquired.

'Yes, we'll see if we can still do it. I haven't been up in a month. I need to dust the cobwebs off myself. You never know when a call will come in. Are you busy yourself Vincent?'

'Fairly busy. The Irish Lights Bolkow helicopter is on its way down from Donegal. They did Inishtrahull and Aranmore today. They'll do Rathlin O'Beirne and Killybegs with the *Grainne Uaile*, and then they'll come here. *Grainne Uaile* is coming down then and I have an inspection. I'll be cleaning and polishing day and night. And I've a Dutch vessel coming in too tomorrow night. They'll send a launch ashore. I think they have maintenance. They want to have it done before that low pressure system comes in from Iceland at the weekend.' He smiled.

'Just in time for us. God you have a busy week ahead. Listen, Vincent, we'll head off. Thanks for the tea. We might drop down again later this week. Sure I'll give you a call to see what day and time suits. If you are still waiting on that inspection, we'll give it a miss.'

'Dónal, I'm here all the time. Day or night. Just call. If I'm not here, Gerry can come down. Safe home lads. Nice to meet ye lads.'

I have always loved lighthouses. There were not many around Tullamore. They fascinate me standing up against the elements and the ocean, red light warning the unwary to steer clear of dangerous reefs and rocks, white light showing safe passage. The lighthouses were unmanned, bar one or two. Vincent was a lighthouse attendant, maintaining and minding the Blacksod light beside his own house as well as the lights on Black Rock and Eagle Island, as his father had done before him. As his son may do after him. I listened to him chat, silently drinking the tea he had made for us.

It took us no time at all to get ourselves ready. Strapping on our PSPs (personal survival packs which were individual survival dinghies we wore, or rather sat on), then our helmets. We went into the hover, a wave from Vincent and away up and over the granite wall leaving the lighthouse compound behind, straight into the inky darkness again. The darkness instantly stole away all memory of the cups of tea, cigarettes and light conversation. It wrapped us up like a leaden weighted cloak as we gradually accelerated and climbed, to the safety of our pre-programmed return route.

Silence on the radio, until we reached our first way point south of Duvillaun Mor, if the wind was south-westerly. A quick check in on the radio: 'Malin Radio, this is Delta Hotel 245 again. Leaving Blacksod for Donegal Bay. Ops normal.'

Vincent would be listening in for us. Always. Always. And before they replied on channel 16, he would call on the aero frequency short and sweet, almost unnoticed. But I noticed.

'*Slán abhaile*,' he would say.

10

DESTINATION HOVER

Success and rest don't sleep together.

Anon.

The lift doors opened. As I and the others walked into the room the lights went out. Over a loudspeaker, we heard the words announced: 'Ready in the module'. In between the time the doors opened and lights went out, I took in and registered the scene. A shimmering pool with dazzling lights above and below the water line. A dripping gantry on which was suspended a rectangular mock up of a helicopter fuselage. Divers treading water in the pool, wearing masks, and hand in the air, signalled OK. When the lights went out we were in darkness, listening to the sound of hydraulic jacks plunging the mock helicopter into the pool, a great crash and splash of water, shouts and yells from the trainees inside before they went under. Then the sound of the hydraulic jacks continued as they rotated the mock-up inverted under the water. Welcome to 'Emergency Underwater Escape Training' at RNAS (royal naval air station) Portsmouth. September 1986.

I think most of us had the same reaction, wondering if anyone would miss us, if we tried to slip out the door. 'Thanks very much. I won't be doing this after all. Where is the naval museum?' was what we wanted to say. When the lights came on, we watched as the trainees came up from the module spluttering, laughing and shaking their heads in disbelief. In military fashion, they quickly lined up in their dripping overalls, and disappeared for their showers and de-briefing. We were next.

The instructors welcomed us. They did this course regularly for any armed forces personnel who flew in helicopters, whether as passengers or crew. The purpose of the course was to teach us how to get out of a helicopter alive if it ditched, as this is an occupational hazard in rescue helicopters.

We were briefed thoroughly and got ready for four 'dunks' – the first, straight in with the lights on; the second straight in with the lights on but deeper; the third, with lights dimmed in and inverted same depth as the second, finally total darkness in deep and inverted. Nerve-racking at first, it became exhilarating. Some timed their final intake of breath incorrectly, sensing the water too late in the dark, breathing in water and were hauled out by divers shocked coughing up water on the pool side, while the rest of us split our sides laughing at them. 'No need for you to wear a Mae West then Paddy. If we ditch, you're fucked anyway!'

Basic lessons and rules that were burned into us. The helicopter is a hollow tube. All its weight, the engines, gear box and rotor blades are on top. If you ditch, it will turn upside down. The only variation is how long it will take to start to flip over. If we do ditch, keep the hand on the door jettison handle. This is called the escape reference hand. Never move it. With the other hand unbuckle, but only when the helicopter stops moving. After you unbuckle with one hand, push the harness straps firmly away from you, so they do not snag and trap you. (We all carried knives on our immersion suits specifically to cut snagged harnesses in a ditching situation.) Follow the escape reference hand to the door. Jettison the door. Swim away. Then, and only then, inflate your Mae West. Happiness. That was the theory anyway. I wondered if I would be calm enough to do it for real.

Whether training or on a SAR mission, we always briefed for every scenario and eventuality. We placed extra emphasis on hovering and hover power, obstacles and what to do if the flying pilot lost visual references at night. But nothing was like the dunker drill, feeling the adrenaline rush as the module dropped into the water at speed, the shock as it turned upside down, and grabbing a lung-full of air while you still could. Then trying to slow yourself and be calm in the water, in the darkness, and follow the drill. It was more than just training. It was a reality check. This is the environment we work in. Be careful out there.

At a subconscious level, the threat of ditching, and finding yourself in the ocean, was always present. Leaving Blacksod behind us, after coastal navigation exercises, we would return to Donegal Bay for night winching. There was a ferry on contract at our disposal. We would arrange a rendezvous and play cat and mouse with them for an hour or so before calling it a day. The game of hovering behind and beside the ferry, winching the winchman or the ship's crew members on and off, over and over while varying the techniques and hover heights as the ferry went in different directions, and adapting accordingly. First though, we had to get down to the ferry. We had to do a transdown.

When you arrive at a ship to do a rescue, you have to go from the cruise to hovering beside that ship. The cruise and the hover are different phases of flight, with different power settings, different attitudes and different responses to control inputs. Changing from one flight phase to another is called a transition. In rescue parlance, a transition down, or transdown for short, is going from the cruise to the hover. The reverse is called a transup.

In between the transdown and the transup is hovering, doing

the rescue, winching, completing the transfer or searching; whatever the situation demands, all the time close to the ocean, watching the engine instruments and our hover height and attitude. Always aware that ditching was a real possibility.

By day, a transdown is done using whatever the eye can see outside as visual references. Watching a ship, for instance, come into view, and then grow bigger and bigger as it gets closer. It can be difficult to gauge the size of a lone ship on the ocean without something to compare it with. Depth perception can be difficult. Scale is difficult to perceive. Very large vessels and medium size vessels are easy to confuse. If you approach too fast, a ship can suddenly race at you as you get closer. You watch your instruments, confirming that the power is reducing as you lower the collective, that the speed is reducing and that you are descending. Over a featureless grey sea, it is not always easy to confirm with the eyes. In choppier seas, the waves themselves are visual cues. You slow down, by slowing the rate at which they go past and under your feet on the rudder pedals.

The SAR helicopter also has the crew. They watch all the time, gauging progress without being able to directly control the helicopter's flight path but they can influence it. The winching circuit, the transdown and the transup, all have checks and calls that include each and every member of the crew. It is carefully choreographed. The years of training and operating the Alouette 3 gave us pilots and crews the experience to do all this as second nature. By day.

In the Dauphin, we had to do it by night. Sometimes there would be a moon. Often the sky was clear and we could see quite well but more often than not, night transdowns were done in pitch darkness: no sense of movement outside, only the instruments inside. Often commencing from being in cloud, only getting sight of the surface when the helicopter reached the hover. It was for good reason that these phases of flight, were called 'Black Hole' approaches.

The transdown is a significant milestone for the night-flying pilot. The Dauphin, was equipped with sophisticated electronics and an all-singing, all-dancing auto-pilot. Instead of flying the helicopter ourselves, we programmed the computer and let the auto-pilot fly. The air-data system, comprising the pitot-static vents and pitot tubes, sensed real-time temperature and pressure variations, using them to calculate the wind, the wind speed and consequently our own speed. This data was then fed to a computer which in turn told the controls what to do, via hydraulic links, jacks and the flight controls.

The result: the helicopter would turn on our command into a race-track shaped pattern, hopefully finishing magically in the hover behind the ship. This would be initiated by our pressing the appropriate button or buttons on a screen menu: *Destination Hover. Hover Fixed Position.* If it was clear, we would see the ship's position and deck lights as we turned and positioned. If we were in low cloud, or if the visibility was bad, we would not be able to see anything. We would concentrate instead on the radar.

As we got closer, the radar return would get bigger and bigger. The co-pilot remained fixed on his instruments, while the captain peered out into the murk, waiting for the ship to appear. He would be helped by the winch-operator who would have opened the cargo door. In theory, once we could see the ship, everything was as we did by day. Standardisation we called it. Everything the same. Brief, patter, practice 'dummy' deck, and then 'live', with the winchman on the wire. That way everyone knew what was going on, and what to expect next. If something went wrong, it would be sensed because it was different, non-standard. The other difference from day was that everything was done more slowly. Much more slowly.

However, it is not that simple, and that is why we trained over and over. This type of flying is very susceptible to visual illusions. The ship's lights moving can momentarily be confused with the stars themselves. The fluid in the inner ear can make you feel you are level when you are descending and *vice versa*. With confusing visual information added to the mix, disorientation is very close by. The height you have over the sea is your safety net. The higher you are, the more room you have for error and to manoeuvre and fly away to safety. As you get closer to your hover height, perhaps fifty feet or so, in your subconscious you know the net is gone. That is why the four man crew is so important. The terse patter and feedback from the co-pilot or the winch operator compensates for the poor visual data available and helps the captain maintain orientation.

A co-pilot might say, 'Watch your height. You are sinking. Nose up attitude high. Are you visual?' If the captain is fixated on some aspect of the hover, which is understandable given the proximity of aerials and so on, this is like a slap on the face, reminding him to do something about it. If he fails to do something, or fails to respond, the co-pilot takes control, staying in position if he can see, flying away if he cannot see anything.

Whether off the Wicklow coast on flights from Baldonnel, or in Donegal Bay, we repeated this over and over again. By day and by night. In cloud and bad weather. In good weather, with instrument hoods fitted to our helmets, to obscure the outside world, simulating night time or fog. There were so many permutations and combinations of normal procedures, different hover heights combined with the ship moving in any number of directions, as well as simply drifting. We also spiced it up with simulated system failures, with warning lights illuminating, EFIS (electronic flight instrumentation system) screens failure, communication and hoist failures, auto-pilot and simulated engine failures. It is important to know how to use complex and inter-related systems when they work normally but being SAR pilots, who have to be prepared for everything, we also trained with many systems failing, and flying without auto-pilot. Murphy's law applied: if it can go wrong, it will.

It got to the stage where just two pilots flew on training exercise, making life as difficult as possible for each other, letting the helicopter sink in the hover towards the sea to make sure the other pilot would take control. Enjoying it too, we laughed at each other's efforts. We were not just flying colleagues but also good friends. We were a close-knit bunch. We knew each others families, friends, girlfriends or wives. Some were co-pilots, some captains, depending on who had started the Dauphin first: Andy Whelan, Dave Sparrow, Seán Murphy, Dónal Cotter, Gerry O'Sullivan, Jim Corby, Dónal Scanlan, Kevin McCarrick, Neil O'Mahoney and Aidan Flanagan. Failing the auto-pilot as we reached the hover. Failing the hover height, so we would sink towards the sea. The Dauphin's auto-hover used to find it hard to stay in synch with the sea swell, particularly in big seas. In real terms, getting out of synch meant sinking onto the crests and climbing high over the troughs. As we hovered, if we did not take manual control, the helicopter could either climb high away from the deck or drop onto the sea. Our practising was for good reason. We ambushed each other just as the sea would.

There were several ways to do the transdown, either using the automatic systems completely, partially, or not at all. It depended on where you ultimately wanted to hover. If a ship had run aground, that would mean terrain was beside it. You would not be able to fly over it to fix and save the position for fear of flying into terrain. There were other ways of doing it. You could use the radar to 'paint' a picture in front of you of the coast, and where the ship was. Using another electronic toy, a 'joystick' just like in a home computer game, you could save a position you had scrolled out to on the radar screen and then tell the helicopter to go there, *Destination hover, hover joystick position.*

There was another reason why this was a better option at night close to the coast. With fully automated transdowns at night, it was very easy to get lulled into a false sense of security. Everything was so smooth. You would hardly feel the helicopter turn or descend. We joked that if you wanted to find the nearest mountain or cliff, just use the fully automated system. The first part of its pattern would involve finding the wind before positioning so that we would end up hovering, and facing into it. This 'finding the wind' element of the pattern, invariably saw the helicopter turn straight towards the coast. We had to watch it all the time. Using the automatic systems let us divert our attention away from the flying but at times that spare capacity was then spent making sure the system behaved itself. It generally did, but not without supervision.

And then the hover. The radio altimeter, sending down a signal to the sea below us, receiving the returned signal, and using it to lock us at a pre-programmed hover height. Anything from 40 feet to 199 feet. The helicopter fixed vertically as if it was on an invisible pane of glass. Lateral movement could be controlled with the cyclic. With the captain on the right, the winch operator behind him, the ship ahead and to the right, we would ideally move forward and right until we placed the winchman on the deck. It worked beautifully in good to moderate sea conditions. The system would literally fly the helicopter for us, hovering, while we prepared to winch.

This preparation started with a thorough briefing by the winch operator and agreed by all of us. All very similar to the Alouette, but this brief was more complex for obvious reasons.

A four man crew not on the same wavelength meant four confused men. When I started to fly the Dauphin, I listened to the brief in something approaching wonder. The winchcrew once more revealing another layer of coolness, another layer of expertise, a Dublin sense of humour pervading the most demanding situations.

The brief, in a nutshell, was to describe the situation facing us, and superimpose on it some sort of order, some method for achieving success. It would identify the dangers to the helicopter or to the winchman. Have a good look at your average trawler the next time you are in a fishing port or harbour, and see if you can find a safe, sterile area where a winchman could be lowered. Not that easy. Finally, the brief would remind us of our emergency options in case the hoist or an engine failed. A typical winching brief would include the following: heading, height, hazards, entry, exit and emergencies. A lot to discuss and it changed each time we trained, adapting to each ship, each cliff, each wind direction. Repetition was building strength and confidence. Training in good weather, preparing for bad weather.

Ben Heron, Dick O'Sullivan, Dick Lynch, Ian Downey; their voices and patter with me forever: 'Hazards to the winchman; on the run in, we have the railings at the aft deck, the flag pole and the fishing gantry on the port side. Same hazards over the deck, and it look like it's not a clean deck. Spilled fish boxes; mind your footing Alan. OK? On the exit, I'll winch in first to get him to a safe height.'

John Manning, Owen Sherry, Dick Murray, Paul Ormsby, Brian Moran, Christy Mahady. 'The aft deck is too cluttered. Best winching area is amid ships. Hazards are … Jaysus lads, you can see the hazards. They are all over the shop: the bridge, the aerials, the fishing gantries, there's some sort of a wire running fore and aft on the starboard side. You'll probably only have sight of the bow when we are overhead. Let's do a dummy deck'.

A dummy deck was a trial run. If you had to winch right into the centre of a ship, the pilot would have very little to look at outside once he was overhead, especially if the vessel was small, especially if there were high obstacles that forced you to hover high. And especially at night. Coming over the ship, the pilot would say a word of warning: 'Lost sight'. That meant that he was unable to see anything and was hovering on instruments. That was one good reason to do a trial run or dummy deck. It might go like this: 'OK, you have lost sight. It's my target. Right two, right one. Steady, steady. Over the winching posi-tion.' Winchman would be on the wire, lowering him to the deck. 'You're descending; up two, up one; height good.' Winch-man would be on the deck. 'Steady. Good hover. Have you any references?'

'Just about got the bow at times. Your patter is good. It feels steady. You happy, Christy?'

'Yea, she's fairly steady. The area is bigger than I thought. Right one, steady. I'll be able to get him on there, but you can't move anywhere … Forward one, steady … until I have Ciaran up above the bridge and that wire. Right one, steady … How's the power, Dave?'

'Power's fine lads. You're pulling just over 50 per cent. You're over head now 90 seconds.'

'OK, Christy. If you want to brief, I'll stay in the overhead and, Ciaran, have a look and see if you're happy.'

'Yea, I'm at the door and watching. I'm happy, but watch that gantry.'

Holding the hover, while Christy, the winch operator, quickly described the obstacles and how we were to get the winchman in and out, on and off the deck, interspersing his brief with patter to help stay overhead. We would retreat then, earlier if it was too difficult to maintain the hover overhead, and get ready to winch. The position where we began to approach the ship would be about a rotor diameter away. This was called the start point. The winchman would be connected to the hoist hook, after his harness and equipment was treble checked. An anti-static lead was attached too, and would dangle below him, earthing any static electricity to the deck the instant it made contact.

Static always built up from the rotating blades and the helicopters hover. Without an anti-static lead, the electricity would be discharged through the winchman himself. Sometimes with a blue flash and a jolt. Not life threatening, but it would certainly loosen your fillings. In training, first-time winchmen were not told about the anti-static lead. Sadistic winch operators loved to watch it happen: 'The face on him. He's after getting a wallop. Did you see the flash!'

The winch operator would ask if he could winch the winchman out to a safe height. The captain would say yes, if he was ready and if all was well. The winchman would be lowered until he was at thirty feet or so above the ocean, the idea being that if he fell from the hoist for any reason, he would survive the fall. When they were ready to move forward to the vessel, the captain would say, 'Running in'. Then the patter would start until they were over the deck. If the deck was so badly cluttered that they had to use the amid ship deck, the winchman would remain in the helicopter attached to the hoist until they got right in overhead.

The dummy deck was your practice hover. If you held an inaccurate hover, you would correct it, learn from it and improve it. Hopefully. You would get the real perspective of the on-the-spot, right-on-the-money hover. If your references were poor, you would use the hover meter more and pay even more attention to the patter. The hover-meter was a display, much like an ILS (instrument landing system), a cross hairs where the idea was to keep it centred.

In the overhead, the winch operator would ask if he could winch out. An affirmative response, and the next thing to happen was the sound of the winch, an electric one with a motor that sounded something between a groan and a whine. The helicopter's centre of gravity would very slightly shift towards the right, countered as a reflex by the pilot squeezing to the left. The winchman would be lowered straight down to the deck, disconnect and we could winch in the cable. Then we would drift back simulating that he was attending to a casualty, returning to collect him when he was ready.

We started with straightforward decks graduating to ever more difficult ones. Once the winchman was *on the wire,* you could feel him in your hands especially if your control movements were not smooth, if you made him swing. The winch operator could dampen the swing manually, with a gloved hand, but this was considered an imperfect technique. The best technique was to not let the swing develop at all. Slow gradual movements. Smooth. The winchman, like a pendulum beneath us, plumb when we got it right.

The more difficult the decks, the smoother we had to be. Hovering high over high obstacles, with barely any deck to look at outside, we became nervous and tense, knowing that a man's life was literally on the line. It was not always possible to be slow and smooth though if the deck was moving a lot or erratically, or if the sea was choppy. The winchman would swing. There were other techniques that the old pros used. Sometimes they used the swing, timed with the forward movement of the helicopter, and a call of 'Steady' to stop the helicopter moving forward, matching the deck's movement, placing him miraculously onto the deck at just the right time. Just when you were anticipating more patter to stay in position, a winch operator would say, 'Winchman on the deck', they were so ahead of the game.

A hi-line was another powerful tool in the armoury. It was a length of rope which could be attached to the hook on the hoist cable end. Using it meant that the deck crew on the ship could pull the winchman onto the deck as he was lowered. This meant that the helicopter did not need to hover right over the ship and was very effective in rough seas and where a ship had high dangerous obstacles. It took a bit longer to do and the deck crew sometimes pulled too hard on the hi-line, breaking its safety weak-link. This meant starting all over again, with or without another hi-line.

Although the casualties taken off ships were often walking wounded, frequently their medical condition was serious enough to warrant the use of a stretcher. The winchman would go on board with his medical equipment, and get the casualty ready. If he needed a stretcher, one would be lowered to him. This was very time consuming and taking him off, with the stretcher as a double-lift was fraught with danger. Invariably the stretcher would spin as they were lifted off the deck. A winchman coming close to an obstacle could use his feet to kick himself away,. With a stretcher to lift and protect, connected to the hoist hook beside him horizontally, he was less able to protect himself. It was crucial to lift cleanly, vertically away from the wires and gantries and aerials, 'Like a cork out of a bottle', was how we used to say we wanted it done.

And that was how we passed the time on SAR duty in Finner repeating the low level navigation flights until we knew every rock and headland in our area; doing transdowns and transups until we were blue in the face; failing as many of our systems, or simulating their failure, as often as possible; winching this way and that, higher and higher hovers; seeking more and more awkward places to winch to and from.

I missed the big calls. I had day callouts and searches and island medevacs and hospital transfers but no big calls. On three occasions I took over duty from a crew that had just completed excellent rescues. A ship ran aground in Galway Bay near Ballyvaughan and I missed it by a few days. All were winched to safety. The crew were awarded the Shipwrecked Mariners award that year: Harvey O'Keeffe, Seán Murphy, Dave Carolan and Christy Mahady. Another ship ran aground at St John's Point, Donegal Bay, the evening after I had finished duty and returned to Baldonnel. Again, all winched to safety. Sitting in Slattery's pub in Rathmines, drinking a pint with my girlfriend after the week's duty, I shook my head in disbelief, as it was featured on the six o'clock news, smiling at my own jealousy.

That was the luck of the draw. You could go weeks and months with no callouts, or modest callouts, while some of your colleagues might be punch drunk with the opposite problem. I did not know it then, but my day would come.

In early summer of 1992, I visited the Skelligs again. Having flown to, and landed on, Skellig Michael, I wanted to see it again. My girlfriend and I drove to Kerry, to Portmagee and caught Des Lavelle's boat. I had a book about the Skelligs written by Des himself, not just a boatman, but an historian, writer, diver and archaeologist to boot. And a member of the Valentia RNLI lifeboat crew, as I later found out. Rising 700ft out of the Atlantic, nine miles offshore, it is an imposing sight. Passing the smaller Skellig, which is a giant sea bird sanctuary, we set foot on the rock, after an hour and a half's sea journey.

The weather was warm and pleasant. After a rough journey

in a strong wind, it certainly did seem to have its own micro-climate just as the guide books said. We walked along the light-house path, leaning over to look at the puffins, past the helicop-ter pad, which looked even more alarming from this perspective around the south of the rock, until we came to the steps leading upwards almost vertically, granite slabs painstakingly laid by the monks hundreds of years before, to the grassy flat area between the two high points on the rock: the monastery site to the east, the south summit to the west. We caught our breath there, at Christ's Saddle, as it is known, and then made our way up the steps to the monastery.

That place, that wild and holy place. Beehive huts suspended in space. On the edge of Europe, on the edge of the world. The raucous sound of the gulls and the south-west wind. Waves crashing hundreds of feet below, as we peered down the sheer drop through the rising sea spray. I wondered if she liked it too, whether its magic was working on her. I wondered if she thought I was crazy bringing her to this place as if it was mine to share. We walked back down to Christ's Saddle. Lying on the grass, looking up at the clouds, the south summit towering over us, we lay in the sunshine, our backs lying on one of the wonders of the world, hands intertwined. I sat up, and asked her to marry me.

That's how I remember it. Rose petals drifting down from the heavens. An orchestra softly playing an accompaniment.

Her version of events is slightly different. She remembers still feeling sea sick after the boat journey and dizzy having looked over the cliff. Her mind focused on the dread of the re-turn journey, she found it hard to answer with any enthusiasm.

11

THE QUEEN RETURNS

Kindness is a language that the deaf can hear and the blind can read.
                                                                    Anon.

Courtesy and etiquette: Our cadet class was given an education on this subject in the cadet school. We sniggered when told how to eat soup and as the correct order of cutlery at multi-course meals was outlined. Having been commissioned as young officers all around the country in different units, corps, battalions and regiments, we learned how much we needed to know the rules and conventions at official uniformed evenings. The end of the meal was the time for toasts. The most important toast, the one that signified that decorum could be relaxed, was the toast to our commander-in-chief, The President: *'A dhaoine uaisle: An tUachtarán.'* Clinking of glasses and a strong murmured response in reply: *'An tUachtarán'*, signifying the loosening of ties, the rising in volume of the table chat, the throwing of boxes of matches and cigarettes lighters across from one table to another as smoking was then permitted. As young officers, we were at the bottom of the commissioned chain of command. At the very top of that chain was the president.

The Dauphin helicopter was a popular choice with government and with the president. I had flown VIP flights on the Alouette over the years but the Dauphin, however, brought me into contact with senior government ministers, the taoiseach and of course, the president. The engineer's preparation would include not just the routine maintenance but also the replacement of the standard 'troop' seats, with cushioned seats as well as carpet on floor. The tension would mount as the day and the departure time drew close, the captain assessing the weather forecast and making his 'Go' or 'No Go' telephone call. Everyone respects the decision of a captain to say 'No' to a flight in bad weather, but the pressure was sometimes enormous. Not everyone involved accepted a negative decision without question. Phone calls would often keep coming back to a captain who had said 'No', trying to pressurise him into changing his mind.

One day in May 1993 I was the co-pilot on a presidential flight. The weather was fine and clear, and we could look forward to a busy but clear and trouble free day. The president was Mary Robinson. We were to collect her and her party at Áras an Uachtarán, the presidential residence in Dublin's Phoenix Park. Andy Whelan, another rugby-playing, beer-drinking friend, was the captain and Colm O'Connor was our crewman. Our destination was the islands off the west coast, Inisturk, Inisboffin and Clare Island. She was to open a community building on one and attend a brief function or two. Mainly her purpose was to bring her presidency to places where it had never been before or not been in a very long time. And also to thank them for their support.

Over the years, thanks to my family holidays in leaky caravans on the west coast, from Cork to Donegal, I knew the islands well. As a child looking out at them on drives or when swimming on remote beaches, my parents used to tell me exactly what their names were and all about them. Not just drawing from their own knowledge, but referring to R.L. Praeger's book, *The Way That I Went*, like a biblical text. Once I left school, I tried to visit the islands, picking them off one by one on weekends away until I knew almost all of them. A few months before taking the president on that flight, my fiancée and I had spent a weekend on Clare Island.

Setting out from Roonagh Quay, we had taken the ferry to the island. There to meet us was our B&B host, Oliver O'Malley. Bearded and cheerful, he took us to his home on the south of the island where we met his wife Mary and their children, Marian and Brian. Over that weekend, they spoiled us and showed us around and introduced us to many of their friends. We ate and drank in McCabes, and walked and talked, with the music, the riddles and the fun of the island, the lapping of the waves on the beach, and the screaming sea birds for company. Weeks later, I phoned that I would be on the flight to them with the president. It was going to be a special day.

We left Baldonnel and made the short journey to the Phoenix Park. The papal cross signposted our way to Áras an Uachtarán. The same cross where I and a million others had looked up into the sky as Pope John Paul arrived. I looked down, not for the first time smiling to myself at the memory of my innocent, smiling and happy face as it looked skywards more than fifteen years before.

A full half hour early, we landed on the lawn, shutting the engines and rotors down. As we took off our helmets, the president's aide-de-camp came over to welcome us. While I stayed in the cockpit and programmed the navigation computer, Andy chatted and reassured him that the weather was fine and that all was well. Colm prowled around the outside making sure that nothing was amiss and placed the double footstep on the grass beside its open side door. A line of garda outriders and soldiers was ranged around the grounds awaiting the president and our departure.

Shifting uneasily from foot to foot, everyone a little nervous for fear of some last minute glitch. I watched their body language, knowing my own was similar, that our departure would lead everyone to breathe a sigh of relief. Kettle on. Light up the cigarettes.

For now my job was to check the navigation for the twentieth time, and the maps and charts too. I decided to get out and stretch my legs. I walked across the manicured lawn over to the gravel drive. As I did, a garda high powered BMW motorbike roared into view speeding towards me. It stopped with a crunch on the gravel beside me. Everyone stopped what they were doing and looked over. The president was due to emerge through the door any minute. The garda pushed his bike back on its stand and raised his sun visor.

'Howaya Daithí! I knew it'd be you.' His voice boomed across the lawn. 'Have you a licence for that thing? Hawr, Hawr, Hawr!' It was Ronan Kennelly, school friend and fellow rugby player from Tullamore. He could not hear me because of his helmet so he continued to shout. 'Where are you taking her anyway?'

If looks could kill. Not mine but the other gardaí, the aide-de-camp. Ronan noticed too and laughed. We chatted briefly and shook hands and he was gone. As the dust settled, the president emerged, smiling, well dressed, radiant, cheerful. I took my place in my seat while Andy saluted and escorted her to the helicopter. Colm was waiting there and saluted too, helping her and the others into their seats. She was sunny and bright, like the day itself. I heard her reply to Andy, something like 'Good morning, captain. Thank you very much', before taking her place. Having seen her on the TV and in newspapers, she was now sitting behind me. I wondered what she would have thought if she knew that I wished my parents could see us. They so admired her. We lifted off and started on our way west. Andy turned to me and smiled, 'A friend of yours from Tullamore?'

The day after our flying visit to the islands the media reports were short and to the point. Just little filler pieces in the bad news of the day, saying that she had visited this place or that, had opened a community centre or met the women on one of the islands. Small news. As a pilot on that flight, I could see that it was not small news. The cliché of taking her presidency to the people was very real and undeniably emotional at times. There was almost something evangelical about her and about our coming out of the skies to the islands and their communities.

Our arrival was anticipated with excitement. The star of the show initially was the helicopter itself. The drone and throb of its engines and rotor blades announced its imminent arrival when we were still out of sight. The gathered crowd searched for us in the east, seeing us as a speck, getting closer and finally alighting. First Inisboffin, where I had been several times before. A warm welcome at Murray's Hotel. After that was Inisturk. It sticks in my mind because it was my first time to stop there without being in a hurry, my first time to look around with no sound of a helicopter, to hear the sound of the island itself, its water, its wind and the sea gulls.

A small island with a natural harbour on its eastern side around which the houses sheltered. A beautiful but steep rocky place, not as frequently visited as its neighbours Inisboffin and Clare Island. The LZ was at the small harbour on a large concrete area known by us as 'The Fish Slab' because basking sharks and whales were caught by the island's fishing fleet in days gone by. The slab was where they used to butcher the fish for their meat and valuable oils.

We approached the 'Fish Slab', avoiding the houses and aerials and fish boxes, landing carefully. Once the engines were shut down and the helicopter fell silent, a magical transformation took place. The helicopter all but curtsied and backed away as the president emerged smiling and waving. All eyes fell upon the neatly dressed lady smiling almost shyly.

A spontaneous round of applause. Words of welcome that I only half heard. The meek standing back as the community elders, eased forward, bowing slightly: *'a hUachtarán, ar son ar mhuintir, tá fáilte romhat go dtí Oileán Inis Torc*. Ma'am, on behalf of us all here today you are very welcome to Inisturk.' More applause and then the president was absorbed into the throng.

Andy, Colm and I watched as Mary Robinson was driven away disappearing among the houses in the village, and then reappearing again. We saw the line of old vans and cars, climbing the steep hill, sputtering and jolting on the narrow road. In the new community centre, overlooking the harbour where we waited, we could hear the distant hum of conversation, inaudible speeches and applause.

We waited for a wave or a shout down the hillside, or the sound of a car engine starting. Someone brought us cups of tea. Stray dogs arrived, sniffed around us, urinated on the wheels and growled at us when we shooed them away. The sound of conversation and starting cars, tumbled down the hillside towards us. It was time to go.

Waving goodbye to the gathered crowd, we climbed up and gently nudged over towards the distinctive shape of Clare Island. Looking east into Clew Bay, our passengers gasped as we flew past the high cliffs and lighthouse. Croagh Patrick towered over the bay in the distance, as we slowed down and made our approach. We landed at the neatly marked helicopter pad beside the intersection of its only two roads. Not far from where the original queen of the island, Grainuaile, built her castle, its ruins still guarding the eastern approaches.

Once more our arrival drew the islanders. As we shut down,

I scanned the faces for Oliver and Mary O'Malley. There they were waving to me. Or maybe it was the president they were waving to. Once the helicopter was silent, the island's quiet and peace enveloped us. Mary Robinson got out and was greeted again with quiet words of welcome, shaken hands and bows, and beaming smiles everywhere.

I stayed in my seat. She walked to the front of the helicopter and stopped just a few feet in front of me. I sat quietly unseen, as she met people and struggled to move forward. I saw their faces all focused on hers, their attention devoted to her presence, her aura, her office. For those few minutes I could sense the magic of the office of An tUachtarán.

When she went to meet people, make house calls and attend a welcoming ceremony, I got the opportunity to meet Oliver and Mary again. A slow moving stream of people was drawn by Mary Robinson's magnetism. Suits and ties. Shined and polished shoes. The boys in neat trousers, with shirts and ties. The girls in pretty dresses. Walking to see the president of Ireland and to hear what she might say. Watching her watch the youngsters as they danced in the sunshine, while curlews tiptoed along the beach, stabbing the sand between the lapping waves. Smiling when she smiled. Their day. I was with them as they watched. Watching them. Mary Robinson was famous for being the first female president, but she was much more than that.

12
—

WILD SALMON

*Criticism is something you can avoid by saying
nothing, doing nothing and being nothing.*

Anon.

The taoiseach, Charlie Haughey, was someone we frequently
flew in the Dauphin. The Boss. At that time, *Scrap Saturday*, the
satirical radio show, was extremely popular. Dermot Morgan's
accurate imitation was known and repeated countrywide.

When we flew him, I had the rare opportunity of being able
to listen to his voice, not that he spoke much to us or to me personally. Dermot Morgan had him off to a tee. I used to suppress
a smile, pulling down my sun visor to hide it. I flew with him
on a number of occasions. The most memorable flights were the
ones when we took him from his home to Inishvicillaune.

Flying the short journey from Baldonnel to Kinsealy, we nego-
tiated with Dublin ATC through their busy airspace, particularly
as our flight path would interrupt their landing traffic flow. Once
cleared to Kinsealy, we would watch the stately home come into
view, make our approach and land on the back lawn. There beside
the small lake, we shut down, and waited.

The sound of a door opening, approaching voices, and then
the taoiseach and his travelling party would emerge. The captain that day, Comdt Jurgen Whyte, was waiting at the front of
the helicopter. Standing smartly to attention, he saluted. And

then the voice: 'Good morning, captain. It seems like a nice day. What sort of weather are you expecting?'

'Good morning, taoiseach. The weather is fine, a few showers, but a nice day.'

Conversation among the taoiseach's party, as bags and belongings were gathered and loaded. The taoiseach walked around to take his seat, nodded at me and accepted the crewman's salute at the passenger door. Our crewman was Flt Sgt Mark Hayden, one of our most senior engineers and experienced crewmen and a former winch operator to boot, just the sort of man you want in case of a technical issue arising on a day like this.

It was not so much the actions or words of Haughey that hinted at his power, but the actions and demeanour of those accompanying him, a certain edginess, a nervousness. Perhaps it was the office of the taoiseach, irrespective of who held it, but Haughey was arguably the most powerful man in the country at the time. Perhaps the most powerful taoiseach ever. You could sense it.

And so they sat in making polite conversation. We started up and called ATC Dublin waiting for permission to start our journey. Even that small pause seemed to crackle with impatience. Perhaps it was just in my mind.

At school in Tullamore, in common with my generation, I had studied *Peig*, the autobiography of an island woman from the Great Blasket, the largest of the Blasket Islands off the Dingle peninsula in Kerry. Our generation had famously been force-fed with *Peig*. The book is in a largely oral tradition of story-telling. The stories themselves were Peig's own of her childhood, her youth and her marriage: her entire life. For boys from the bogs of Ireland, written in an Irish dialect, it was hard work.

Br Eoin Rossiter was our Irish teacher. A Wexford man, from Carnsore Point, he overcame our lack of home-spoken Irish and the difficulty we had understanding *Peig*. He overcame the peer pressure to reject her story and brought it to life. I could imagine the islands and the waves, because of his patience but also because of those leaking-caravan holidays. He brought the islands to life and helped us appreciate it. Our class devoured the book.

By the time I was flying the taoiseach, I had already flown to the Blaskets and landed on Tearaght, the most westerly lighthouse in Europe. In the Alouette 3, I had been down there a couple of times in security roles. One flight had been with one of our operations and management gurus, Flt Sgt Jim Martin. Escaping for a day to Kerry and the Blaskets, Jim and I relished the freedom, the wildness and absence of formality.

Flying the taoiseach to Inishvicillaune was like bringing life to the islands again, to the stories of old. His house, built from stone on one of the smaller islands. Because I was facing forward, I could not see our passengers. Nor could I hear them as the intercom isolated them from us. Mark sat with them in the back and would tell us if they needed anything. Otherwise, I busied myself with whatever had to be done, checking our progress and our fuel burn, where we were and what time we were due to land. Soon we saw the spine of the Dingle peninsula pointing west. A flick of the intercom switch as Jurgen spoke, the familiar landmarks passing by underneath us. 'Taoiseach, we'll be there in a few minutes. Tralee Bay beside us. I'm sure you don't need me to tell you where you are from here.'

Flying at 3,000 feet, paralleling the long undulating spine of the peninsula, we saw the windmill at Blennerville, then Slieve Mish, Caherconree, between Castlegregory and Stradbally Mountain, as we made for Mount Brandon. The Magharee Islands floated in Tralee Bay beside us. Staying at the same level we got closer to the ridge from Ballysitteragh to Brandon and on to Masatiompan blocking our way south-west. We could see the hump of the Great Blasket herself, as we neared the gap at

Ballysitteragh. The Owenmore river valley beneath us, Brandon's knife edge ridge to our right, with cars parked and people waving to us from the top of the Conor Pass on our left.

The taoiseach might be on the intercom then looking out and admiring the view, narrating in his unmistakable voice, describing and admiring, the places where I hill-walked when I could, places that I loved.

Mount Eagle blocked a full view of the Blasket Islands but it shrank as we continued south-west. The sharp point of Tearaght was further west and Inishtooskert, popularly known as 'An Fear Marbh', the dead man, north of the Great Blasket. I had loved this area, these islands, ever since *Peig* had introduced me to the Blasket writers. The Alouette 3 had given me rare and wonderful views. The sense of history and culture was tangible to me. I was a bit of a dreamer. Still am. These deserted places were walked by the ghosts of long departed communities.

Scrap Saturday and other commentators parodied his notion that he was the chieftain, the taoiseach, the boss, but as we landed on the grass beside his stone house on Inishvicillaune, that term seemed an appropriate one to me.

We only stayed a short three-quarters of an hour. The helicopter would always have another task, or maintenance awaiting it at Baldonnel. Time stood still. Jurgen had flown the taoiseach before, as had Mark. Not quite on first name terms, but almost. The taoiseach and his party disembarked and I busied myself with preparing for the return journey.

Once that was done, I waited and walked about taking in the scene. The house was stone and blended into the surroundings. Jurgen and Mark accepted the invitation of a cup of tea. The conversations drifted from the helicopter to the house, reducing to faint echoes as they disappeared inside. I looked at the Blaskets from my new vantage point.

Looking north-east towards Slea Head, the full majesty and length of the Great Blasket was revealed, rising steeply out of the sea, basking in the morning sun. I followed the line along the grassy ridge and its path east/west looking down at the cliffs where the islanders had fished and placed their lobster pots from their currachs, rowing below this very cliff towards where I stood now. The highest point, the Cro, looked more elusive than ever seen from further west.

Someone approached me, asked if I wanted a cup of tea too, and led me into the house. It seemed dark inside compared to the bright sunlight outside. A large window looked south, a view of heaven through it, constantly changing. In front of it was a rough wooden table with high-backed chairs, a sheepskin thrown over each one. Taking the cup of tea, I retreated back to the sunshine not wanting to get in the way, a little shy of the company.

Looking east towards Dingle, the expanse of the bay in front of me, I stood drinking tea, smiling to myself, that it was made for me in the taoiseach's house. South was Valentia Island, the coastguard radio station, just visible on the north side white in the sunshine. Inis na Bró, beside us at the end of the Great Blasket, near enough to touch. The point of Tearaght to the west, closer and yet untouchable and out of reach, as it always is.

Time came to go. As we readied ourselves, their conversation slowed and stopped. The taoiseach came over and handed Jurgen a package, and said words I did not hear. Jurgen smiled and stepped back to salute.

Then the noise of the Dauphin starting dominated. Quiet and smooth at first, then the beat of the blades and the sound of the engines. We took off across the sea and then turned back to make a low level pass, a salute to the taoiseach. Standing slightly away from the rest of his party, he waved in reply. And we were gone.

'What's in the package, Mark?' we asked as we settled into the cruise. 'Salmon. Three wild salmon.'

13

—

PIGEONS TO MOTHER

You learn the rules by study, and the exceptions to the rules, by experience.
Anon

The Dauphin was capable of many roles and was impressively equipped. Its hoist and instrument and navigation fit were intended for its night SAR role. It could carry stretchers for air ambulance, VIPs in quickly fitted seats and troops when necessary. Two out of the five helicopters came equipped with naval modifications so that we could embark with *LE Eithne* on naval patrols. These consisted of a harpoon fitted under the belly of the helicopter which gripped the lattice grid steel deck having landed, securing the aircraft in rolling seas, as well as crash-proof fuel tanks. Fire on a ship at sea is feared and can be catastrophic. These crash-proof tanks were for the protection of the ship itself in the event of a helicopter mishap on deck as well as for the protection of the helicopter and its crew.

The navy prepared for helicopter operations with gusto. The design of the *Eithne*, the flagship of its day, was centred around the helicopter deck at the back of the ship. All the ship's procedures and organisation of the crew were dedicated to the helicopter.

Like any new aircraft coming into service, there was a honeymoon period when everyone wanted to fly in the Dauphin. Journalists, air corps and defence force hierarchy all wanted to see the marvellous new sleek modern machine in action. When this honeymoon period ended, and when the nitty-gritty of night SAR training and operations got into full swing, naval operations became relegated to a subordinate role despite extensive joint navy, air corps and French navy deck landing trials and training in the Bay of Biscay that year.

When this was completed we prepared for naval flying operations. I was flying the Alouette 3 at the time, by the time the training conveyor belt had brought me forward, naval ops was third in the hierarchy after SAR and VIP operations. The navy could have been forgiven for getting the impression that we did not want to go to sea, a suspicion exacerbated by some of our pilots mysteriously developing seasickness, preventing them going on patrol.

That left a cadre of Dauphin pilots who could go to sea. I became one of them. I enjoyed the sea and developing an understanding of being a part of a ship's crew. It was an eye-opening experience and gave me a greater insight and understanding of another arm of the defence forces.

Typically we would gather our crew of six, two pilots, two winchcrew and two engineers, in Baldonnel, and find out where the *LE Eithne* was headed. Usually, she was already at sea and we would rendezvous with her. It was generally easier to land on deck when she was under way than in the confines of the naval base or Cork harbour. Meeting her off-shore, also kept her and our movements far from prying eyes. Our joint mission may have been fishery patrol and protection, but the security of the state was always our primary role. That could mean armed intervention into anything that cropped up. The *Eithne's* information technology allied to her armour, her armed boarding parties and the stealth the helicopter provided, made her a potent and formidable asset.

On one occasion, *LE Eithne* was off the west coast. Flying a member of government the previous day had delayed us and we arrived in Shannon airport in the morning to refuel before heading west to meet up. I took the opportunity to go into the airport shop, negotiating my way through security, feeling conspicuous in my immersion flying suit, to get copies of every newspaper I could find for the ship's crew. The captain was Dónal Cotter. Owen Sherry and Tommy Gannon were the winchcrew. Nick McNulty and Fintan O'Donoghue the engineers.

We departed Shannon and tracked west to where the *Eithne* was due to be. We called them on their marine working frequency: 'Echo India Yankee Sierra, good morning, this is Delta Hotel 247. Request your position, Over'.

'Delta Hotel 247, Echo India Yankee Sierra at position 52 30 North, 010 25 West. Pigeons to mother, 265 degrees at 45 miles.'

Naval radio procedure included many slang words and expressions. We were the pigeons being given a course to steer to the mother ship, the *LE Eithne*. When heading west, next landfall America, hearing the radio crackle with 'Pigeons to mother' was very reassuring.

We were about eighty miles offshore at that point. Shannon ATC did not ask us where we were going and we did not say. All very cloak and dagger. Our approach was carried out using our on-board navigation systems, as well as following the helicopter control officer's (HCO) instructions to us. We saw her on our radar. Then she appeared, her grey shape, almost camouflaged against the Atlantic, with her white wake behind her. We tracked in closer, descending all the time, completing our pre-landing checks.

The ship's HCO handed us over to the flight deck officer

(FDO) who took over once we were in visual contact. We could see him in his white suit on the right of the flight deck. He wore a helmet and transmitted to us via long lead and hand held radio, watching us all the time. The ship maintained its course, rolling and pitching with the movement of the ocean.

Once the pitch and roll settled within given limits, and when his checks were complete, he cleared us in to land. Owen, the winch operator, opened the cargo door and watched the deck and the wheels as we touched down. We could hear him give a running commentary, his normal patter, while the FDO called out the wind direction and the pitch and roll values. I was the co-pilot and called out engine parameters if they seemed high, but mainly watched for high temperatures or signs of an engine failure.

A green light above the deck, signalled that we were cleared to land in case we had a communications failure. We came closer and closer to the deck, our blade clearance from the closed hangar doors less than ten feet. The silver fireproof-suited fire crews knelt on the left side of the deck, fire extinguisher at the ready in case the unthinkable happened and we crashed onto the deck in flames. The priority was to contain the fire on deck and not let it threaten the whole ship.

Every pilot, no matter what aircraft type he or she flies, aims to make a smooth landing. Landing on a ship is an exception. Unceremoniously, the helicopter is landed positively and firmly on deck. The captain pulls a trigger under the collective control firing the harpoon into the deck, gripping firmly, and then we feel ourselves pulled slightly downwards, the engines and rotors still running. We were locked onto the deck as much a part of the ship as its crew. We moved then as the ship moved. Our shoulder straps stopped us from compensating for the ship's movements and so we impatiently waited for the word to unstrap, to get out of our seats. Having landed on deck, the rotors slowing, one of the ship's crew would emerge holding scorecards above his head, revealing their judgement of our landing. That was CPO Gerry Cusack, the chief mechanician, a man with a huge responsibility that he carried with a smile, a sense of humour and a teak toughness.

And senior CPO Mick Veale, the highest ranking non-commissioned officer on board. CPO Barney Quirke, the invisible man who maintained all things electric and electronic. Without him there would be no flying. After a while I could see that they were like us. No matter what rank, high up or low down, no matter what the professional duty, the team, the ship's crew, the helicopter crew, were all inter-dependent.

Unclipping our individual emergency flotation packs, we emerged onto the deck, smiling and saluting the ship's crew who smiled back at our unsteady legs.

'Welcome aboard lads! Hello sir, welcome aboard'.

I was introduced. Hello and first names. The FDO's job of getting us safely aboard was done, but he then had to complete a list of other checks, to secure us and all the associated equipment. The hangar doors opened with a whirr. The ship's crew busied themselves with securing the deck. We unloaded our bags and flying gear and stowed them temporarily in the hangar. The ship's heli-deck crew, assisted by our own engineers, started to secure the helicopter. It was a hive of activity.

We were in a new world. Public address announcements split and punctuated that activity, shepherding the crew to move this way and that. A shrill two tone whistle blast followed by *'Eist le seo, eist le seo* (Hear this, hear this)', followed by an instruction. And then another closing announcement, the words '*Sin a bhfuil* (That is all)', and the same whistle again. Announcing that flying stations were complete.

We became used to these public addresses announcing that a meeting or briefing would take place, or that it was time to eat, and to go to the galley or the wardroom, announcing whatever needed to be brought to the ship's crews attention. We made our way below decks to our cabins or briefing rooms. We now had a new language in this new world. The toilets were called heads, the mess was the wardroom, the bedrooms were bunks, the front of the ship was fore, and the blunt end was aft!

The railings around the heli-deck were put up again, so we knew there would be no flying for a while. The ship resumed her course to whatever her designated patrol area was. The ship's senior officers, Cdr Frank Lynch, who was the captain, and Lt Cdr Pat McNulty, XO, met us and briefed us on the patrol plan and flying operations. It was classified up to that point so that the ship's movements could be kept as clandestine as possible to stealthily arrive at fishing grounds and catch illegal fishing trawlers. Our stealth and secrecy was also a weapon against subversives and drug-smuggling.

While the ship ploughed through the sea, and while those on duty on the bridge plotted our course, monitored the engines and listened to the emergency channel 16, we were formally briefed. I was introduced as it was my maiden voyage. Then I listened with pen in hand, noting co-ordinates and timings, smiling to myself as I recognised the names famous in sea and maritime lore and weather forecasts since I was a child listening to a crackling radio, on family holidays in a caravan in Round-stone, to the RTÉ weather report, and being told to 'shush' by my parents if I interrupted: the Great Sole Area, Porcupine Bank, Rockall Bank and so on.

We briefed. We questioned. We noted and then we calculated how much fuel we would have for each patrol at each position, taking into account how much fuel we would need to dash back to the coast in case we could not get back onto the *Eithne*. We did worst case scenario calculations in case the weather changed, in case we suffered an engine failure, or in case *Eithne* herself had a problem, checked weather forecasts for each airport on the west coast area, Waterford, Cork, Shannon, Galway, Donegal, Derry, or maybe Scotland, depending where the patrol was. And of course Castletownbere and Blacksod as well, our trusted and reliable helicopter refuelling sites.

The operational and intelligence data on board the *Eithne* was supported by state of the art Information Technology. They were able to track large numbers of fishing vessels with satellite data and radar, all without their knowledge. They could check fishing permits, licences, country of origin, species being fished and all against up-to-date Irish and EU legislation. Essential as the crew and its officers are an arm of the state, enforcing the law of the land and the sea. Our job was to gather data on ships that were suspicious in terms of their location and activity, as well as to scan over the horizon in the area blind to the ship's radar. Our daily plan would be made, and weather permitting, we would fall into a routine of patrolling, reporting, debriefing and then after a rest and a meal we would repeat it again, all the time trying to provide more data, to help the ship's crew enforce the law.

The plan was to patrol northwards, just inside the outer limit of the Irish fishing grounds. We would spend the next couple of days tracking from the Great Sole Area all the way up to the Rockall Bank. Once we were settled in, the helicopter was pulled into the hangar and secured. I went down to watch and offer help. It was fascinating to see one of the large attachment pins from each blade root removed so that they could be swept back along the fuselage and locked neatly in position. The helicopter then slowly and carefully was pulled through the hangar doors by an electric winch. I watching it slowly inch forward, its black radome, housing the radar, easing forward first. With its sleek attractive lines, its folded blades, and its streamlined fenestron shrouded tail rotor, it did have the graceful shape of a dolphin.

Once in position, the hangar doors were closed. It was a snug fit. There was barely enough room to walk between the helicopter and the hangar sides. I marvelled at how it had been done. They ship's crew and our own crew worked as a single unit, all while the ship was under way, rolling and pitching all the time. Anything not secured properly, any deviation from their procedures, and the helicopter could have been damaged. No helicopter was ever damaged going in or out of the hangar on patrol.

The rhythm of the ship was in my bones as I wandered it that evening. I knew Brian Fitzgerald, a lieutenant, and one of the officers, from rugby matches between the navy and air corps. He welcomed me for my first patrol. He explained the watch system and how the ship's crew had a working rota of sleeping, eating, watch duty and other duties too.

He introduced me to the ship's officers, people I would come to depend upon in all aspects of life on board, not just for flying. The HCOs, unseen in their operations' room below the bridge, deep in the ship, turned out to be Peter Twomey, Eugene Clonan or Martin McGrath. The anonymous yellow helmets and dark sun visors of the FDOs on the heli-deck, materialised into Seán Crowley, Tom Roche, Colm McGinley, Brian Nolan and Pearse O'Donnell.

Taking out admiralty sea charts, Brian showed me where we were going, and explained the geography of the ocean floor beneath us, the contour lines, denoting the ridges and valleys, and the edge of the continental shelf of Europe. Michael Byrne of the Tullamore Historical Society had introduced me to J.R.R. Tolkien's *The Lord of the Rings*, years before it was popular.

Echoes of my childhood followed me again as the names of the ocean floor beneath us had been used by Tolkien as placenames for Middle Earth. We tracked along a line where the continental shelf fell away to an abyss. We were working our way north along a precipice deeper than we could imagine, with elemental forces at work beyond our comprehension.

He brought me to the bridge, entering first on his own, to ask permission for me to come in and look around. His serious and professional style made me grasp the etiquette of the ship, and the interaction of the various ranks. From captain to cook, they were all locked in, cheek by jowl, for weeks at a time. Doing often dangerous work, mutual respect was as important as respect for rank. As an ignorant first-time sailor, a land lubber, his tutelage helped me to settle in, to observe and respect centuries' old maritime decorum.

The following morning, I sat in the Dauphin again. Blades unfolded, she sat on deck like a faithful dog, wanting to go for a walk. We got ready to fly. Engrossed in our own preparation, we failed to notice that others on the ship were preparing too. Four different teams, each with specific tasks, interlocking with each other and with us, slipping into both their tasks and gear. A flight deck crew, comprising the FDO, a designated captain of the watch, four of the ship's company as lashing crew (to tie and untie the helicopter thankfully, and not to administer the cat-o-nine), two fire-suit men and a swimmer of the watch.

In the operations' room, in the belly of the ship, were the operations room officer, the HCO and the helicopter tracker. The crash boat was ready, with a coxswain, a mechanician and a bowman. The ship's medic was on standby too, helping in the hangar and on the deck.

Strapping in, we were once more locked into the motion of the ship, the slow movement, side to side, over and back, up and down; slow and easy but inescapable, because of our five-point harnesses. The hangar doors whirred closed in front of us. As we completed our cockpit checks, the FDO checked in on the intercom.

The engines started, the blades accelerated to full RPM with their distinctive beat. Completing our checks, the winch operator checked the hoist and we announced that we were ready. The FDO passed the call to the bridge. While we were getting ready and starting up, the ship would maintain its patrol course and speed. Only when we were ready to go, would it alter for us. The ship started its turn, rolling slightly as it did. There were times, when the ship took up an into-wind course for us to take off, but held it for the minimum time due to sea room or reducing sea depth below. When they had to turn aggressively, we rolled noticeably away from the turn. As a result, the centrifugal force in the turn made us strain against our shoulder straps.

The helicopter held firmly in place with the harpoon. 'I like some things, but I hate that', from one of us on the intercom. Sitting on the left as the ship turned right, or starboard, I felt like I was going to fall out over the deck and into the sea. Looking at our instruments, the artificial horizon confirmed that we were rolling sharply and we were not even off the deck and flying yet.

The FDO checked that the pitch, roll and heave deck movements were within the laid down limits. Then he cleared us to go. Harpoon released with a thud, the helicopter lifted slightly as the undercarriage oleo struts extended. Then the wheels breaking contact with the deck, as we lifted to the hover. The lift-off positive, so that we would not hang around close to the moving deck, we saw the FDO drift downwards and to our right. We moved up and slightly back, away slightly to increase the blade clearance, checking all the normal engine and power parameters. If an engine failed now, we would land straight back on the deck. Below us the ship rolled lazily as we could see the upturned visor-obscured faces of the deck crew looking at us. The ship's funnel now in front of us, the exhaust plume giving us a clear indication of the wind direction.

A gentle application of rudder to turn us into that wind, the ship swivelled to the right and the ship slowly disappeared from view. Wheels up as we climbed. We turned to have a look at mother ship before starting our patrol. We could see the wake behind her, where it had altered course for our launch, and where she had already turned back onto her original course. A determined and attractive lady, *LE Eithne*, alone on the Atlantic.

Our own patrol started immediately. It was defined by a number of variables. How far offshore we were, what the weather was like where we were and at the nearest land alternate, where the ship's captain and executive officer (XO), wanted us to go. On that particular patrol, each flight lasted an hour or so. We set off with the co-ordinates of an area of ocean that we were to search. The area was north-west of *LE Eithne*. She would scan the area in front of her with her own radar while we would cover just over her horizon. Anyone east of her line was legal anyway. We approached the area at about 3,000 feet, scanning with our radar and looking out. The busiest person in the crew was the one operating the navigation computer, the nadir. He also operated the radios, as well as keeping the flight log. As the co-pilot, I was very busy, especially as it was my first patrol.

Dónal laughed as multiple radar returns appeared on the screen. 'Jaysus, Dave, I'm glad it's you and not me doing the radar today. Sure there must be thirty trawlers there already.' Owen and Tommy joined in the laughing as I cursed and started working. I started to log the positions of each vessel as we went past, plotting each position, creating a way point designation for each one, keeping them in sequence, both in the computer and on the flight log, and, finally, remaining orientated as we flew around the grid, trying to fly low and slow enough to see the names. With radio calls thrown in for good measure. 'I'll take the radios, Dave,' said Dónal, with a smile.

We could patrol through a fleet of thirty trawlers from several European countries in half an hour and pass on their positions and names to *LE Eithne*. As we flew, the data base of fishing licences would be interrogated, compared with our real-time activity report, and then the fun would begin. Illegal fishing vessels were ordered to stop, either by *Eithne* or via ourselves. No vessel could outrun her and she was armed, heavily armed. A boarding party would be prepared then. An arrest would be made if the offence was confirmed. It certainly was busy but like anything in flying, or in any work, it got easier, with each flight, each patrol. It was great to leave *LE Eithne* behind us, take to the air again, and work our systems to the limit. There was a feeling of satisfaction that came, from doing exactly what the ship's captain wanted us to do, and more.

Our flight would finish, and we would return to 'mother'. It was very easy to get disorientated. *LE Eithne* would give us her current position, and we would enter the co-ordinates into our computer and turn towards her. Following the course back to her, it was common to get an uneasy feeling that we were going the wrong way. The monotonous grey ocean sucked confidence away at times. Then she would appear again, on the radar first, and then we would see her wake and her impressive grey shape again. An inward sigh of relief, at least for me on my first naval patrol.

There were three methods of getting back onto the ship. The first being to simply fly towards her when the weather was clear, and make a visual approach and landing. The second was when we were in cloud or poor visibility where we were given a ship's controlled radar approach. This was similar to a radar controlled approach on land with slightly different terminology used. 'Pigeons to mother' being the most memorable and the one I liked to hear the most, particularly when fuel was running low.

One day, we had to use the third option; the ELVA or emergency low visibility approach. Irish weather is fickle at the best of times. West of the Atlantic coast, it can be even more unpredictable. With weather systems queuing up, one after another over an ocean, heated from below by the Gulf Stream, low visibility could quickly and unpredictably turn to fog. We always kept enough fuel to fly away to the nearest land alternate. But if there was fog onshore as well, the ELVA was our saviour.

Initiated by the officer of the watch (OOW) in the bridge broadcasting over the public address, 'Recover Helicopter by ELVA' when the ship or the helicopter went into fog. It was straightforward in principle. On the ship, all the upper deck lighting, navigation and fog lights were switched to full brilliance. The largest signal projector was shone vertically by night or down the approach bearing, that is, backwards off the back of the ship, by day. The ship's speed would be increased (they could technically go as fast as 40 knots, but a lower speed was a compromise, so we could catch her in the hover drift forward mode), by the time the helicopter reached a distance of one mile. This would increase the ship's wake, making it easier for us to see from above.

We would position behind the ship with a ship controlled approach. Once in position behind the ship, we drew closer and used the auto-hover transdown system. This brought us to just behind the ship, at our lowest hover height of 40 feet, with a residual forward speed of ten knots, increasing if the ship was going faster. Our radar would show a large red return in front of us, unseen to our eyes in fog. We increased our forward speed to fifteen knots and watched the red return grow on our screen in front of us. The winch operator would have opened the door, peering out to get sight first of the ship's wake and then the ship itself. At an agreed point, the deck crew would drop illuminated floating flares over the stern from the deck behind and below the helicopter deck, still known by its ancient name of the poop deck. This line of flares would lead us back to 'mother'. As we got sight of the ship's wake, we looked for these floating flares appearing out of the fog bobbing and floating gently past.

'Flare in sight. One o'clock, twenty yards.'

As each flare was dropped overboard, the FDO would make a radio transmission: 'Second flare dropped', and so on. We looked for each one, and lined up on them. Moving cautiously forward, the fog parted and we found ourselves looking straight out at the poop deck. The ship rolled ever so slightly in the sea and fog, the upper parts of it completely shrouded in the fog and low cloud, grey and ghostly. We climbed slightly and slid over the deck landing, once the FDO gave us permission. We shut down and took off our sweat-sodden gear as quickly as we could. One of us joked that we must find the man that gave us the last weather report. 'Well done lads. Thanks. Nice flare path', we said to the deck and fire crews, as they started to take off their helmets and gloves. The divers started to get out of their gear too, smiling at our relief, somewhat relieved themselves. For every take-off and every landing, they were fully kitted and ready to launch in a Sea Rider RIB in case we ditched. Amazing how we never knew them but trusted them with our lives.

14

PIGEONS TO MOTHER – PART 2

*A pessimist sees the difficulty in every opportunity:
an optimist sees the opportunity in every difficulty.*
                                                    Winston Churchill

No newspapers. No television. No radio. No mobile phones. No contact with family. The monotony of watch duty and sleep. Fly or wait to fly. Or just wait. Getting used to life at sea, seeing how the crew coped with heavy seas. Pouring water from a jug onto the tablecloth at a table set for our dinner. Then each plate of food unmoving as the ship rolled. At night, strapped into my bunk, restrained, my pillow on top of my head, not under it, so that I would not bang my head against the bulkhead or fall out. And all the while, the ship's crew working, watching, patrolling ploughing through the ocean in the dead of night, while their families slept in their homes in Cobh and Ballincollig, Carrigtwohill and Cork City.

I often roamed the ship at night when I couldn't sleep, if the swell was big and sleep impossible. Peering out into the darkness from the bridge, listening to the weather reports being transmitted by Valentia or Cork or Clifden radio. The dull red light of the navigation and engine instruments all around, carefully walking and trying not to stumble into one of the watch crew.

Outside I often stood in silence, holding the guard rail, spray and wind and salty brine. Thinking of my father. He would slip into my thoughts like a friend calling unannounced. But welcome. The jumble of stories and half-remembered memories would come to life for me. In the monochrome of moonlight or faint starlight, I saw him looking over the side of a different ship. A converted merchant ship during the war. Its decks crammed with troops. Watching silently, shoulder to shoulder with his comrades, as they watched France draw closer.

Smoking cigarettes, hoping that the battle was really over. The flashes of artillery further inland, as Arromanches and Normandy awaited them. The continuous drone of bombing aircraft overhead, lining up invisibly on their targets. The shadows of the concrete break waters and scuttled merchant navy ships that protected the beachheads, slipping past as the tension rose. The rising and falling metal behemoths, the Mulberry piers, where they docked, and started to course over the pontoon bridges, until they set their vehicles and feet on French soil. And liberated it. He went ashore a couple of days after the big day, D-Day. And because of that pause, that gap between D and D plus whatever day he arrived, he lived and I was born.

He used to say that his life and survival were accidents of fate. It upset him at times, the memories still raw and fresh, of stepping over the bodies as they advanced inland. The bodies lying on the sand or in the hedgerows, sea gulls pecking at their remains, white identification papers blowing in the wind. Young men, their blood staining the French sand, some intact with neat fatal wounds. Others cut in two, dismembered or decapitated by remorseless machine gun fire. Or simply strewn about the place by bombs, grenades, mines or shells. 'It could have been me. It could have been me.'

But he was almost taken once or twice. As all survivors surely were and are. As I shaved at the sink in my cramped cabin,

holding on as the *Eithne* rolled in heavy seas, I used to look in
the mirror and see him, not me. Using a horse hair brush, he
lathered his face. Then the tap, tap, tap, of the razor against the
side of his metal mess tin. In his other hand, a small mirror. He
was a young man. Twenty-four.

He knelt in a wood, looking around like a deer sniffing the
wind. Birds chattered in the trees around him. And then fell
silent. The flapping of wings as they flew away, darkening the
sky as they left. I hear the muffled shouting in the background
that he used to describe. He paused and looked up. Hearing
incoming mortar rounds. In the mirror he held, I see the impact
behind him. Earth explodes fifty yards away as the first hit. The
mirror fell and all was dark. I imagine the feeling of the shock
wave as six more rounds exploded.

'And what did you do then dad?' I used to ask him.

He picked up the mirror. It was shaking in his trembling
hands. Someone ran up behind him. They were laughing. My
dad knew he was laughing because he could see it, but he could
not hear it. Because of a ringing in his ears that stayed until
he died, sixty-one years later in Co. Clare. Still in shock, he
tried to continue shaving. It was July 1944. They were attack-
ing Caen. He recorded the dates in spidery neat pencil, in the
leather bound pocket bible that he used to read each night. And
which I keep safe forever: 'Caen taken'.

The image fades as I stagger back out of the gloom, into the
ship once more. Arriving as the plot is updated. 'Where are we
now lads?' I asked.

'We're off the Bull Rock, sir. West of Castletownbere. Heading north-west.'

They showed me their plot on the admiralty chart, positions
plotted meticulously, timed and dated in fine pencil, a chain
link of dots, pointing north-west. This was a manual plot in case

the computer navigation failed. I went back down through the galley ways, making my way to the hangar and the heli-deck. The Dauphin was well wrapped up and secure for the night inside its hangar. Seawater sloshed under the door. I walked through one of the side doors, staggering as I stepped out onto the heli-deck.

I could see the glow of a cigarette and the shadow of one of the crew standing at the railing. The swell was making for a rough ride, but it was clear, windy and dry. As I put my hand on the railing beside him, he turned and said 'hello', his cigarette cupped in his other hand. We could not really talk because of the wind. He must have known I was one of the aircrew but I could not tell who he was, and did not ask, assuming he was tired and in the middle of a duty, but we had a couple of cigarettes together. He told me we were west of Castletownbere where Michael Quinn had died a few years before. Leading Seaman Michael Quinn who had died in a rescue in the bay in January 1990 and was posthumously decorated for gallantry by the king of Spain himself, Juan Carlos.

The man beside me in the darkness had been on the *LE Deirdre* that night. No helicopter could have gotten through, he said. A Spanish fishing vessel had run aground at Roancarrigmore Rock, so near and yet so far from safety. I didn't know what to say. 'The sea will take you', he said then. We fell silent for a while, smoking our cigarettes, thinking of that brave young man, as we shivered in the wind. We were over a hundred miles west of that watery grave where the masts of the Spanish vessel that sank that night still stick out above the water in Castletownbere, a reminder to all who passed her of the dangers of the sea and of Michael Quinn's heroism. In later years as we flew by to refuel the Sikorsky at Castletownbere, before or after long range rescues, those masts sticking out of the water were a reminder of danger, a reminder to pray for Michael Quinn and those he left behind. And maybe even pray for ourselves.

When we could not fly, and I tired of reading whatever books I had brought or borrowed, I asked to go on a boarding party. At first they smiled, then they realised I was serious, and went off to see about it. Cdr Lynch said 'yes', as there was no chance of flying stations at the time.

The boarding party was the navy's inspection team. They would launch a Sea Rider RIB over the side, crewed by an officer and four crew. The crew carried a waterproof radio and each man could be armed with the standard weapon of the day in the defence forces, the Austrian made Steyr rifle, if the vessel was acting suspiciously or fishing illegally. Their job was to inspect every aspect of the trawler's fishing activity, to make sure it was legally compliant with EU and Irish law. The inspections were time consuming and thorough – logbooks, licences, fishing permits, nets, fish holds, anything and everything. It was a serious job, taken seriously by the trawler's crew who co-operated and waited nervously for it all to be completed.

I joined the boarding party at the heli-deck, a convenient place for us to brief and get ready. Suiting up with a heavy duty dry suit, with built-in boots, I put on the lifejacket and helmet that I was given. I waited, as the standard orders for firing their weapons were repeated, and acknowledged, the same orders wherever defence forces personnel carry arms. The details of the trawler were discussed: Spanish trawler, long-liner, at sea four weeks, previous convictions and offences, what to look for and so on. Aviation is full of procedure and briefing and information. I found it a revelation listening to the amount of knowledge these men had been given courtesy of the ship's information technology, and also the comprehensiveness of their preparation. I had thought it was just a case of hopping over the side into a boat and away. I was in for a surprise.

'And lads, we're bringing one of the pilots with us. Make sure we bring him back. The captain said to make sure he doesn't fall into the tide.' Smiles all around as the seadogs looked me up and down. They readied themselves to board a Spanish trawler, 160 miles west of Mizen Head as they had done countless times before, as countless other navy vessels have done over many years, largely unseen by the Irish public. Well, I was going to see anyway. The crew helped me into the RIB, wondering if I would get sick on them or fall over the side. I was determined not to let the side down.

'*Eist le seo, Eist le seo.* Boarding stations, boarding stations.' The gantry that held the RIB in place was lowered. Other deck crew held it steady with guide ropes as one by one we filed in and sat down. Then we were lowered, out and down to the ocean. As we fell away slowly from the ship's side, I looked up at the onlookers. My own Dauphin crew laughing at me, and telling me to bring back a fish. The RIB crew had no time for looking at the ship. They focused on the swell as we were lowered onto it. The RIB's engine was running, ready. The man at the helm twisted the throttle a couple of times, making the engine race and then quieten, making sure it was good to go. As gently as possible, we were lowered onto an approaching crest. Timed beautifully, we sat onto the crest, avoiding the trough behind it. As the RIB was released from the gantry, the engine roared. As gently as a butterfly landing on a flower, we were on the ocean.

We raced away dropping straight away into a trough. The *Eithne* disappeared from view as I held onto the hand line on each side of me. We turned away so that we would not hit 'Mother', a very real and dangerous possibility. While I got used to the bumpy ride, like a man riding a horse at a canter for the

first time, the others were already at work, radioing a communications check, and pointing out the trawler.

I could not see it. I couldn't even see *LE Eithne*. I was disorientated as we climbed each swell and dropped into each trough.
It was a white knuckle ride. The RIB crew turned to see how I
was getting on, smiling at me, as the freezing spray washed over
us. Before we left *LE Eithne*, I had looked across at the Spanish trawler. It was less than a mile away. Now that we were in
the RIB, it seemed a much bigger distance to travel. I realised,
judging distance depended on the vessel you are in. Just like
aviation.

When we were about half way across, I could see *LE Eithne*
again. Her grey hulk appearing and disappearing, solid, powerful and seemingly motionless in comparison to us. The trawler
drew closer. It pitched and rolled in the 25 foot swell, rusty and
old, weather-beaten and ominous. As we came alongside, some
of the fishermen looked down, waved and nodded, and then
reappeared with a scrambling net. Thrown over the side, it clung
there and they stood back, waiting. That was the way up.

Once again, the RIB crew timed their movement with the
swell and the trawler's rolling. Skilfully positioning themselves,
one by one they jumped off onto the trawler's net. They did it
so expertly, it was more like a step. As I waited, I could see into
the bowels of the trawler, into the lower deck and fishermen
standing there, watching me, watching them, as they baited the
long line that trailed behind their vessel. They came in and out
of view as the swell dropped the RIB and raised it again.

When three were gone, it was my turn. Drawing alongside,
the RIB helmsman shouted to me, 'You can stay here if you
want. It's up to you. I'll be going back to *Eithne* until the inspection is finished.' I gave a thumbs up and pointed at the
trawler. I jumped as we came level. I did not get on board with

the same grace as the others but I managed and was helped by several hands. Hauled up smiling, I took in my new surroundings.

I was a silent witness from then on. They opened proceedings by reading the trawler captain his rights, informing him very formally, that he was being inspected by the Irish navy, in accordance with Irish and EU law, and so on. For the next hour or so, I stumbled after the boarding crew as they inspected and probed. I listened as they asked for logbooks and licences, and checked safety equipment. Communicating with *LE Eithne* and passing back fish catch details, and licence serial numbers. On a gloomy day off the west coast of Ireland. Just another boarding party. Just another days' work for the navy. But it was very impressive. I was very proud of them.

Some professionals train for situations they never encounter. The navy routinely encountered situations that you cannot train for. Another underlying and unspoken aspect of the interaction of the navy and the fishermen, was mutual respect. Everyone doing their job. Each at the mercy of the elements and the ocean. Making a living. The naval team were firm in their work, but patient when the Spanish captain did not understand. The Spanish themselves, co-operating and offering coffee in the bridge, and fish from their catch. Out of a respect for the uniforms and the formality of the team but also, I think, because they were well aware that the navy would be their closest means of rescue if the worst happened.

In the bridge, the trawler's captain was asked for the vessels plans. Taking them with us, we navigated below decks, inspecting the holds and sometimes even looking for hidden compartments. Into the belly of the beast. One of the tools the boarding party had was a measuring tape. Having counted and moved about thirty boxes of fish, the petty officer I was with, measured the depth and height of the hold. Then compared it with the plans. Even though it was freezing, we were sweating with the work. Our breath steamed in front of us. We were below the water line and moving around like a fairground ride.

Just when I thought it was over, we would lift more boards, move more fish boxes, probing and kicking the ice out of our way. I said I was going up top, and with a nod and a reassurance that I felt OK, I made my way upwards. I ended up on the long line deck at the aft of the trawler. I stood unseen at first, watching the flashing hooks as they went by, being expertly baited by the fishermen. Like a conveyor belt at a factory, the lines trailed past them, and into the ocean. They worked by hand, wearing ordinary clothes, as the sea water washed around them in the swell and sea spray blew around them.

Standing in my layers of warm, waterproof gear, I was in a different world to them. They saw me, nodding, nervously, thinking I was inspecting them, I suppose. '*Hola, Buenos Dias,*' I said, using the only Spanish I knew. They replied in kind turning to nod at me. Mind your hands on those hooks lads, I thought. They wore Nike tops, flip-flops, track-suits and tee-shirts, an FC Barcelona football jersey or two, a Spanish jersey and one or two I did not recognise: colourful once, faded now. Some of the men looked Spanish, some north African, Moroccan maybe, all sorts of skin tones and ethnic backgrounds so far from their homes.

Music of the Souk started to play in my mind, God knows where it came from, as I watched the black African deck crew at work. *Sean nos* Irish style singing that sometimes drifts around me, became intertwined with African melodies, sad and mournful, lilting and changing key, rhythm folding back on itself unexpectedly, music from different places, different peoples, celebrating life but lamenting loss or loneliness. The fishermen looked dishevelled, cold and bedraggled. Holding onto nothing, as the deck rolled and dropped beneath them, they baited their steel hooks, sure-footed and silent. What music played in their minds? Whose faces smiled at them in their day-dreaming?

Years later, I used to hear SAR colleagues bemoan the regular callouts we got to Spanish vessels. A natural enough human response to being roused from a warm bed in the middle of a stormy night. I would not have disagreed but the image, of those men that day, stays with me forever, looking at me and through me, haunting me, never allowing me to doubt the urgency of their call. Whenever it came.

15

LAST ORDERS

You live longer once you realise that any time spent being unhappy is wasted.
Anon.

Pilots have to keep accurate flying logbooks. A logbook is a legal document and records your flights, your training, your instrument ratings, simulator training and all that sort of professional stuff. Some pilots take great care with their logbooks. Some don't. Some logbooks are bare and impersonal, and consist of pages and pages of perfectly added flying hour numbers, totals and sub-totals.

Others have scribbles, newspaper clippings, photos of themselves smiling in faded photographs beside long forgotten aeroplanes and helicopters, even photographs of babies and children. Logbooks record the change in the personality of the pilot too. The exactness of each entry at the beginning of a flying career: the totals, the underlining, the verifying signatures and stamps from management or National Aviation Authority; the gradual slip from print to hand writing; from clarity to errors and corrections, coffee stains and dog ears; the evidence of a pilot's personal life and experiences, intruding on the recording of flight time. The logbook tracks the change from the entry out of devotion to the entry out of obligation.

In the space of two years I got married and retired from the air corps. Two of the most momentous events of my life. I have to look back through my logbook, to try to jog my memory, to try to remember. Among the dates, crews names, types of flights, as well as where the flights took place, I try to read between the lines.

It does not take too much calculation to see that half of my working life was spent away on duty. I was not alone in this regard. I spent a week at a time in Donegal on SAR duty, often twice a month, then navy patrols and flying VIPs here and there, all of which I enjoyed but all keeping me away from my family and my fiancée. As I approached my thirties, I must have begun to think of leaving.

Civil SAR was up and running in Shannon. I had visited there with the Swiss air force when they were in Ireland. As we arrived, the Sikorsky S-61 was departing on a rescue. It was huge and impressive. I had hoped to meet one of our former winch-crew that day; John Manning, but he was on the departing crew. The chief pilot was there, a cheerful Englishman, about fifty years of age, called Al Lockey. I introduced the others to him, and we stayed for a chat. We left after half an hour. Pilots have very short attention spans when there is no aircraft to touch and ogle. As we went away, Al looked at me mischievously: 'Would you be interested in joining us, Dave? We need more Irish here you know.' I think I laughed and said, 'You never know.'

The West Coast Action Committee had been formed by that time and became famous in the circles I worked in and in marine circles. They were Joan McGinley, Joey Murrin and Peter Murphy from Donegal. Joan, from a fishing community, Joey the head of the fisherman's organisation, and Peter, a solicitor. Fergus O'Connor, an ex-air corps helicopter pilot himself, Paddy Kavanagh and Eamonn Doyle, both ex-naval officers, were also there and Dr Marion Broderick, a medical doctor from the Aran Islands. They battled against much opposition to get the state to put in place a medium range helicopter SAR service.

While the media discussed their report, and whether civil SAR should be in existence in the first place, I was trying to decide what starter and main course to have for the wedding meal. As my colleagues started to leave and join airlines, I was wondering where to go on our honeymoon. We tried once more to win the defence forces rugby championship. Who else but the navy knocked us out, with Brian Fitzgerald and some of the *LE Eithne* crew, applying the *coup-de-grâce*.

Tullamore was home. My parents' home was my home. My bed was always made up for me, even though I was in my late twenties. I could call and say that I would be down for the night, and I knew that a meal awaited me: a casserole in the winter, baked potatoes or bacon and cabbage and boiled potatoes. I was fussed over as if I were still a child. The baby of the family, but I was getting married and leaving this behind.

I look back and reminisce, and see 'movie trailers' in my mind of that time of my life. Recent enough to retain, unlike childhood memories that have to be scratched out carefully. Snippets of my life, that memory has preserved. The senses jostle with each other to bring to life some essence of the past: the smell of my father's match being struck, how that smell and colour changed as I watched it flare, the sound of the puff, puff, and the draw, to get first his pipe and then my mother's cigarette lit. I can almost taste that tobacco still. The sound of a stylus being lowered gently onto a record, the hiss and scratch, as it found the hidden groove. 'Hold it by the edge, mind it now', he would say, when I was a child. I carefully did what he said, the record seeming almost sharp enough to cut me.

I had been the youngest. My brother and sisters, already out

in the world working and living separate lives. Me left drinking
in my parents' lives. Badminton on Tuesdays, he would come
home sweating, with a towel around his neck, tucked into his
jumper with all the latest from the school hall and friends,
Regie Morris, Joe and Isobel Mulligan, Geoffrey Kennedy and
Greg Strong, while I finished my homework. 'Don't overdo it,'
she would chide him. 'You're not as young as you used to be.'
His bragging that he could still beat the youngsters.

Meals-on-wheels, with my mother, collecting the food near
the hospital on the Arden Road. What days did we do that? To
the old couple who lived alone, out by Ballydaly. 'Will you have
a duck's egg, gossun?' they would ask me each time. Jimmy, the
man who lived alone down the lane, where, years later, we built
our house. I would walk into his dark house, feeling his dog's
wet nose sniffing at me, his face as he looked up, half-lit from
the glow of the turf fire where he sat. The smell of the turf,
cut a couple of hundred yards from his own door, by Trevor,
his neighbour and friend, later ours. 'Thanks very much missus,
thanks very much.'

In those couple of years around the time I got married something in me changed. Some cog fell into place. Some connection
made. The decade since leaving school had passed so quickly. It
was not that I made a decision to do this or that differently but
at a subconscious level something was happening. I was getting married, and starting to contemplate leaving the job I had
dreamed of as a child.

Another piece of my childhood jigsaw had always been the
Tullamore Gramophone Society. My parents were always in it.
The idea was simple. People took it in turns to do a 'recital'.
This evening consisted of them playing whatever music they
liked over a two hour period or so. There would be a break in
the middle for tea and sandwiches, or alcohol if preferred. The

music tended to be classical, but could include jazz, blues and carefully chosen pop music of the day. The evenings were very social with plenty of chat about the backgrounds of the music, why they were chosen, and so on.

One evening, down for a couple of nights' visit, I went along to one. The person giving the recital arranged the turntable, the speakers, the connecting wires and cables, and carefully prepared hand-written notes. 'Hello again everyone. Welcome to David down from Dublin. And Ann and Peter who have moved to Screggan from Galway. And Father Joe, back from his holidays. I'll get straight into it. I am going to play Rachmaninov, concerto number ...' He carefully took out a black vinyl long playing record from its sleeve, its distinctive yellow colours, showing that it was *Deutsche Gramophone*, the real deal, top-of-the-range, the latest recording from a series in Chicago. There were nods of approval and a hum of chat in anticipation. It was at one of those recitals that I listened as my father played his selection. The man who I always remember smiling, perhaps leaning on his spade in the garden, taking a break from digging potatoes, talked about things he normally would not mention. 'This is the Red Army Choir. Russian folk music, adapted and made into marching music. It starts off slowly. You'll have to wait for it to build up. I heard the Russian soldiers singing this in Berlin at the end of the war.' Hard to hear at first, building to a passionate and patriotic fervour. Filling the room and our minds, with our own imaginings of the Russian steppes, or wartime Germany. Then Spanish classical guitar, Rodrigo and his music of the mountains. While it drizzled outside, the room filled with the sound of strings accompanying John Williams.

I would love to say that later, on evenings like this, we discussed my future, my life, marriage, love. I would love to say that, over a settling pint of stout, my father said something that

I could quote for evermore, but our conversation is blurred now. No sound bites. The reality was that I was lucky to have an entire lifetime of shared anecdotes and times. I just did not realise it at the time.

Those last visits were my farewell to my parents, farewell to childhood. The apron strings cut, slowly. They would wait patiently as my car lights came down the lane, only knowing it was me when my lights entered the small drive. They would stay in their chairs if I was late, smiling and standing up to hug and shake my hand in welcome. 'It's all right. It's in the oven. It'll still be warm. How was the drive? We opened a bottle of wine. Sit down and tell us all your news, and I'll pour you a glass.'

And when I told them one evening that I was thinking of leaving my job, leaving our house and leaving Dublin, they listened and did what they always did. They told me that it was a great idea. Whether they meant it or not, I had their support. It was not as significant to me then as it would be later.

My father was fond of The Bridge House in the town. The restaurant had always been held in high esteem and had a reputation countrywide. Like anything excellent, it was not cheap. We would go there, now and again, and feast, and eat and drink too much. I went as a child when my brother Philip returned from London or Hilary or Ruth returned from Dublin and France. Before I married, we went there again. We settled into a table, a couple of drinks, a few cigarettes, and then Jimmy O'Sullivan, the gracious Kerry manager, returning with a flourish to take orders. My mother tried to order the cheapest thing on the menu. Jimmy seduced my father and me into getting one of the specials, shifting from foot to foot, looking furtively over his shoulder, as if he was offering us something illegal. The after dinner drink. Jimmy used to bring us an Italian coffee. Like Irish coffee, but instead of being made with whiskey, it had Amoretto. Leaving home, leaving Tullamore, saying goodbye to life as a son, about to embark on life as a husband, for me that meal was my farewell banquet.

Back to Donegal. Seeing the county again in darkness in moonlight and starlight. We had navigation flights to Letterkenny, all the way around the coast, the way we would have to fly in winter to avoid ice, following the lighthouses beams, relentlessly flashing their coded identities into the Atlantic infinity, all the way from Finner to St Johns Point, south of Killybegs, seeing how many fishing vessels were in, seeing the navigation lights blinking at dusk. Then past the 2,000 foot cliffs at Slieve League. Keeping well clear, watching the radar return as it mapped Rathlin O'Beirne Island on the western edge of the bay with its own lighthouse. Feeling the tickle or the rumble of turbulence, depending on how strong the wind was, as it reflected off the wall of the cliffs.

To Aranmore Island Lighthouse. Then Tory Island. Along the top of Ireland, looking east at the shadows of islands, where once people had lived: Cruit Island, Owey Island, Gola Island. Then Fanad lighthouse. Its beam guarding the entrance to Lough Swilly. Turning carefully we lined up the lough on our radar. Flying at night, at a couple of hundred feet above the sea, below the SSA, safe sector altitude. The Urris Hills, rising to just under 1,500 feet, lurked inland, east of us, on the Inishowen peninsula, littered with the wrecks of the Second World War aircraft. The Mamore Gap with its false promise of a safe route home, slightly lower than Urris, hiding Slieve Snaght, at over 2,000 feet, further inland. How those pilots and navigators must have been relieved to be almost home, exhausted and using poor charts, concentration lapsing after u-boat patrols, sometimes under fire, some struggling to keep damaged aircraft in the sky. The hidden Donegal hills finished them off.

Enjoying the company of people I would never fly with again:

Ciaran Murphy, Kelvin Duffy, Ken Skelly and John O'Rourke. We flew south, past Fort Dunree, past Buncrana, then Inch Island. Finally turning south south-west, to see the lights of Letterkenny, and the hospital. A sigh of relief. A landing and then repeat it again in reverse. Or stopping off for a cup of tea and a chat with the radio operators and rescue controllers in Malin Head Radio. Right at the top of the country, at that beautiful desolate place, led by Mick McGarry, watching and listening all the time. Another group of unsung heroes, hiding out of sight, ex-lighthouse men and ships' radio officers, listening constantly to the crackling radios. Just as they do at Valentia, Dublin and Belfast.

To Blacksod. Past the beautiful Stags of Broadhaven again. To stop and meet Vincent. To hear him talk about storms, about the wild geese returning from the Arctic and wintering on the Iniskee Islands off the Mullet Peninsula. About when the islands were inhabited and which local people were born and raised out there. The whaling station. The lighthouses around the coast, where he had worked. He had served on each and every one when they were manned.

One day we went to Blacksod, and shut down the engines, stopped for tea and conversation. When you are training, it is possible to stop, to talk and take a few minutes' break. Not everyone does stop though.

The captain that day, Dave Sparrow, went in to phone operations or to check the weather. I was left outside as the P2 to supervise fuelling. The noise of a helicopter around Blacksod draws local people, especially children, especially in good weather. They could tell the helicopters apart. Which was the air corps Dauphin or the Sikorsky. Whether it was a training flight or a rescue. Refuelling or stopping for tea.

I found myself at the helicopter, surrounded by local children, Vincent's children, David, Simon and Erika, as well as their cousins Dermot and Fergus, and friends. I listened as they mixed Irish and English in their chat. Blacksod is a Gaeltacht. Vincent's wife Doreen is the local school principal, in a school where all subjects are taught through Irish. I started to tell them about the helicopter. I answered their questions, showed them how the winch worked, fitted a rescue strop on them, while drinking a cup of tea, that Dick O'Sullivan, the winch operator had brought out. Dick continued: 'So when Dave is looking out, he can't see what's underneath him. I open this door, I look down, and I tell him what I can see. Then I talk to him, so that he hovers where I want.'

'And could you fall out? Is it scary?'

An acre site surrounded by an eight foot wall. A lighthouse and a rescue helicopter. Two of us and ten children from the parish. The sound of the sea on the shore outside the lighthouse walls. The wild kids from the parish. But they weren't wild. They listened. They asked questions. They put on rescue strops as we demonstrated this or that. And over the next ten years, I watched those children grow up. I got to know their names and they knew mine. I knew when they were leaving school. And when I was older, and worn out from rescue, they were often there, helping Vincent to refuel, saying 'hello' and wishing me well. Such a fragile and tenuous friendship. Refuelling the helicopter in later years, so that we could push out 200 miles west. Recharging and renewing my spirits, giving me encouragement and strength.

In between trips home and to Donegal and to the navy, we used to fly out to the east coast for training. A new bigger launch was on contract to us, *The Wicklow Research*, owned by Gordon Hunter. Just as we had done with the Alouette and Mick Purcell, so we did again with Gordon. The idea was to keep night-current, not to lose the night winching skills.

I remember dinghy training that we did each year in Dublin

Bay. In the Dauphin, we wore PSPs. In an emergency, we would carry out the escape drill and be able to inflate these packs and get into them. It was not that easy though, and that is why we practised it. That year we went to the bay at dusk. Gordon Hunter and *The Wicklow Research* were there as safety. It was autumn and the sea temperature was cold. We got into a choppy sea, fumbling around as it got dark, trying to overcome the numbing cold of the water. Mentally deciding, to buy neoprene diver's gloves at the next opportunity, we struggled into each dinghy, trying to tie them together and then closed, to preserve the heat, hearing the splashing in the dark, as others failed to get in, seeing the flash of the torches, and the sound of laughter, as one of the supervisors said, 'Ah, sir, will you get into the fuckin' thing!'

That year I was with a fellow Tullamore man, David O'Flaherty during those dinghy drills. When I finished flying the Alouette 3, I had given him all my detailed border maps, carefully marked and high-lighted. For some reason I remember clearly, the two of us bobbing around in the semi-darkness that evening insulated from the cold in our fully deployed PSPs, lying back and chatting about home.

'Were you home lately?'

'I was. I was home two weeks ago. There's a lot of building going on out your way. Come to think of it, there's a lot of building going on out our way too.'

Asking each other if any of our old school friends were around, which pubs had been sold or done up, who was going out with whom. Same old town gossip that we shared and traded. Both understanding that our lives were probably not going to be lived there again. In the town we loved so well. Laughing at the changes. Floating in canvas survival packs at night in Dublin Bay 200 yards from the Forty Foot. Not knowing that that was one of the last conversations I would ever have with him.

One night we were called out after flares had been sighted on the north-west Donegal coast. With Ian Downey and Brian Moran as winchcrew, we set off after midnight to the Rosses. We spent about three hours searching up and back along the coast between the many islands. It was a clear night, with a full moon, making our task not just easier but enjoyable. It turned out to be a hoax but we did not know at the time. We searched using every pattern stored in the navigation computer, adjusting the leg lengths and the track spacings so that we flew in between the islands that came up on our radar screen, gliding between them like a slalom skier. My obsession with islands made me enjoy it even more, trying to count the ruined houses as we slipped past.

It's all very well to read in a manual that searches are best done 'down sun', meaning with the sun behind you, and 'up moon', with the moon in front of you. However that mission stands out for the clarity of the moonlight and the way we adjusted the search tracks, to line up facing into the moon and darkness as we turned away. A ghostly clear light as we turned back into the moon. There were other lessons that night too. A hoax is a nuisance, but you can still get training value out of it. And a friendly crew, one that not only respects each other, but enjoys each other's company, can achieve an awful lot. Dave, Ian and Brian were always a pleasure to fly with.

1994 saw me leave the air corps. Kevin McCarrick was the first of us to go to Shannon and civil SAR. I followed him a year later. Some pilots stay, some go. It is a personal choice everyone makes. I loved rescue and relished learning more. I was afraid of becoming desk-bound, especially as I seemed to be doing more frequent stints in the operations' office. Anyway, leaving is never seen as disloyal. Leaving creates opportunities and promotions for those left behind, keeps the whole place fresh. That is what they say anyway.

I left, with enthusiasm and apprehension. From the sanctuary of my familiar helicopter wing, I went to a civil unit staffed by ex-RAF and royal navy Sea King crews. Would I measure up? I was in touch with Kevin who was in Aberdeen in Scotland flying the Sikorsky S-61 to and from the oil rigs. He was there to accumulate flying hours. He was enjoying it all but was candid about the adjustments he was having to make, the challenges he was facing.

One day, I returned home to my wife in our new house having been away yet again on SAR duty. There was lots to do around the house, inside and outside but Lynda stopped me and said she had something for me. I did not take much notice. She repeated her words again pointing to the table, which was set for dinner, to a dish cloth, folded in a triangle. 'Guess what's underneath it.' I guessed incorrectly that we had won the lotto, that she had bought us concert tickets or a voucher for a weekend away somewhere. 'Have a look', she said. I lifted the dish cloth to see a slim tube or stick. I picked it up, not knowing at first, what the hell it was. She squeezed my hand as I saw the blue line, clearly visible on the side. A positive pregnancy test.

'Looks like this family is getting bigger,' she said with a smile.

16

STICKY TOFFEE PUDDING

You only see your parents love when you become a parent yourself.

Anon.

Summer 1994 went in a blur. Chopping and changing my retirement date. Trying to arrange ground school, simulator time and a start date for flight training on the Sikorsky. There was so much to miss at home. So much to feel doubtful about. Was it a good idea to leave? So much tradition. So much a part of it. A secure job and good company. I doubted myself. When the official response was a delay to my retirement date, I protested but inwardly breathed a sigh of relief. Two more months' service. Two more months' flying. Two more months saying goodbye.

When the date was confirmed, my training in Irish Helicopters fell into place. They would be my new employer, and I would be in Shannon working on contract for the department of marine. I would find out later on who everyone was and their backgrounds. Most were ex-royal navy or RAF crews, as well as former civilian North Sea helicopter crews. Some were ex-Irish air corps.

The date of my departure drew close, and I suddenly did not have time to say goodbye. Where was Sgt Matt Hanley, the man who ran the parachute shop? The man who won the javelin championship for twenty years or so, before an upstart of a pilot took his title and then shook his hand and became friends? Where was Flt Sgt Jim Fortune, the engineer from the

Fouga squadron, who I battled in vain against in badminton? Or Sgt Matt Crowe, the winch operator who got his rating the same day as me? Or Sgt Mick Arthur, the prop forward on our victorious rugby team?

Or Jarlath Connerney? The retired engineer who instructed on airframes, engines and aeronautics. He was a member of the Royal Aeronautical Society, a space travel devotee who had attended several Russian and American space launches over the years. Soft spoken, modest, unassuming, he knew everything there was to know about flying, and passed it on almost lovingly. He proudly followed the careers of all his protegés over the years, never taking personal credit, instead praising 'the corps'.

Some I met before I left. Some I did not get the chance to meet before taking off my uniform for the last time. Not being able to say goodbye made me realise that whatever opportunities and challenges lay ahead, I was leaving great camaraderie behind.

Being in Aberdeen for the ground school, prepared me for working and flying there. Aberdeen is one of the busiest heliports in the world. As I walked along the airfield fence from the Skean Dhu Hotel, I watched amazed, the number of helicopters coming and going: Eurocopter Superpumas, Dauphins, Sikorsky S-61s and S-76s, as well as smaller types. All very well to say I was looking forward to it, but I could see I had a lot of work to do to adjust.

Irish Helicopters was part of Bristow Helicopters, one of several offshore helicopter operators in Aberdeen. The Irish pilots, who were already working in SAR in Shannon, had all been sent to Aberdeen because it was the quickest way to accumulate flying hours before converting to SAR. Carmel Kirby, Dara Fitzpatrick and Kevin McCarrick, had all been there.

I arrived in November. The baby was due later that month.

The only thing I managed to do before returning to Ireland was to get my UK licence validation so that I could fly in the North Sea, that, and a night rig landings flight to a rig called *The Aberdeen Explorer*, a line check for day and night deck landings, before flying 'the line' out of Bristow Aberdeen.

The training captain for that flight was Capt. Tim Noble, not much older than myself, another person with whom it was a pleasure to fly. Having come through months of training, travelling, ground school, exams and tests, doubt and relief, that flight sticks in my mind. We briefed as it became dark, going over performance, and what the classroom theory meant in real terms to the pilot: how to fly an approach, so that we could guarantee landing on the deck even if we had an engine failure; how to take off and fly away in the event of engine failure. All previously covered but repeated because this was a night line check.

The rig got closer and closer in the dark, and then we started the approach: manual night flying, no auto-pilot. Our anti-collision lights reflected off the metal around us as we sank gently onto the deck. Taking off again meant lifting to the hover, pitching forward into the darkness, the instant adjustment from visually scanning outside to the instrument scan inside. It reminded me of coming and going from Blacksod at night. We repeated it half a dozen times then back to Aberdeen airport. I was buoyed by Tim's encouragement and the simple enjoyment of getting it done and 'ticking the box'. I left a few days later for home to wait for the arrival of our first baby.

All thoughts of restricted decks, PNR (point of no return) calculations and flying off over the North Sea before sunrise were put on hold, but there was no sign of the baby's arrival. Finally in early December our first baby was born: Alyson. Our parents and families rushed to see the new addition. Seeing her arrive put all my concerns about work and flying into perspective.

Seeing my own parents holding her, smiling and with happy tears in their eyes, made me realise that this was a new phase of my life. I had become a father. This little perfect, fragile baby would be depending on me to keep us afloat. We settled into our house with her, but four days later, I was gone again.

With hundreds of oil rigs and platforms to support, as well as on-going exploration west of the Shetland Islands, the training school was always busy. My target was to adapt both to the S-61 and to offshore public transport flying which was quite different. The Sikorsky S-61 weighs ten metric tonnes when fully laden. From blade tip to tail, it was 73 feet long. It could carry nineteen passengers. It was nicknamed 'The Queen of the Skies' and was being phased out of public transport flying because of the 'Tiger', the name given to the Superpuma. However, about eight of them still flew in the North Sea to rigs and platforms within 150 miles distance offshore.

I used to check in at the main reception, and then go to the operations room. It seemed vast to me when I first walked in. The entire North Sea area chart was displayed on one wall, with hundreds of different coloured pins denoting rig or platform positions. The opposite wall held data for each and every one of them, in neat compact pigeonholes. Each and every offshore installation had a set of equivalent notes, or 'plates' as they are known, which list physical descriptions of the installations: their height, orientation, helicopter pad position, as well as frequencies, dangers and other information.

Computers were lined up with access to the national meteorological system, as well as offshore weather reports from the individual rigs. Weather data for the other side of the North Sea was also available, in case diversions were necessary to Norway. Other computer terminals were used to calculate performance, by inputting the variables of the day and of the flight: number of passengers, temperature and pressure, as well as offshore rig restrictions. The computer would spit out a recommended fuel load to get us to the rig, with an on-shore alternate, while also keeping our take-off and landing weight within the legal limits. Another notice board displayed information that was graded as essential to know, good to know or nice to know. Also updated on a daily basis.

Training captains like Bill Woods, Jonathan Milbank, Peter Whyment, Lemmie Tanner, Pieter du Pon and Bill Noble, patiently walked and talked me through all this new routine while the room buzzed with activity. An engineer would walk in and shout, 'Who's doing the ground run on Charlie Golf Lima?'

Someone from the radio room would announce, 'Brent Alpha is closed. That's you John, is it? I'll have an update for you in about twenty minutes. Just standby for the moment.'

When all the paperwork was done, which for seasoned veterans took ten minutes, compared to my forty, double and treble checking, we changed into our immersion suits and made our way to the aircraft.

There was no time to be nervous. The trainers got straight into things. The flying operation was vast: no time for small talk. They were great company, very positive and encouraging. With their help, I enjoyed those months in Aberdeen. They passed on as much as they could from their vast store of experience of North Sea flying, or flying with the UK military. They shared their experience from years spent hovering by day and night, with sonar equipment suspended below their Sea Kings, hunting Soviet submarines during the Cold War. Walking out to our helicopter in the dark each morning became enjoyable, despite waking up feeling lonely in dark cold Scotland, miles from home. And I was lonely. I missed home. I missed my wife and our new baby.

I had to get on with things and put those feelings aside.

Having already spent about an hour preparing up to that point, the next half hour was busy. We had to find the helicopter in the rows of parked aircraft, inspect it externally, do all the checks, talk to ATC and get permission to start up. Then we would taxi over to the area where the passengers boarded, call the company and get the passengers strapped in, giving them a safety brief. Then we taxied to the runway, joined the queue and took off climbing as the heavily-laden old lady accelerated.

I struggled with the routine at first. It was an eye-opener for me. After a while it became easier and smoother, and I started to enjoy it. I was fortunate to be working with pilots who had been doing the job for decades.

When I started, they still used rolling Decca navigation charts on the S-61 fleet. We loaded up our rolls of colour-coded charts, which plotted our course as we flew. It was back to basics in every sense. Flying at our assigned flight level, we flew past the 40 and 80 mile distances, changing frequency to Highland Radar, and giving them our ETA or another check distance off-shore. During the cruise on the outbound leg, the navigation log was checked and written up every twenty minutes. This was done in a very rudimentary way using a 'whizz wheel' computer, which is a flight computer, but uses a rotary sliding scale rather than electronics.

The information we gleaned from the helicopter's progress, enabled us to calculate the actual winds, rather than the forecasted winds. This information, used on the 'whizz wheel', helped us to calculate revised timings and fuel burns at destination and at alternate. This was especially important given that we always had to have enough fuel in case we could not land at the rig because of some problem or other.

Next we radioed ahead getting permission to make an approach, and passing on passenger numbers and loads, as well as more crucially, confirming the load we would be taking out. The pilot flying would have to be able to see the rig and its obstacles when eventually coming into the hover and then landing. It was often necessary to switch pilots and completely change the approach if the wind direction changed subtly. The final choice could only be made when we knew the wind. If there was low cloud, we would do a radar controlled cloud break and approach. This was a procedural way to land when unable to see the rig which we had practised over and over in the simulator.

By the time Christmas came around, I was looking forward to getting home to a traditional Christmas, to our baby, and all that goes with family. I had been out and back to the Tartan platform which the S-61s served and a variety of rigs and platforms and semi-submersibles in the North Sea and the east Shetland Basin oil fields.

Between Christmas and New Year, I had to work but I did not care. I got home. I had Christmas and New Year at home, one in Tullamore and one in Monaghan. We travelled the meandering country roads between Offaly and Monaghan, bringing Alyson with us like the baby Jesus himself. She was our baby, and was welcomed with mistletoe and holly, turkey and ham, wine and whiskey, but most of all, hugs and kisses. The cold of the North Sea gave way to the warmth of home.

1995. Back to Aberdeen. Flying further afield now, further offshore, east and west of Shetland. I lived just outside Aberdeen. One day I had visitors. I went to the airport to meet them. I could scarcely believe my own reaction when I saw Lynda carrying our tiny baby Alyson. All the trouble of travelling. All the disruption of leaving home, its comforts and warmth and security to be together in the granite city.

For the next month and a half, we were in Peterculter. I worked early and got back in the afternoon. We traded stories of oil rigs and flying, with a sleeping baby and morning walks. Together we explored the town, and the area: afternoon tea and buns, 'haggis, neeps and taties' (haggis, turnips and potatoes), and maybe a malt whiskey if Alyson was asleep. It was there I discovered sticky toffee pudding. I never thought I had a sweet tooth but in those afternoons I found that sticky toffee pudding was just what I wanted.

We were away from everything we had ever known, in a different country, different job, married and with a baby but we were happy. Watching Alyson sleep in her buggy, as I leaned back in a chair beside a roaring fire, while it snowed outside, I felt far from anything I had done before. We both did.

The priority in Aberdeen was to get the flying time, build up hours, hurry home and get to work as a SAR captain. I had to work as many hours as I could while I was there. I pestered the operations staff to let me do more. I volunteered to go to the Shetlands for the flights out of Unst. Lynda and Alyson had returned home. I was missing them but warmed by having them to miss.

They sent me north to work out of Unst for a week. The northernmost Shetland island, on the top of the UK, with the most northerly lighthouse called Muckle Flugga. Bleak, boggy and rocky islands. Just like Connemara or Donegal except not as mountainous. A unique culture and music and tradition, blended from Scotland, Ireland and Scandinavia. Sheep and Shetland ponies, tractors and long-horned shaggy-haired cattle. Music in the pub in Lerwick, just like our own traditional music. The small airport had a short runway, big enough for the aircraft that brought the 'Roughnecks', the oil workers, from cities further south. Then we would bring them onwards to the rigs and platforms.

I was met by the chief pilot, Capt. Valentine. I took a room in one of the company houses. It was, for all intents and purposes, like an air force billet: bed, toilet, and a kettle and a hotel bar roughly two miles away on unlit roads.

I was flying further north than I had ever been before. Still winter, we arrived at a rig one evening as it was getting dark. The flare tip burned brightly in the overcast cold cloud as we emerged to see the rig before landing. The flare, burning unusable gases, lit the underside of the cloud at dusk, like Dante's inferno. We slipped forward to the deck, restricted by generators and air conditioning vents, blowing hot air across our landing pad, robbing us of power and lift just when we needed it.

But by that stage, I had become *au fait* with the vagaries of the Sikorsky and its performance. We had planned all eventualities. We reached the hover. It was just a moment, but it was a demonstration of extracting the last ounce of power out of a 10 tonne machine, in harmony with the environment, that left an impression. The precision of those calculations, done hours before, in the humble operations room in Unst, allowed us to respect the invisible wind, the fickle changes in air temperature and pressure, and come and go in darkness from that rig.

With rotors turning, I got out as it was my turn to monitor the refuelling. The scene was surreal As I stood beside the helicopter, its anti-collision light flashed in the darkness, reflecting off the metal monster beside us. At the deck's edge, I peered over the side, down to the sea below. The rig's legs had lights which caught the white water, foaming over a 100 feet down. Stretching away from where I stood, was the enormous gantry, at the end of which was the burning flare, waving like a giant Chinese silk dragon, its colours changing from yellow to orange with hints of purple and blue. Mesmeric. Fuelling finished, I strapped in and we departed.

Bristow Helicopters were very good to me in Aberdeen. They

adjusted my working days as much as they could so that I could get home. They allowed me be there when Alyson was born. They gave me as much varied flying as they could. But there was one flight they would not let me do. I kept asking the operations manager, Dave Smith, for permission. Each time he said no. The flight was once each week to the island of St Kilda.

St Kilda is 50 miles west of the Western Hebrides, over a 100 miles west of the Scottish mainland and inhabited until the 1930s. Its history mirrors the Blasket Islands. They are frequently compared in books. Bristow Helicopters' flying there each week was an opportunity to visit a mystical place.

The island is part of a group, including Soay and Boreray, that rise to 1,000 feet cliffs, almost straight out of the Atlantic. Inhabited now only by seabirds, seals and UK military personnel maintaining a radar control site for a weapons range. Special security clearance was required and it was a notoriously tricky place to land. With about a week to go before I was due to return to Shannon, one of the operations' staff winked at me as I came in from the apron at Aberdeen. He told me that I was rostered for St Kilda.

The other pilot was Eric Pashley, an experienced S-61 pilot with many years' SAR under his belt, as well as North Sea flying and trips to St Kilda. The weather was lousy, we went around the coast anti-clockwise avoiding the icing conditions. The coast had cleared as we made our way across the North Minch, to the Isle of Harris and Stornoway where we stopped to refuel.

The following morning we were up early, flying down the Minch to Benbecula. Like Stornoway and the other western isles' airports, I had encountered them previously, when planning land diversions on patrol with *LE Eithne* and read about them too. We flew low under an overcast sky, our screens and windscreen wipers building up ice. We stopped briefly at Benbecula to refuel and collect our military passengers, their equipment and supplies.

As we drew closer, the islands came up on our radar, and then appeared on the horizon. The highest points were covered in snow and cloud. Flying just below the cloud and hugging the terrain, we came over the bay, flying along the island of Dun, past the chasm that separates it from Kilda, then the rocky beach, finally landing at the helicopter pad.

Village Bay or Hirta Bay as it is known, was sheltered and quiet. Soldiers took away food and supplies, and chatted to their comrades who were staying. Once they were away from the helicopter, the familiar silence of islands returned: wind and sea birds, sea waves and the crack of rock on rock on the shore. We were surrounded by cloud topped hills. Looking at the sheltered bay in front of the helicopter, the wild beauty was laid out all around me. It must be heaven on a summer's day, I thought. We had a few minutes so I went for a walk. The deserted village was beside us. A larger building that I recognised as the old schoolhouse. Paths meandered up towards the snowy mountain. I could only imagine the sea cliffs that day. It was like the Great Blasket with the same feeling of desolate beauty, human life that became exhausted by nature.

It was soon time to go again. St Kilda disappeared behind us, swallowed up by the cloud and the ocean, and the curve of the sphere of the earth itself. Over a malt whiskey that night, a peaty Talisker, in a hotel in Stornoway, speaking a mixture of English, Irish and Scots Gaelic with other hotel guests, I raised my glass and saluted Scotland and looked forward to returning home: *Sláinte Mhaith.*

17

BLACK MAGIC

The best way to cheer yourself up, is to try to cheer somebody else up.
Anon.

I left the noise of Aberdeen airport, and the drone of the helicopter traffic behind me. It was nice being free again, free from the North Sea work pattern, free to return home ready for the next step. Shannon was waiting but Irish Helicopters continued to be patient, and I had some time to be at home.

It had only been a month since I had seen the baby but she was bigger and brighter already. We were a family, doing all the things first time parents do, like trying to keep the baby fed and happy, trying to keep ourselves fed and happy too. We looked in at her when she slept, admired her as if she was the only baby in the world, showed her off to our friends, slept when she slept.

I started to work in Shannon within a week of returning from Scotland and spent the next few months adjusting to civil SAR. The crews were a mixed bunch, some civil, some military. Although the captain of the helicopter was the legal commander, there was no rank structure and everyone was on first name terms.

The new aspect to the work was the daily pattern. Duty was split into three periods. The first was from about 1 p.m. until 9 p.m., during which we were immediately available at fifteen minutes notice. The second duty period was from 9 p.m. until 7 a.m., during which we could go home and were on forty-five minutes notice which was why we had to live within twenty minutes of the base. The third period was the morning from 7 a.m. until 1 p.m., and was once again, fifteen minute readiness.

The reason was that as civilians we were legally bound to be rested. If we were called out from home, another crew could replace us when we returned. Rest is built into military operating procedures too but not as formally. The day off between duties was something completely new to me. It seemed like an easy arrangement until I was called out regularly at night and struggled to get my sleep pattern under control again.

I settled in, was introduced to everyone and prepared for flying. I would start as a co-pilot, learn the ropes and gradually be promoted to captain. And that was it. Off we go. Up, up and away over familiar territory once more. This time in EI-BHO, the Irish Helicopters' Sikorsky I had admired on the odd occasion I had seen her. I was flying it and trying to do my best to look as if I knew what I was doing.

There were some familiar names there. Kevin McCarrick, whose path I had followed and who was then a SAR captain, and John Manning, Noel Donnelly and John McDermott, winchcrew, formerly air corps. Also Carmel Kirby and Dara Fitzpatrick, both co-pilots. Amongst the engineers were several from Baldonnel that I knew before: Shane Leonard, Mick Whelan and Liam Hannon.

I quickly got to know others. Winchcrew – Mike Horton and Peter Leonard, formerly royal navy, Al Clapp formerly RAF. SAR captains – Nick Gribble and Martyn Rayner, formerly royal navy, Rob Torenvlied and Simon Cotterell, formerly Bristow pilots. Engineers – Dermot Galligan and Paul Husband, formerly royal navy, and Pat Joyce.

The Shannon SAR base covered the entire Irish coastline out to a range of just over 200 miles. This was before the establishment of Dublin, Waterford and Sligo SAR bases. In my first few months in Shannon, I was called out frequently, by day and night, all around the country. It was valuable experience. I got used to the nitty-gritty of flying, how the crew split up the various tasks on the ground and in the air, to the personalities and the differences between my former career and my new one.

The Sikorsky S-61 is a big machine and it could carry over two tonnes of fuel, giving it an endurance of five hours. The cabin was cavernous. In the North Sea, it was fitted with seats for nineteen passengers. In rescue, most of these were removed, and a large auxiliary fuel tank fitted instead with a stretcher and medical equipment. The winch operator sat at the front of the cabin, plugged into the intercom, listening to all that was going on and plotting our course on a chart. This was called 'follow nav'. It kept all of the crew involved in knowing where we were, and provided rudimentary navigation information in case we lost our electronic systems.

The winchman at the back of the cabin operated the marine radio, the high frequency (HF) radio for long range, over-the-horizon missions, as well as the forward-looking infra red (FLIR) camera. That was the magic sphere-shaped camera mounted on the front left side of the helicopter. In a search, the winchman could move and adjust the camera by using a joystick guiding us to what he saw on his television monitor. The camera displayed a live person as a bright red and very obvious target. It supplemented the eyeball search the other members of the crew would do.

The winchman would move forward from his FLIR monitor once the search was completed and the rescue began. Our method was to lower a winchman to a casualty in case the casualty was unable to manage, due to hypothermia or injuries or shock.

The winch was electrically powered. It could lift three people, or 600 pounds weight, or a winchman and a stretcher with a casualty. It had a speed of 150 feet per minute. The faster the winch the less time the pilot has to hold the helicopter in a difficult hover over an erratically moving deck.

The aircraft was all-weather and could take moderate ice. It also had a full auto-pilot and auto-hover system called the LN450. Operating was similar to the Dauphin but with some differences. In between the two pilots was the centre console, with radios and the LN450 auto-hover control panel. If we pressed 'Overfly', it would save the latitude and longitude of that position at that instant, add in its own calculation of wind velocity, and fly a racetrack pattern to arrive just short of the position, in the hover, actually a hover that drifted forwards slowly at ten knots. The drift forward was incorporated because we anticipated that most vessels would move forward at that speed – a forward speed of ten knots would give us some free lift over the rotor disc, using less torque and giving us a better power margin. All worked out over years and years of accumulated experience.

We used the transdown and transup controls to manoeuvre the hover. We could select a hover height from 40 to 200 feet. The winch operator also had auto-hover trim (AHT), a joystick beside the cargo door so that he could manoeuvre the helicopter over survivors in the water who were out of the pilot's sight.

This was all very similar to the Dauphin system, but it felt different due to the sheer size and the way the system worked, which meant that it seemed to fly slowly. It seemed to sink to the hover with a sigh, and just sit there, stable and happy. The AHT was not twitchy. It seemed to follow the sea beneath it smoothly, keeping at the set hover height in all but the roughest or most chaotic conditions. It felt in harmony with the ocean.

Taking various rescue scenarios, breaking them down into their component parts, and training for them, is the bread and butter of helicopter SAR. The sadistic and the masochistic can invent very wearying training flights. We would simulate fog with an instrument hood fitted to one of our helmets, then fly along the Shannon Estuary at low level, with the auto-pilot off. We would make manual approaches and transdowns, to cliffs or buoys until finally taking off the hood from the helmet, bathed in sweat, hands shaking, and cursing the other pilot.

Not every flight was like that though. On other days we would fly lazily around the coast, passing Labasheeda, 'bed of silk' in Irish, Kilbaha, Loop, the Bridge of Ross, Kilkee, Doonbeg, Miltown Malbay and Lahinch. We winched onto cliff edges or passing trawlers, admiring the views and saying 'good morning' to the familiar voices on the marine radio.

One was Tomsie O'Sullivan, devoted to the sea, watching us through binoculars, from his living-room in Lahinch. Marie, his wife, could not swerve him from his gaze. Channel 16 was always tuned, the volume turned up. Like a lighthouse keeper himself. Truth to tell, Marie was just the same, one of many people along the west coast who had campaigned for the helicopter service and supported the base at every turn. He ran a voluntary rescue boat in Lahinch for years, collecting for the RNLI, and serving his local maritime community.

There were others too: Odron O'Looney also in Lahinch, Manuel di Lucia in Kilkee, John Walsh in Ballybunion and Noel Kellegher in Ballyheige. People all along the coast often called in when we appeared. We got to know them and their friendship and assistance was valued highly over the years.

In the summer we would fly above the ferry to the Aran Islands, as they ploughed across the bay, winching first our winchman and then volunteers on and off the aft deck.

'Winchman is on the deck. Steady. Good hover. Steady. Winchman has the strop over the passenger. I don't believe it. He's got that blonde girl. Her boyfriend doesn't look too pleased. Good hover. Steady. Strop on the survivor. Winching in the slack. Steady. Ready for lifting; up gently. Winchman and survivor are clear of the deck. Winching them in. Clear forward and down.'

We drifted away from the ferry as the winchman and his damsel in distress came to the door. The other passengers on the ferry waved and took photos. We flew back to the ferry and got her to point out her boyfriend. Plucking him skywards, he came aboard and we could hear the shouted conversation, the excitement in the girl's voice. We told them to stop kissing, that we had to put them back on the deck. Big smiles and 'thank yous', 'goodbyes' and 'good luck'.

On other days when it was too rough to winch passengers, we would winch members of the ferry crew. And always, always, Seán Rowntree would cheerfully volunteer. Rain, hail or shine, wearing his distinctive dark-peaked cap, the John Hurt lookalike would swing upwards on the hoist cable, to the helicopter. Sitting behind us on the cabin floor, as we flew away and back again, a big smile on his weather-beaten face. And then the deep voice, booming over the noise, as he shouted a hello.

It was wonderful to share the helicopter with people like that, and to sense their excitement and elation. So much SAR training has to be dull, repetitive and not all that enjoyable. That is why flying in good weather, over the beautiful Atlantic coastline, on exercises like that, was special.

The mountains were nearby again. Kerry and its mountains. The Gap of Dunloe and Beaufort village. Our original family home. The family name all over the place, but disconnected. History, famine and two world wars had dissolved our family tree and forced us apart. Like so many other families, I found out later. The Magillycuddys Reeks, Mount Brandon. Galway and the Twelve Bens or to Cork and the Galtees. And the Comeraghs; all close by and easy to reach for training. The islands that I knew and loved were closer again too. I flew the navigation routes to each and every one, squeezing the oversized Sikorsky onto the small landing pads. It felt great to be back.

One crucial aspect of the training was night flying and in particular night winching. In the summer months, with so little darkness, it was proving difficult to get the training done. I had to wait but had plenty to keep me busy. I was driving up and down to Dublin each week to my wife and baby trying to organise a place to live, and reorganise our lives. The summer months were coming and I hatched a plot.

We decided to christen Alyson in Tullamore and at the same time I set about arranging a surprise family reunion for our parents' forty-seventh wedding anniversary.

The week of the christening arrived. Family and friends were ready in Tullamore. We took our parents to The Moore Hill House restaurant, for a quiet meal on the Saturday evening, before the christening next day. Hilary, my sister, drove our parents and walked into the restaurant, where a full hall awaited them. My mother said later, that as she walked in she saw a boy walking towards her who looked just like her grandson, Kieran, from France. Then she saw a woman like his mother, Ruth and Armand her husband. As she realised that it was them, the tears came.

The room rang with applause. The first risk was overcome: they had survived the shock. My brother Philip, his wife Lyling and their daughter Sarah were there and many of our family, along with the Gramophone Society, neighbours and friends. Oliver and Jean Toner gave us a night to remember: good food, good company, a few drinks, stories and laughter. Father and sons drank at the bar. Mother and daughters drank wine at the table. My mother worked the room like a pro: 'Don't tell me you were in on it too, you wagon.'

The following day we christened Alyson. The yin and yang of a perfect weekend: the craic of the surprise party, the anointing of a baby. It was one of those occasions you want to preserve forever.

There was another distraction that year. It was 1995, Clare, one of the most fanatical of hurling counties in Ireland, was on the verge of history. We lived in Newmarket-on-Fergus but everyone knew I was from County Offaly, who were facing Clare in the final. Rugby had always been my game but that didn't stop me from telling any Clare person who asked that they hadn't much chance.

The whole county, every village and townland, prepared for the final as if nothing else mattered. And nothing else did matter. It was infectious. It was mad but not as mad as when Clare won and their captain Anthony Daly gave one of the best acceptance speeches ever made in Croke Park: 'We love our music, and we love our dancing, but we love our hurling too.' He paid compliments to the Offaly team also. And didn't my neighbours love saying 'Hard luck' to me with a smile. And to top it all, wasn't the weather great too? How could you not love being there?

Since it started in 1991, as the civilian replacement for the air corps SAR, Shannon had evolved, based on the model of the UK Coastguard and the service provided by Bristow Helicopters elsewhere. By the time Kevin McCarrick and I arrived, the first air corps pilots to join, Shannon had taken a motley crew, and successfully adapted to the west coast and all that went with Atlantic SAR. Their operating procedures were an amalgam of Bristow Helicopters, Irish air corps, royal navy and

RAF experience, the best of each, blended to make the ideal set of SAR procedures. That was the theory anyway.

The battle had not been without some cost though. While I was in Aberdeen, the helicopter had been called to a Spanish fishing vessel in distress. In the middle of the night, in huge seas and storm conditions, a crew comprising Nick Gribble, Carmel Kirby, Pete Leonard and John McDermott, struggled to hold position over the *FV Dunboy*. A slack winch cable, which had to be played out because of the swell size and the vertical movement of the ship, caught on something on the deck and snapped, whipping back up into the darkness, seriously damaging the main rotor blades. They limped away to fly to Galway leaving John McDermott marooned on deck.

The air corps Dauphin in Finner was alerted. Crewed by Dónal Scanlan, Mike Ryan, Dick O'Sullivan and Tommy Gannon, they too were defeated by the conditions. Finally, John was winched up by an RAF Sea King after daylight when the storm passed. All the crews were awarded citations. That incident scarred Shannon. It was a reminder that ultimately the forces of nature are unbeatable.

Other rescues that took place before I arrived, were recounted as horror stories and fables over cups of tea in the crewroom. The night in Clew Bay when the standby helicopter, which had no auto-hover, rescued the crew of a foundering trawler while a south-westerly storm blew across the bay. The long range missions which stretched the capabilities of the aircraft and crew to the limit. Or the famous mission where they joined in a search of the Irish Sea along with a royal navy Sea King helicopter whose crew broadcast a Mayday and then ditched. The Shannon crew then rescued them. I wondered when I would get my chance, if I would be up to the task.

The shortest days in winter translate into the longest nights.

With a five-hour fuel endurance, and a range of over 200 miles, I found myself in new territory. My body clock would start to trigger an uneasiness after an hour's flight. Turn back. Check your fuel gauges. Check your fuel flow. Calculate. In the dark, I checked and re-calculated. After a while, I got used to being only half way there.

The Shannon helicopter is an ambulance service for those in distress at sea out of reach of lifeboats. Crewman with chest pains: call Shannon. Crewman with suspected appendicitis: call Shannon. Fishing vessel drifting with rudder problems: call Shannon. We were busy. Up to Blacksod again. '*Dia dhuit* Vincent. *Cén chaoi bhfuil tú?*' Refuel and head north-west to where I had only ever been on the back of the *Eithne*.

Or to Castletownbere again to pick up a man who had fallen and broken his leg. Crews still testing me, teasing me out. 'Do you know where we are, Dave?' as we reached landfall again. The winchcrew laughing on the intercom, waiting to see what I would say. I peered out into the darkness, and said, 'Well that's the Fastnet on the right, Mizen on the left. Roaringwater Bay straight ahead. Those islands on the radar, that's the three Calf Islands, and Hare Island. Schull over there. That's Baltimore. Sherkin Island and Cape Clear on the right. And do you see that dim light over there lads? That's O'Driscoll's B&B.'

The Spanish crewman on the stretcher probably wondered what we found funny.

'No it's not, Dave,' said a strong English accent on the intercom. 'That's Mrs Murphy's house. Oh and look; the curtains are open. Look what she and Mr Murphy are doing.'

At 4 a.m., tired, and relieved to be back over *terra firma*, we found it so funny, laughing hysterically, as we prepared to land at the University Hospital.

The summer weather was good. We had lots of visitors, and

together we explored Clare. My parents drove down from Tulla-more, arriving in their white 'OY' Lada with gifts of meat from Tormeys, and bottles of wine. A pint with dad in The Weavers while the dinner cooked. How I miss those pints with him.

Fussing over the baby. Day trips to Lahinch, where we sat with a cold beer watching the surfers. Or ate seafood chowder at Monk's in Ballyvaughan or Vaughan's in Liscannor, my parents reminiscing about their visits to Clare when I was a child. Lynda's family too, her parents, walking through Bunratty folk park, seeing all the types of houses from bygone years. Trying to find one that matched their own childhood memories.

The west coast was our playground. We flew anywhere we wanted to, as long as it could be justified and had a training value. And everything did. Low level navigation to Castletown-bere. Mountain approaches to the Eagle's Nest at Carrauntuohil in Kerry. Search patterns west of the Aran Islands. Instrument flying training at Shannon or Cork or Kerry. Waiting for the opportunity to fly at night myself and do night deck winching. The final exercise before getting command again.

After six months flying for the United Nations, Al Lockey returned to Shannon as chief pilot in the autumn along with another pilot from Bristows, Phil Tonks. Both in their fifties and coming to the end of their flying careers, both supremely experienced, they had been involved in the set up of the early UK Coastguard bases. I found them both cheerful and prag-matic.

Within days of his return, I was flying as captain at night, training in every possible manoeuvre and winching. Finally, Phil flew with me, doing the same exercises and then signed me off. I was a civil SAR captain at last. I was congratulated. Kevin and myself allowed ourselves a night out or three on the strength of it. And of course my family and Lynda were pleased too.

Phil and Al congratulated me too. Nodding in agreement at each other's comments and advice, they wished me well.

'You've done it all before Dave. You'll have no problem. Just get out there and do it. These guys will help you. They're not perfect, but they'll help you. And anyway, this is no black art. It's not black magic.'

18

THAT SINKING FEELING

One great cause of failure is lack of concentration.

Anon.

December 1995 was a busy month. The crews were patient with me, putting up with my enthusiasm and desire to train twice each duty shift, on as many of the SAR disciplines as possible or visit the helicopter refuelling depots at Castletownbere and Blacksod.

At Bere Haven Dónal Holland was on the radio at the refuelling pad, 'How are ye lads. We're all ready here. Wind is southwesterly at about fifteen knots.' The harbour was often busy with the Atlantic fishing fleet, local Irish vessels or the Spanish ones, tied up and off-loading their catch to the waiting refrigerated lorries. The exhausted fishermen would wend their way in through the narrow channel between island and mainland to their paymasters. The bay between the town and the island was often full of moored vessels in stormy weather, sheltering until the conditions abated.

The landing pad at Castletownbere is just outside the small town and, built up about 20 feet above the water's edge, is big enough for the S-61 and RAF Sea Kings. We knew Dónal from having refuelled helicopters for years. His children Nevin and Gavin, helped out as they got older. After refuelling, and a cup of tea, we would depart.

With the sun setting on the picture postcard scene, we would climb towards the narrow gap between the west edge of Bere Island and the mainland, past the lighthouse at Ardnakinna Point. I would time it to depart at sunset. I wanted to see the scenery and get acquainted with it, not just the data that we stored in our computer. I wanted to get a feel for the rocks that guarded the coast, the cliffs and the mountains behind.

We never called the water beneath us the ocean. We called it the sea or else just described its qualities: light swell, small swell, calm, heavy swell, tidal current, and so on. Privately, I liked to think of it as an ocean. I liked to think of it as having no end, the notion of infinity, spoiled only by the waving palm trees of Jamaica or Cuba thousands of miles away to the west. Calling it the ocean was my mark of respect. I loved it but I feared it. As the sun set, it darkened to ink, the cliffs by Black Ball Head, Crow Head and Dursey island, veiled by darkness as we approached. Past Dursey Island, the Bull Rock, the Skelligs and then Tearaght, one of the Blasket Islands, before turning into the Shannon Estuary. Loop Head lighthouse first, atop the cliffs that poked out like a dagger into the Atlantic. Then Kilcredaun Lighthouse near Carrigaholt, guarding the mouth of the Shannon Estuary. And then following our radar, our navigation route, superimposed on the channel markers that led the way in. Checking the flash identifications of each and every one. Tearaght: two white flashes every twenty seconds. Loop Head: four whites per twenty seconds.

We repeated the whole exercise in reverse a few days later, picking our way in slowly from the west, following our pre-programmed route along the centre of the bay, flying below the safe sector altitude, knowing the hills and mountains were waiting for us to err or drift in strong crosswinds. Facing east at night with nothing to see, our winchman on the FLIR camera, reassured us and talked us in.

The helicopter followed its navigation route, and we used every bit of our equipment and wit to make sure it was using reliable data. Slowing down to 60 knots, we turned north-west towards the helicopter pad. Sometimes using the transdown as we got closer to simulate fog, and get to within 200 metres of the pad, and a 40 feet hover. The flying pilot wore an instrument hood, the winch operator giving dummy patter as if we were in fog. The flying pilot took off the hood inching forward and landing, or simulating an engine failure and flying away on a reduced power setting, seeing just how close the bridge there would get, as we limped over it.

There are hundreds of islands off the Irish coast, of which about thirty are inhabited. The population varies but it is estimated that there are 3,000 or so living on them. Their cause is championed by the islands co-operative, Comhdháil Oileáin na hÉireann, and by people like Dr Marion Broderick on the Aran Islands. Because they have the largest population, the Aran Islands in particular, need the helicopter service. Marion looked after the Aran islanders when they were sick, campaigning for improved medical facilities and highlighting the need for a rescue helicopter. She knew a lot of us from the air corps. As Shannon evolved, the new crews came to know her too. She always rang Dublin to look for permission to get the helicopter, if it was needed. But she often rang us directly, to give us what we called 'a heads up' immediately after.

The island population swells each summer, and with it the number of medical emergencies. Being at a distance from a hospital, and being marooned in bad weather, the Aran Islands depended on Marion and on the Shannon helicopter. Getting people to Galway hospital rapidly, at any time of the day or night, no matter the weather, became something we were proud of. We could take off in fog, climb up and descend into Galway

Bay, using our radar and auto-hover to creep forward, until we could see the shore beside each of the three islands' airstrips.

In winter, when there was icing conditions, we would go all the way around the coast if necessary, west past Kilrush and Loop Head Lighthouse, flying at 200 feet until we reached Black Head and then position for Inis Oirr, Inis Meáin or Inis Mór. If the cloud was not too low, we could get to the bay by heading north along the road to Ennis, Gort, Kinvara, then Ballyvaughan and onto the islands.

Their RNLI Lifeboat helped us a lot too. They were the nearest lifeboat to us and used to come out when we needed to train, particularly at night. The ferry to and from the island was used frequently for training, but you could not guarantee that the wind direction would suit. Failing that, we could do 'opportunity decks', which was winching onto fishing vessels that we might encounter, a bit of a hit or miss affair. We used to try to co-ordinate with the lifeboat crew, so that we could fly when they were exercising at sea as well.

On such an exercise, we would establish radio contact first. The radio calls back and forth, quick and slick. We would confirm the lifeboat's position and go there, pressing the overfly button as the helicopter came over the lifeboat, visible ahead of its white wake, illuminated by its deck lights. Once we got just behind the lifeboat, it was business as usual.

The lifeboat was small. The Sikorsky was huge above it. Those exercises were critical to our success on missions far offshore. Going past the lifeboat meant that you would be looking at darkness again: no sense of movement, no depth perception or height perception. It could mean disaster and because it meant disaster we practised it. We practised all the possible permutations and how to cope with them, so that in the event of the real thing we would be ready.

Collecting troops at a border checkpoint, Alouette 3.
[Photo: D. Courtney]

Alouette 3 approaching Clare Island from the north.
[Photo: D. Courtney]

Alouette 3 winching training in Glendalough.
[Photo: D. Courtney]

The clean lines of the Dauphin as it approaches, the winch and shrouded tail rotor, clear to see. [Photo: Air Corps]

Dauphin winching training with Wicklow Research.
[Photo: Air Corps]

*View of a ship, from inside the Dauphin, while winching training by day.
Pretty close to those masts!*
[Photo: D. Courtney]

Just about to land on LE Eithne.
[Photo: D. Courtney]

Lashing crew removing tie downs before flying stations.
[Photo: D. Courtney]

Blades folded, putting the Dauphin to bed at night in the hangar.
[Photo: D. Courtney]

The Dauphin on Inshturk.
[Photo: D. Courtney]

Gazelle, Alouette 3 and Dauphin formation near Baldonnel.
[Photo: Air Corps]

S-61 landing on an oil platform in the East Shetland Basin.
[Photo: Rex Features]

View from inside an S-61, as we approach an oil platform for landing.
[Photo: D. Courtney]

Shannon S-61 at Blacksod refuelling site.
[Photo: D. Courtney]

RAF Sea King training in the Welsh Mountains.
[Photo: CHC Shannon]

RN Culdrose Sea King deploying rescue diver/swimmer on training exercise.
[Photo: CHC Shannon]

Air corps CASA Top Cover, overflying fishing trawler off the west coast of Ireland. [Photo: Air Corps]

Shannon Rescue 115, approaching a trawler on a rescue.
[Photo: Air Corps]

Shannon and Dublin S-61s together over Aran Islands.
[Photo: Irish Coast Guard]

RAF Nimrod Top Cover, in flight. [Photo: CHC Shannon]

Shannon S61 winching onto a trawler near Dingle.
[Photo: Anna Heussaff]

Shannon S-61 flying away from Hags Head near Cliffs of Moher, winchman on the wire, cliff winch training. [Photo: Irish Coast Guard]

Doolin unit at Aill na Searrach, training. The stretcher party and Cliff Top Man. [Photo: Press 22]

Doolin Coast Guard Unit, gardaí, Irish Cave Rescue, civil defence and ambulance staff removing casualty from a cave after hours of effort.
[Photo: Press 22]

S-61 training with Doolin again, Mirror Wall Fanore, west Clare. Cliff Top Team, luff tackle and a view of heaven. [Photo: Press 22]

The Arosa *lies dying at Skerd Rocks and* [left] *an empty life-raft and life-jackets at the rocks.* [Photo: Press 22]

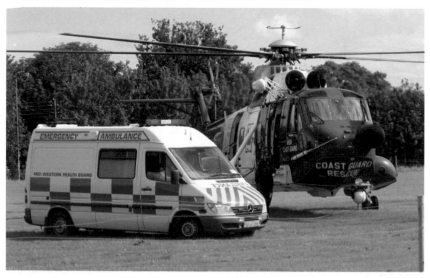

An S-61 meets an ambulance with a casualty for transfer to hospital. Not every hospital has a helicopter landing pad. [Photo: Press 22]

Shannon S-61 approaches surfers at the foot of Moher cliffs. Aill na Searrach.
A member of Doolin unit at the cliff top. [Photo: John Kelly]

S-61 interior. Two pilots look out at the world. [Photo: John Kelly]

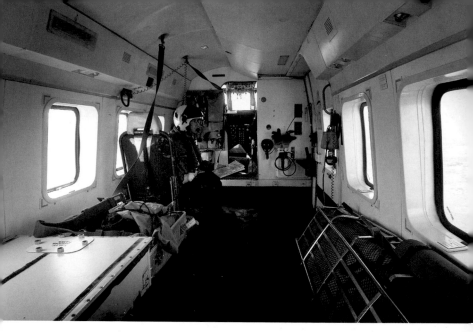

S-61 interior. From the back forward towards where the winch operator sits. Long range fuel tank and medical gear and sea tray. [Photo: John Kelly]

Shadow of the S-61 on a beach in west Clare.
[Photo: John Kelly]

Just before Christmas, we got a call to a vessel south of the Fastnet Rock. A crewman had to be airlifted to hospital. There was no problem with distance or fuel. It was misty and foggy. Wind was light and it was a dark and moonless night. We climbed up and headed south. The crew was Phil Tonks, Graham Goosey was winch operator and Mike Horton the winchman. We checked in as usual on Channel 16, and updated our navigation computer with the latest position of the vessel.

We saw the Fastnet Rock Lighthouse flashing as we continued south. We arrived at the vessel and positioned ourselves behind it, as it made its way northwards towards Cape Clear and Baltimore. Another 'black hole' approach: zero light, zero references, zero sense of movement. We hovered behind it, getting ready and briefing. The torque indication higher than we expected. The wind had died off, and the long swell was making the helicopter struggle to hold its hover height. Every now and again we sank down towards the sea. Graham kept alerting me and silently wondering why it was happening, I am sure. Silently I was wondering why too. Mentally I had to start at the top. Was I over controlling? Was I stirring the cyclic in an effort to hold position, changing the angle on the blades too rapidly, making them inefficient, and dumping lift from the rotor disc?

With these thoughts in my mind, I watched and listened. The vessel was not holding a very steady course, seeming to travel in a straight line and then meander as it met the swell again broadside. The ship's crew were finding it hard work too. I observed, tried to relax and learn from the deck's movements, trying to mirror the trawler's movements smoothly. We had about forty minutes fuel available to use on scene.

The trawler is a creature of the sea. The sea caresses it or slams against it, washes against it, slows it and nudges it this way and that. The air is my element. The two elements are not in harmony.

That night, in my hands, the helicopter skated and slid, drifting sideways when the trawler slowed. I had a balancing act to master that everyone in SAR encounters at sometime or other. Flying decisively, with punchy, positive control movements would dump my lift, and we would not be able to hover safely. Flying too cautiously would waste fuel and be too slow if we needed to move quickly. I started to feel a tiny nagging doubt, that I had not enough experience or finesse on the S-61 to do it. And I knew that if I was wondering then the rest of the crew would be wondering too. Sensing my doubt like a dog senses fear.

Ten minutes gone.

The helicopter did its best to hold a hover for us, using the radio altimeter, a signal bouncing constantly off the sea below us, to keep us at the same height. When the helicopter sank below the height we wanted, I would manually use collective to climb to the desired height, as smoothly as possible, so as not to over-torque the engines. While the collective was raised manually, the safety net that the auto-hover provided was removed.

The direction that we faced, was fixed by the auto-hover and auto-pilot. It would stay locked onto the heading, only moving when pressure was applied to the rudder pedals. The advantage of this, particularly at night, was that there was one less thing to do, one less control to worry about, and more attention could be devoted to the other controls. The disadvantage was that if the trawler slewed off its course, your view of the deck below you would change. Your choice was to accept the change or else apply rudder pressure, keeping your view of the deck the same. No two situations were the same. No two pilots would agree.

The additional concern, particularly on a night like we were having, was that pedal turns against the tail rotor torque, would rob us of a little more power. We did not have much to begin with. A small adjustment, like not sitting squarely in your seat, could help, and sometimes mean no rudder pedal pressure was needed. Sitting slightly to the right, effectively leaning towards the deck, could increase your peripheral vision.

As well as that there was cyclic control. On the top of the cyclic control stick, was a 'cooley hat' which was spring loaded to a centre position, that you could use to trim out the forces on the controls, so that when you took your hand away, the helicopter remained in the hover. In practice, you would trim slightly, so that if you got disorientated, or just plain tired, releasing the cyclic would result in the helicopter drifting away slightly to a safe hover position. So as not to fly into the trawler. Flying backwards, especially at night, is undesirable. Rearwards trim was to be avoided. Moving towards the deck laterally, would be accomplished by applying pressure to the cyclic control. Pilots differ, but most would quickly work their way through the controls, one at a time, trimming, as the brief was being done. End of brief, end of trimming, action.

In the hover, the co-pilot can see the instruments, but not the deck. The winch operator can see the deck, but not the instruments. The captain sees both. As captain, you come to know that the perfect hover is an illusion. It is a trade off between the hover the winch operator wants, what the instruments tell you, what the movement of the deck outside tells you, what the co-pilot tells you. And what your own intangible sixth sense tells you. Constantly reviewing those different sources of information, averaging them, and acting upon them. A flesh and blood computer. Sometimes you get it right. Sometimes you get it wrong. Practice increases your chances of getting it right.

Hovering beside a tree or a cliff is one thing. Hovering when everything is in a state of flux, moving constantly, is a different thing. Nothing to hang your hat on. If it was not going well, it is better to admit it openly, communicate.

The briefing was done by this time. Graham had pointed out all the obstacles on the way in, on the deck and on the way out. As he talked, Phil interspersed Graham's patter with encouraging comments and the odd caution for hover height.

We were in a higher hover because of the deck movement and the lack of wind. We timed the deck, something we almost always do, watching for a pattern. There usually is some sort of a pattern, believe it or not. A vessel will obey the sea that governs its movement. Waves come in trains. Swells have periods and frequencies, all affecting the vessel. Having timed the deck, getting its rhythm, we could predict a time to winch. The period of relative calm might be only twenty seconds every minute. If that was all we had, then we had to make do with it.

The calm period came and we moved into position for a dummy deck, slowly moving forward with no winchman on the cable. I saw the trawler's deck crew looking up in expectation. When we were right over the deck, I could see the masts in front of me and the deck lights below me. I could see the torque meter in my peripheral vision, but Phil was watching it and was silent, so I looked away from it. I eased in collective power as gently but as positively as I could, when Graham told me we were descending. I could hear the blades whack outside, picked up by Graham's microphone as he leaned out the door, as I moved the cyclic control a little too nervously. We moved back to go 'live': to put the winchman 'on the wire'.

Twenty minutes gone.

I could not see him but I felt his life in my hands. My throat went dry. My hands started to sweat. In the dark, a trickle of sweat ran down my face and into my eye. The trawler rolled and pitched as a bigger swell went through. I responded, coaxing the helicopter cautiously closer. The blades travelled in different paths as they too adjusted, agitating the air, mixing and condensing it, just as a river going over rocks makes white water. My nervousness and fear of injuring the winchman transmitted through my hands, through the controls, through the blades and sensed by the humid air. Instead of a trace of mist in front of me, the nervous blades were making a small cloud. In front of and above me, the blade tips drew a line in the air, marking the divide between the black infinity of the sky above, and the illuminated deck of the trawler below. Like steam. Like a kettle boiling in front of and above where I sat.

We waited. The small cloud remained. Then as the trawler returned to its stable rhythm, the cloud ghosted away. The blades travelled in a smooth circular motion around us, making no more cloud. Harmony had arrived. I could feel my hands' tight grip on the controls loosen for whatever reason. Perhaps the wind had increased slightly or maybe the man on the helm below us was making a better job of keeping a steady course. Maybe I was getting better at flying the deck. Maybe the Man Above had decided to smile upon us.

I matched the deck's movements and we were ready to put Mike down. No time for further analysis. No time to talk. JFDI. Mike was on the winch cable then, a 15 stone pendulum swinging out of sight beneath me. My movements had to be smooth so that we did not turn him into a human wrecking ball. We moved forward and put him on the deck.

It felt right. But how did it feel right? Why? How do you describe just knowing? How do you explain, 'feeling it in your water'? It is a Zen-like state. I drifted away from myself, like someone having a near death experience might describe. For a moment or two, I was outside myself, watching, listening. My thoughts had become slow. Calmness had spread from without to within, from my head to my heart. The helicopter blades became an extension of myself. They responded to my thoughts which were patient and calm, and that calm spread to the crew. The initial doubt was replaced instantly by confidence, as if there had never been any doubt.

Thirty minutes gone.

Listening. To the tone of each other's voices on the intercom. To the speed of our conversation. It may have been the darkness or tension, but our sense of hearing became heightened as it always does. We sense tension and unease or calm or fear. The helicopter speaks to us too in its own way. Just as those bygone aviators listened to the heartbeat of their machines in the note of the wind in the rigging, I felt it in my hands. I saw the instruments in front of me, responding to the wind and the unseen swell below. I saw the rise of the engine's RPM and temperature, our height above the sea on my altimeter, my artificial horizon showing me whether my hover was level or not. How quickly each instrument changed, its rate of change, told me even more.

We positioned back over the trawler, and winched both winchman and casualty off with the minimum of fuss. All's well that ends well. It is hard to remember the rest. We climbed away and made for Cork University Hospital. There was a landing pad then. Flying over Cork city, I stole a glance over towards where my two dead sisters, Linda and Angela, were buried. Died at birth. And where I was born in St Finbar's hospital. The chance of life and death. Two babies die and one lives. My mother the only one who felt their lives kick. I might not have been born, if they had lived.

The casualty was handed over to the A&E staff, as I sat, holding the controls. Looking across the road beside us, down towards where we lived, not responding to questions being asked of me. Because of the dark. Because of tiredness. Because of the mesmeric rhythm of the rotor blades. Because of the family

photo albums of my mother, as she would have been, around
the time those sisters of mine were born. And died.

Then we went to Cork airport to refuel. My logbook says we
arrived in Shannon, checking in with ATC in the early hours,
landing and shutting down at our own hangar. Engineers met
us, red-eyed from waiting up, snoozing in the crew room or
watching *Sky News* for the twenty-fifth time.

'Any snags, Dave?'

'No, she's fine Paul. No problem.'

'What was the job?'

'Head injuries. One of the crew fell earlier on and was unconscious for a while. They wanted him checked in hospital.'

'How many winch cycles did you do, Graham?'

'Three Paul. Who won the match?'

Knowing that we were still on SAR readiness, and had to be
on the base again at 7 a.m., we stayed on, using the beds and
sleeping bags that were available. I think that night, I stayed
outside for a while, drinking tea and smoking cigarettes. I sat on
a plastic chair that I dragged outside, feet up on another, in the
dark, in the carpark, looking up at the stars thinking it all over.
It was not my first SAR, nor my first night SAR and not my
worst SAR. However it was my first night SAR on the Sikorsky
as captain. My mind spun as I went over it from beginning to
end, scrutinising the hover again, from my plastic seat in the
dark, 150 miles from where the trawler had been, chastising
myself for taking too long to get the hover sorted, but allowing
myself a private smile for getting over the doubt, and getting it
done. I was tempted to drive home and go to bed, thinking of
home and the baby curled asleep, picturing her toys beside her,
the pink blanket with the teddy-bears and butterflies. Graham
joined me after a while. We drank tea and chain-smoked. We

exchanged stories about rescues done in the past. We may even have said 'well done' to each other. I'm not sure.

19

PAVLOV'S DOGS

Motivation is what gets you started. Habit is what keeps you going.

Anon.

I peered into the rain. In the darkness, the windscreen wipers moved back and forth, revealing nothing. The helicopter shuddered in the low-level turbulence. The radar picture was cluttered with bright red blobs signifying either islands or heavy showers. Our dilemma, at high speed at night, was distinguishing one from the other. We had to be low under the cloud to have any chance of seeing the sea and finding this vessel, if indeed there was a vessel.

Carmel Kirby was flying, staying on instruments. John McDermott was the winch operator, kneeling between us, looking out above the instruments panel. Just behind him, stood John Manning the winchman, kitted, prepped and ready to go out into the night. Having given up looking into his FLIR monitor, rendered useless by the horizontal rain, he silently waited for something to appear.

We had slowed down so that we would have time to climb to safety if an island appeared in front of us. Our airspeed may have been low but our speed over the water (groundspeed) was still racing. The south-westerly gale was thrusting us forward.

'Surface visual John. We're visual here all the time. Got about a mile visibility'.

I spoke on the intercom, to no one in particular, narrating our progress, so that they knew that I was not like a rabbit caught in headlights and I was happy with clearance and conditions. As happy as I could be. Breaking the silence with narration presented some semblance of normality. The radio crackled as the coast guard asked us for an update.

Hard to believe that it was June. The winter storms had not been too bad that year. It was something of a reprieve to get past winter unscathed. Not everyone had had a quiet time though. Kevin McCarrick had hit the news twice. A vessel had run aground in foul weather at night at the entrance to Cork Harbour. With Phil Tonks, Graham Goosey and Peter Leonard, they had winched the crew off. That was early January, and was a job to be proud of.

For some reason, the response amongst our own crews was muted. It was my first encounter with ego, or perhaps the flip side of ego. Others did not want to praise them. They themselves shied away from praise. Privately, I clapped Kevin on the back and congratulated him. In Baldonnel, a good rescue, a good job, would have meant a trip to the officers' or the NCO's mess or both. Maybe it was the mix of the different services we were drawn from, but praise was not often or publicly given.

After another of Kevin's callouts, he ended up telling the nation about it all on *Morning Ireland* on RTÉ Radio 1. A small boat had gone missing near Dingle. Along with Dara Fitzpatrick, Noel Donnelly and Al Clapp, they found the missing men holding on to the cliff beside the sea north of Mount Brandon. From a precarious position, they winched them to safety. In a matter-of-fact way, Kevin described what had happened, leading to plaudits in the media. There was a spring in our step after that. There was in mine anyway, and I was not even there.

Being on call, waiting for the phone to ring, builds tension. The phone in Shannon, we called it the 'Bat Phone', had its own distinctive ring tone. When it rang, we would gather around, trying to appear nonchalant, while beginning to sweat and palpitate. I even found, if I was away from Shannon, and heard another phone ring with the same tone, that my body would react the same way. Whether it was a friend's house, a shop in town or a restaurant. I was Pavlov's dog.

On another call out to the Aran Islands, a baby was born in flight above Galway Bay at night with the winchcrew acting as midwives, while the pilots flew, listening as a new life arrived. Delivering the baby in the back of the helicopter, then delivering mother and baby to the hospital in Galway. Safe and sound. All well. Such a change from searching for the missing, the injured, the dead, the men overboard.

When you start learning to fly, you have to learn the ground syllabus. It comes as a disappointment, to find that you cannot just sit in and fly around the sky, a magnificent man in your flying machine. The years of study, committing vast amounts of information to memory, answering questions and passing exams, finally lead to a licence in your hand. The earth's rotation. Magnetism and compasses. Meteorology. The making of maps and charts. The significance of the moon's cycle. Weight and balance. The relief that you will never have to read the stuff again. But it all comes back. Gradually.

The earth's orbit around the sun, taking 365 days, as against Mercuty's 88, or Pluto's incredible 248 years. The divisions of our orbit into seasons. The way that our winter in the northern hemisphere, is colder than the southern hemisphere, simply because of the 23° inclination of the earth. And because it's not plumb, we have winter in Ireland. In November, December and January.

The earth spinning all the time, eastwards, towards the sun and away again, the air on the surface heating and cooling all the time. Regions on the earth's surface where the sun lingers longest, warming most. And where it visits least, remaining coolest. And then those air masses, meeting and fighting like gladiators, all year round, but especially every winter off the Irish coast. Warm and cold air doing battle for supremacy, lining up as warm or cold fronts, churning up the sea below.

The complexity of the forces that make it rain, or not rain. That made it difficult for us to winch a man off a trawler, or that made it easy. The forces that are always at work, the forces of nature that we name, trying to tame them and understand. Coriolis Force, that makes all weather systems spin anti-clockwise in the northern hemisphere, because of the earth's rotation. Kepler's laws of planetary motion.

In Shannon on SAR, knowing when the sun would rise or set, how long you could stay and hover, how much fuel you could take, could mean the difference between success and failure. For each degree west of the Greenwich meridian, the time of sunset or sunrise is four minutes later. Crucial information, when deciding when to take off to rendezvous with a ship coming east. You would allow a little more time, a little more fuel, because a hover would take longer at night. No point in taking off in haste in the daylight at Shannon only to be overtaken by the inexorable turning of the earth as the sky darkens around before you arrive, earlier than you expected.

And winter seas. And winter swell. Waves and wave theory. A branch of science in itself. From the classroom days in Tullamore, when John Pareira drew waves on the blackboard. The Atlantic coast of Ireland was where I saw those waves again. With 3,000 miles of open ocean, the waves have time to grow. That 3,000 mile distance is called a 'fetch'. With a predominantly south-westerly wind, our waves, born in America, are moulded as they travel east. How big they are and how many there are per minute, depend on a myriad of factors, the size of the fetch being one of them.

And when they do arrive, that ever present weather front generating ocean would add a twist or two to make our lives more difficult, turning a nice predictable swell that we could manage, into something chaotic. A confused sea is what the scientists and meteorologists call it. A sea that does not know whether to obey the forces that were moulding it while it travelled, or the forces that act on it when it arrives off the Irish coast. Different wave heights. Different wave frequencies. Sometimes coalescing and cancelling each other out. Sometimes joining forces and making monsters. Often, as we peered out into the search lights beam, we wondered what would emerge from the darkness.

June arrived and with it the longest day. The earth was approaching its furthest distance from the sun, its Aphelion. Not quite the Irish summer yet. The primary schools holidays had not started but secondary schools were on holiday. As the longest day passed by, just after midnight at home, I got a call from the marine rescue co-ordination centre (MRCC). It was a Mayday from a fishing vessel off the Galway coast.

After a hurried explanation to Lynda, I looked in on Alyson. She fidgeted as the light from the hall spilled into her room, the wind whistling outside, rain lashing against her window. Blowing her a kiss and an 'I love you', I left. The others arrived pretty much at the same time at our hangar. Waiting for us as usual was the SAR area weather forecast. Prepared for us by the Shannon met office forecaster each and every time a mission took place. Using all available data to provide us with what was always an incredibly accurate prediction of weather and sea conditions where we were headed. Invaluable in helping us succeed. Invaluable in preparing us and improving our chance of success.

Once we confirmed the position of the vessel, we made a

rough plan and decided on the fuel load. We brought more than enough. There was a very strong wind blowing, so being heavy would not be a problem if we had to hover. We wanted lots of fuel because the on-scene weather forecast was saying all the wrong things: 40 knot winds, visibility down to less than a mile, choppy seas. We also wanted the fuel in case the Mayday position was wrong and we had to search. It was better to have it and not need it, than need it and not have it.

We changed into our immersion suits. The normal routine swung into action. Carmel listened as we got the information, and once she was happy with the plan outline, she went out and started the helicopter. John Manning went with her to prep the SAR equipment and the cabin. That left me and John McDermott in the operations' room, running quickly over the plan. We could not hang about. We had to be in the air within 45 minutes of the call at home. More importantly, we wanted to get going because the ship's crew could be in the sea already.

It was warm so we went straight to the scene, climbing up into the cloud, not concerned about icing. After a while we dropped down, getting back into visual contact with the sea, at about 200 feet. We had a gale behind us. We were racing to the opposite side of Galway Bay. Racing north-west towards Slyne Head, passing Golam Head and Roundstone on the way. At Slyne, the lighthouse light revolved like a cartwheel. Towards us and above us. Spokes of light, struggling to penetrate the misty rain. We approached into the light, before turning north, the white water of the breakers crashing on the rocks. Phosphorescent creamy water, dreamlike as we passed. The cartwheel of light, like a mill wheel, straining against the darkness and the rain, as if it was treacle. Then north towards Inisboffin and the rocky islands beyond. We slowed down and made ready. As we got closer, Shannon coast guard radio gave us an updated position for the vessel.

It had made one Mayday call but they had no more information. We were going to have see what we could find.

We got everything ready in case we suddenly saw anything. We slowed right down and peered out through the wipers, checking the islands, one by one as usual, one pilot flying and the other monitoring. With the auto-pilot engaged, Carmel took us through the gaps in the weather and the islands, slowing as the visibility dropped, locked at the set radio altimeter height. While I looked out through our light's beam, and at the radar screen, in hope.

The next island was Inishturk, a 630 feet lump of rock dead ahead. We were at 200 feet. Our speed over the water was about 80 knots, thanks to a 40 or 50 knot tailwind. We could not see it. It has no lighthouse. The radar showed it ahead, we banked to the right slightly, the silence saying more than any words, that this was not anyone's idea of fun.

As we turned, the radar showed two smaller islands ahead, Caher and Ballybeg. The position where the Mayday had come from was just ahead. Then we were clear of Inishturk. As we approached Ballybeg, things started to happen. Real fast.

The vessel was aground on Ballybeg Island. We had the wind behind us, and as we approached, a lot went through my mind. Very quickly. I could see the vessel and the rocky island she was aground on. I reckoned I had enough room to turn and stop right beside her. I didn't want to waste time using the overfly function, haring off to God knows where in the darkness, in a racetrack pattern that might take us into even more danger. I knew the island was not high. I feared that the ship's crew were in the water and a racetrack would take four minutes at least. But to take control and position manually, would demand a lot of trust, instantly, from the rest of the crew.

'You have control,' replied Carmel. Cool as you like.

We turned and banked and slowed. Carmel calling out the power, the height and speed, as the rocky shore ghosted beside us and then around until it was in front of us. Stopping in the hover, we were illuminated from below. The ship may have been aground, but its deck lights were still powered. I stopped in a position where I could see the ship in front of and below me. It was shuddering and lifting with the waves. We knew that the hard work was already done. It was unsaid, but we were there.

'OK, good hover,' said John. 'There's two crew on the shore. Another in the ship, being helped off. We can take them off right here from the shore. John is attached to the cable, equipment checked. Check clear to winch?'

The winchcrew sprung into action. There were three in the crew of that vessel. Their engine had failed. They had drifted and their generator had been swamped. They lost their radio although the deck lights still worked. They only had enough electrical power to make one Mayday call. They had not received a reply. They had drifted onto the shore of Ballybeg Island, not knowing which it was, not knowing when they first hit it whether they could make it ashore. When we arrived, their life-raft was in shreds, ripped by the rocks and the waves. Less than an hour after their Mayday call.

The winching took minutes. John McDermott pattered me, so that I stayed locked in position. It was still lashing rain, and the waves were crashing over the trawler, sending spray into the air. Our wipers were washing a combination of rain and sea water off the screens. John Manning did what John Manning always did. He cheerfully went on the wire, was lowered down to the men below, and sent them up one by one. The deck lights and our own searchlights dancing around him, the waves washing over his boots, as he waited for his turn to be lifted up too. John McDermott even enjoyed the crashing waves.

The crew were wet but more embarrassed than anything. They were lucky and grateful. We climbed up rapidly, with the help of the strong south-west wind until we were well clear of the islands and local high ground, before turning towards Blacksod as we had done so many times before. The light at Blacksod was a welcome sight.

As was Vincent Sweeney, who was waiting for us when we arrived, tea already brewed, smiling. The fishing vessel's crew did not want to be taken to Galway hospital, and to be honest, they did not need to go. We drank tea as the darkness gave way to grey, saying 'goodbye' to Vincent, not wanting to waste much more of his time. Then we departed for Shannon, agreeing to drop the three men at Cleggan, their home, if the weather was clear enough.

And like many rescues, the peripheral events are faded now. I can imagine what might have happened that day. I like to wrap up my memories with a decorative ribbon. One that says, 'And they all lived happily ever after'. The way I remember it, we got back to Shannon at about 6 a.m.. We could have called the next crew to come in early, but we probably didn't. We probably decided to stay on duty until lunch time, so that the roster and duty pattern was not disrupted. We probably decided that we could sleep later on.

We might have gone to the Great Southern Hotel for break-fast. Mulling over it all, I think we thanked each other, and said well done. It had been a good job. Sitting together eating a full Irish breakfast, drinking coffee and telling Mary, the waitress, where we had been. We only ever went to the hotel after a call-out.

'And where were ye last night lads?'

'Where?'

'Where's that Carmel?'

'Aw, it was a shocking night last night. You wouldn't put a cat out in it.'

'What sort of a summer are we going to get at all?'

'Do ye want any more toast?'

Back at the base, we would have relaxed in chairs, or slept a few hours in the beds, handing over to the oncoming crew at 1 p.m. We would have been tired and would have gone our separate ways. Arriving home, I might have met a neighbour, who might have said something I would get accustomed to over the next few years: 'Don't you have a great job. Another half day. Sure that isn't a job at all.'

I would have smiled and agreed. It was easier. Then I see myself being welcomed at the door with a kiss. And after that I imagine myself, snoozing on the couch. Instead of strapping a 20,500-pound helicopter to my back, I imagine my 20-pound baby daughter, asleep on my chest.

20

HOVERING IN SPACE

*There are only two ways to live your life. One is as though
nothing is a miracle. The other is as though everything is a miracle.*

Anon.

The illusion of the hover fascinated me. That there was no such thing as a hover. You cannot be fixed in space relative to everything. If you looked at planet earth from space you would see that each hover was moving. If you were at the end of a transdown, and drifting forward at 10 knots, you were not hovering in the conventional sense, but from space, from some other place that moved at exactly the same speed, 10 knots, you were indeed hovering.

One night, we stopped our transdown east of Inis Meáin. We ended up drifting forward at 10 knots. We were in thick fog. I remember watching all the normal things, the height, the power, the wind direction, waiting to see if we would be able to see the island. But there was a flash of some other perspective in my mind. I imagined looking down from outer space from an old satellite that was slowly dropping out of orbit. Instead of being stationary over the earth, it was moving at 10 knots. Over us. As the earth rotated beneath us, it could see, that as well as us inching forward to the island, Inis Meáin was inching towards us. For our delectation: 'Ladies and gentlemen, I give you, Inis Meáin.'

The helicopter base in Shannon was visited frequently by rescue teams, school children and passers-by. Some of us grumbled when they visited. Others patiently showed them all the equipment, sat them in the pilots' seats, and posed beside the helicopter for photographs.

Firemen came from Limerick and Ennis and Kerry learning how to operate with a helicopter and where the dangers were. We practised carrying their firefighting gear, and dropping it to them on deck, training like we did with young soldiers. We took them flying, and winched them on and off a stranded old deck on the nearby Fergus estuary. I think they enjoyed it. It was a different day for them.

We visited the Bord Iascaigh Mhara training school in Castle‾townbere each year. Told them what we could do. Told them how they could save themselves, or try to. How the length of time they could survive in the water, depended on what they were wearing. And that we would get to them. If they had flares to hand, and a life-jacket on, when they worked on deck. Then we used to do training out in the harbour, winching them on and off one of their own vessels.

Mountain Rescue got wind that we were friendly too. The south-east mountain rescue association (SEMRA) started to visit under team leaders Roy Johnston and Terry Brophy. The visits turned into full blown exercises in the Comeraghs and Galtee Mountains once or twice a year. Mike Sandover and Mike and Tim Long of Kerry MRT, arranged great exercises in the Magillycuddys. A couple of the Shannon helicopter crew were even invited on MRT training programmes.

It was all fun but it was all serious. Every year the Shannon helicopter gets called to mountain incidents usually with an MRT team on scene, helping or directing the helicopter. Know-ing each others' strengths and weaknesses is essential to success where saving lives is concerned. Ireland may not have very high mountains, but the combination of inexperienced walkers and climbers, rapidly changing weather, very strong winds and low temperatures, can put lives at risk.

An example of one exercise that was slightly different was one we did for a couple of years in Ballyheige, in Kerry. We would visit the long beach there in the middle of December. Arriving in darkness, we would swoop in over the town, descending into Tralee Bay. Then we would hover beside the cliffs, inching our way along, and carry out night cliff winching. Bloody good training.

The final part of the exercise was our departure. From the top of the beach at the town, a crowd would have gathered to watch us. We would transition away, disappearing into the darkness, and make our way to the unlit side of the beach just south of the crowd. As we got closer to the top of the beach again, a donkey and cart would appear below us. The children did not know that it had been waiting in the sand dunes and thought we had delivered Santa to them, because that was who was driving the cart. That worked successfully for a couple of years, thanks to Noel Kelleher, the local inshore lifeboat fund-raiser.

One summer, my sister Ruth, her husband and son Kieran, visited from France. At around that time, a song was number one in the French charts called 'The Lakes of Connemara'. The wild unspoilt mountains and lakes near Maam Cross, where we flew so often, were *de rigeur* in France. She loved being home, and showing her son Kieran what the song was all about. Families do not mean to be apart. Life just does that sometimes. No matter how long she has been away, no matter that she now thinks in French, phrasing her sentences differently, she is instantly recognisable as being Irish when she says, 'Thanks a million'.

The Shannon helicopter was invited to display at all sorts of festivals during the summer months. One was Cruinniú na mBad at Kinvara, the Festival of the Boats. Ruth and her family went with Lynda and Alyson. And best of all, I was flying the display. The festival celebrates the Galway Hooker, a twin sailed boat with distinctive reddish-brown sails and black hull about 30 feet long.

The day of the festival was beautiful. The boats were lined up in the bay as we appeared over the Burren. Easing across the water, their red sails filled, I could imagine them creaking and swelling with the sea water. They criss-crossed the bay, tacking and gibing, their crews waving and shouting greetings to each other and paying their respects to the patron saint of the Galway Hooker at the island that bears his name, St McDara, dipping their sails in the water as they passed. It seemed a shame to bring the noisy helicopter into such a serene place, but perhaps people appreciated the message of the old and the new. The Doolin coast guard rescue RIB waited for us in the narrow confines of the harbour. There was not much room to move. We arrived suddenly, swooping over the town, dropped down to the water, standing the helicopter on its tail, and then started the exercise. Winching on and off a few times before the RIB ran out of sea room. Then away again and returning from a different direction.

We came. We saw. We showed off a bit. And then we Foxtrot Oscared. The helicopter is impressive when it does a display. As we flew by the pier, I wondered where my family was and hoped that Ruth, Armand and Kieran would remember days like this whenever they heard 'Les Lacs de Connemara'.

It was impossible to get to each and every shark festival, regatta, and naming ceremony, but we certainly tried. Those amongst the crew whose idea of a busy day was checking the results of race meetings or doing the crossword, would groan to see the diary full of exercises.

'Oh no!' we'd groan, as the diary pages were flicked through in disgust. But we would manage. We'd find a solution, teasing each other, cajoling. Agreeing to take off after the two o'clock results were in, finishing before the four o'clock race at Sandown. It didn't always work out though. Sometimes we had to go when we all wanted to stay on the ground. The others used to love to see my plans spoiled too, missing Ireland and Munster rugby matches because of exercises or displays. Sauce for the gander and all that.

Once we went to Clifden in Connemara for some pre-arranged exercise but there was some sport on TV that we all wanted to watch. And there might have been a government minister involved too, meaning we had a fixed and definite timing to stick to. We made our way across the Aran Islands, on a clear day, all of us grumbling. I looked down as we flew, gradually withdrawing from the intercom chat, participating only with automatic replies. I watched the coast drift by. We were at 2,000 feet or more which was high for us. I looked ahead to Slyne Head, and all the indented coastline and bays and inlets and islands in between.

Lettermore Island, not quite an island since it had long been linked by a series of bridges. But an island nonetheless. 'Seo libh Pegin Leitir Mor', the song I sang along to, as a shy teenager, when I had gone there to practise Irish, played in my head again. I saw the same stone wall I sat on during the mass. *San Aifreann, is féidir leatsa fanacht anseo ar an mballa* (during the mass, you can stay here on the wall)', because I was Church of Ireland. Sitting on the wall, thirteen years of age, I listened to the beautiful music of Ó Riada's mass as I looked out to sea, a sea gull perched beside me. The sea gull did not know I was Church of Ireland. Neither did Ó Riada. Or the wall. Or the wind. Or the music. Or God himself. Although sitting alone on the wall was a bit of a tell-tale sign.

We seemed to slow. The sun made the rotor blades seem

slow too. They flickered above my head, beating a reassuring rhythm, a heartbeat, a pulse. A pulse that was absent from the deserted islands below me. I scrambled for a map. I had seen them all before but it was as if I was seeing them for the first time. Inishmuskerry, the map said, where only a holy well and the ruins of low stone huts remain. Used in bygone days by the gatherers of seaweed. Finish Island, its line of neatly arranged ruined houses, built after the Great Famine – grassy perfect plots. Where once trees stood and bent with the wind, gone now, as its people are. Then Mason Island, another island with its own deserted village, built by the Congested District Board. Each a plot in paradise in good weather. Forlorn in bad. Not congested now.

McDara's Island – its perfect chapel. Solitary all year round. Except on its pilgrimage day. That rang another bell. Summer holidays in Roundstone. The caravan site throwing up new people each year. The McMahons from Galway, never seen since, talked us into going by currach, on a pilgrimage to McDara's Island. From Roundstone, a fleet of twenty currachs, put-putted out into the sea, a wicker picnic basket on my mother's lap, my father smiling as the breeze reddened his cheeks, the chat above the noise of the outboard motors. Did my memory play tricks and make each day sunny? The currachs drove onto the beach, one by one, crushing the sand with a swoosh and a splash. The adults went to mass at the ruined chapel. The children explored, and swam, and fished in the shallow water with nets on bamboo sticks. The island silence was broken by the hum of prayer, the lapping of waves on sand and our playful noise. We ate our sandwiches and left.

I was looking down at my past. As we flew on to Clifden, I imagined I could see our currachs returning to Roundstone. There I was, leaning over the side, trailing a hand in the water, looking down to see any fish. My mother held my other hand while my father smoked.

Called out more regularly now, I was starting to wallow in the sheer beauty of it all: Galway, Clare, the Doolin ferry, the cliffs of Moher. We flew along the cliffs at any height we wanted, stopping further down near Hag's Head to do cliff winching. Everywhere we went, up and down the coast, more treasures to be revealed: the Caha Mountains near Kenmare, Skellig Michael, the saint's fields on the north side of Brandon, Dun Aenghus on Inis Mór. An endless list.

Rescue is not all about scenery. Because we went out so frequently, we often encountered the other side. We encountered death as well as life. Sometimes in the emptiness of the vain search for a man overboard, or a body in the water, floating lifeless, while swimmers splashed a hundred yards away, shielding the sun with their hands, wondering why we were hovering. Or the relatives at a hospital, overcome with emotion, as we took their loved one away in a stretcher. The tears flowing, as they wondered if they would see them alive again. Having to ignore their tears, as politely as you could, you did your job. Cliff rescues that were not rescues at all. Wondering why.

Some of the winchcrew used to be very hard about it all in a humorous way, half in jest, half serious. A coping mechanism, I guess. Often, inside the helicopter was seawater mixed with blood or human tissue after a rescue. There was a blue 'sea-tray' in the cabin, stretched across and fixed to the floor. Made of a plastic, its purpose was to prevent the helicopter itself getting wet, so that it would not rust and degrade. It had to be cleaned. They would set about their task cheerfully, wearing protective gloves, armed with a mop and detergent and bucket of hot soapy water. Then they would come in and ask how many of us fancied a curry. We would wince, but it was funny and it helped.

The night we went to Inis Meáin, the crew was Kevin Mc-
Carrick, myself, Al Clapp and Graham Goosey. Someone had
to get to hospital. Middle of the night. Weather bad. We took
loads of fuel. We asked Marion, Dr Marion to you, if the casualty would survive long enough to get to the Isle of Man because
there was fog everywhere. We might not get into Galway, or even
Shannon. Or anywhere in Ireland. She said yes, after a pause.

And so we went for the loaf of bread, six eggs and a pint of
milk, or, over the Burren and Black Head and down into Galway
Bay if you prefer. The approach was difficult because we could
not see a bloody thing, not even the sea 40 feet below us. The fog
was as thick as it gets. Unable to stop and hover, without enough
power and nothing to see, it was better to keep moving forwards,
keeping a relative airflow through the rotor disc above us. It is
easier to ride a bicycle slowly, than balance it stopped.

That was when I imagined the geo-stationary satellite above
us. Thinking of it helped. We could not see but if we had to we
could do a transup and fly away, have another go, think it over,
make another plan. Then we began to make out the surface of
the sea below us. Like an illusion. Dreamlike. Becoming real.
As the door opened and the patter began, the moisture from
the fog and sea, whipped up by our downdraft, permeated the
helicopter cabin and cockpit. Dampening our foreheads slightly,
telling us this was real.

The satellite above us watched as we waited for the Good
Lord to move planet earth east, just a little bit. And the Good
Lord moved the island, and the shore was revealed to the faithful. And the Good Lord revealed himself to the faithful, as white
waves were caught in the searchlight's beam, saying: 'Blessed
are ye that wait for the turning of the earth, in the darkness,

'Blessed are ye that have faith and believe that the earth will
turn below your feet, though many doubt you.

'Blessed are ye who believe that you will see, when others cannot.'

We drifted over the beach, not sure if I was being blasphemous, or actually praying. We landed and collected the casualty. As fog was all over Galway Bay, we did an instrument landing at Shannon, and handed the relieved patient over to an ambulance from Limerick.

21

—

MY CREWMAN IS DYING

*People do not like to think. If one thinks, one must reach
conclusions. Conclusions are not always pleasant.*

Anon.

You could either take John Willie's boat, or the *St Kieran*, which
was the mailboat, if you wanted to get to Sherkin Island or Cape
Clear. Once he had finished his pint in Salter's pub, John would
set out from Baltimore with the visitors, and the stores and gossip that ran the islands. Once on Sherkin, my brother would wait
impatiently for my sisters and our mother and father, as they
dragged their bags up the hill to the house given to them for a
couple of weeks. No water, electricity or toilet. An island summer idyll. Fishing, the only thing on his mind.

He used to stand on the beach with my father, fishing for
bass with Toby spinners, laughing excitedly as the mackerel
arrived, the water boiling yards from where they stood. He
feared the dark water of Horseshoe Bay, and the spirits of the
pirates that lurked there. Being the youngest, I was, as one of
the Christian Brothers used to say, in God's pocket at the time.
Born years later, I had never been there. Those are my brother's
memories, not mine, sustaining him in London, when he was
making his way in the world.

I had always wanted to visit, to see for myself. So before I
went to Scotland, I visited Sherkin and Cape Clear. John Willie
was long gone, but the magic was there all the same. We walked

along the grassy island road, passing the places that were part of my family's lore, recognising the white marine markers that stand on each side of the narrow strait, separating the mainland from Sherkin, recalling the black and white photos of our family holidays, faded and dog-eared, smiling faces, short trousers and cardigans.

Having flown past Cape Clear on the way to the Fastnet Rock several times, I knew what it looked like. Going there the next day, our visit coincided with a change in the weather. It was roasting hot. We walked to the harbour on the south side, listening to the echoes of a canoe instructor's voice, teaching Irish students how to Eskimo roll in Irish. Cape Clear is a Gaeltacht. It was alive with young people, with bees buzzing in the wild flowers, but quiet as every island is. The day was so clear that the distant Fastnet looked close enough to touch.

I had a mental checklist that year of islands that I had never visited. We went to Mayo after that. Having spent so much time with Vincent Sweeney and his family over the years, refuelling helicopters and having short hurried conversations, I wanted to see it from the ground. There are numerous islands off the Mullet peninsula and Vincent promised us a trip to one of the Inishkee Islands, Inishkee South with its deserted village and a once busy whaling station beside a perfect sandy beach and a small pier. We wandered on another perfect day. Standing on the island's highest point, I pointed out the islands, the huge cliffs at Achill, just south of us, the dark forbidding Black Rock to the south-west, the Mullet Peninsula stretching north towards Eagle Island, which we could see just over Inishkee North, beside us. Then we returned to Blacksod, following the same route through the water, that the helicopter would follow above.

We stayed a few days, jumping off the pier and snorkelling in the freezing water with Vincent and Doreen's children, David,

Simon and Erica. They were disappointed to see that I was flight-less. I managed to go to Vincent's local pub in *Each Leim* (Horse Leap) for a drink. Sitting at the bar in *Teach John Joe* listening to the conversation in Mayo Irish (this was another Gaeltacht area), we passed a few hours, as men do, talking about nothing in particular. I spoke Irish as best I could, listening to the rapid perfect Irish that I struggled to follow, flowing naturally between Vincent and his friends. I had never heard Mayo Irish before, never knew it was different.

Old photographs of football teams adorned the walls. The proprietor himself, John Gallagher, proudly standing in the Mayo team line-up against Dublin. The local team, Belmullet, today's generation in colour, were beside yesterdays' men, in black and white. There was John Joe fielding a ball. There he was again tackling a Dublin player. I walked around the bar before it got busy, looking at each glimpse of the past.

Vincent introduced me to Theresa and Peter Murphy, from the nearby fishing village of Cartron, before they set up for music in a corner. I wondered whether the music of their duo, 'The Murphy Movement', accordion and tambourine, would be drowned out by the sound of a helicopter overhead. It depended on the wind, Vincent said.

'Do we want top cover?' asked John McDermott, nodding at me as he took a call from MRCC Dublin. I nodded and gave a thumbs-up in reply. He hung up the phone and rattled off the details: 'Spanish fishing vessel, injured crewman, out of range at the moment, north-west of Blacksod. He's heading south-east now to shore. They want us to go to Blacksod and standby. Should be in range by the time we get up there and refuel.'

There was no a rush: the vessel was out of range for the time being. We had taken over duty at lunchtime as usual, and had time to eat and settle in before the phone had rung. In a leisurely way, we got dressed and soon we were asking Shannon ATC for take-off clearance.

It was mid-afternoon in December: darkness was only an hour away. The longest nights of the year were upon us. The journey to Blacksod took us an hour. During the flight, we got more and more information on the marine radio. John McDermott was busy crunching numbers on his hand-held computer, trying to calculate when the fishing vessel would be in range, and what time we should take off from Blacksod to meet it.

Pete Leonard, winchman, was doing the same calculation using an admiralty chart, dividers and a slide rule, just like a navigator in the Second World War. It was our way of checking everything, using the old and the new. Mark Robson was the co-pilot. A new addition to Shannon's crew, he was over from Aberdeen, working for a few weeks

Gerry, Vincent's brother, was holding the fort. As they re-fuelled I used the phone to get Dublin to tell me the latest news. I looked at the admiralty chart, which was pinned to the wall showing the positions of rescues and their dates, and how far offshore they had been, Vincent's rogues gallery. Those rescues were as much the Sweeney's as our own. Over time, Vincent and Gerry and their children, had seen the faces of helicopter crews before and after rescues, seen the thin veneer that covers tension, and the subsequent scars of stormy ordeals.

'You're now declaring this a life or death job?' I repeated, loud enough for the others to hear. Cups of tea were put down. Conversation stopped. We drew together, listening. 'And they are at 220 miles now. Making ten knots. And top cover is on the way. An RAF Nimrod from Kinloss. We are now tasked. OK. OK. Give me a few minutes to talk it over with the crew and the met forecaster, and I'll let you know.'

We already had the weather forecast both for the Mayo area in general, and the position of the fishing vessel in particular. We just had to agree on what range we would meet the vessel, and then work backwards to decide our take off time.

All vessels fishing off the Irish coast have medical back up. In the case of Spanish fishing vessels, they were in HF communication with Medico Madrid in Spain where a doctor could respond to enquiries. From sultry Madrid in the evening, to a ship on the Atlantic off the Irish coast. If one of their crew fell ill or was injured, they would radio with the details, the symptoms, and await instructions. The more serious the medical situation, the higher the priority given to the mission. Changing the medical status of the casualty to 'life or death', meant the worst possible situation. It meant we would push to our outermost limit of range to get the casualty to hospital as soon as possible.

We all reached the same conclusion, give or take a few minutes. If we left in about half an hour, and if the vessel continued east as promised, then we would get to them as they reached our limit. We decided to delay an extra half hour, just in case the vessel was slower than expected and because there was a big swell.

Half an hour later, the helicopter groaned as it eased off the ground and into the air, full of fuel at its maximum weight. We cleared the granite wall around the lighthouse and shuddered into the darkness again. We climbed to 500 feet and then turned west, over *Teach John Joe*'s in *Each Leim*.

I paused in the checklist as I imagined the smoky conversation in Irish in the pub below where I had been not so long before. Used to the sound of helicopters, they would take up where they left off in their paused conversations as the throb of our engines faded away. On maximum range rescues like this one, the next part of the flight would take us almost two hours. We settled into the cruise in the dark, a sense of anticipation building.

Once we had cleared the invisible islands below us, we descended to 500 feet where the westerly wind against us would not be as strong. The friction of the wind on the water, would slow it just a little. Each knot reduction in wind speed would help us to move faster, help us reach the vessel sooner, using less fuel. Using less fuel to get there would leave more fuel to hover. At critical maximum range. We hoped to meet the vessel, position over it quickly, winch the man off within the time our fuel allowed, and then return home.

It is good to have a plan, so that as it starts to unravel, you notice that something different is happening. You start to become uneasy. Unease is a symptom of the sixth sense. Except for taste, SAR uses all the senses, but that sixth sense is the one that is hardest to quantify. Yet it's probably the most important.

The unravelling began as we flew along our unerring northwest track, listening to the top cover after it arrived. Rescue helicopters that travel long distances are protected by communications links. Coastal radio stations, like Valentia and Malin Head, maintain a continuous listening watch on marine radio frequencies, used by ships, ocean-going vessels and rescue helicopters which operate at too low an altitude to be able to talk to ATC. ATC Shannon, that watched over us like a shepherd, making sure we were always safe and well, and talking to someone. Just as they do with all aircraft. Their reassuring transmissions getting fainter and more distorted as we headed offshore. Then fading altogether. Until we worked solely with the marine coastal radio stations. But there comes a point, a distance offshore, when coastal stations can no longer continue to communicate with helicopters. The radio wave used is a direct wave, and cannot curve over the horizon.

An alternative is HF communication, used to cover greater distances and able to bounce back off the ionosphere. However

HF comms are susceptible to weather and atmospheric pressure interference. At distances of 100 miles offshore, the coastal radio becomes useless, but HF may be useless too. That's where top cover comes in. Aeroplanes from either our air corps or the RAF are given the task of flying over us and providing a communications link. They would fly down low over the fishing fleet, scouting for us, telling us which vessel was ours, giving instructions to the ship's captain, and getting weather information for us. Ideally, they got the vessel to change course before we arrived, adjusting so that it was into wind, or better still, 30 degrees off the wind direction to the right.

Those top cover crews tried to search before we arrived to save time. And God forbid that we would have a technical problem ourselves, but if we ditched, they could drop life-rafts to us, and direct others to come to our aid. At high altitude above cloud, two pilots up front flying, with numerous crew behind them, in dimmed green or red night light, sitting fixed to radar screens and hissing radios. A flying battle controller. Our guardian angels.

We listened as the RAF Nimrod from Scotland came on frequency. They started to talk to the Spanish vessel. The unravelling began. The radio operator on the Nimrod had a very strong Scottish accent. We kept hearing him repeat his messages. We were unable to hear the fishing vessel reply. The curve of the earth separating us from the fishing vessels in front of us.

'I say again. Fishing vessel *Santa Cruz*, this is Rescue 11. Request your position, course and speed. Say again the condition of the casualty. Over.'

We trundled along, getting closer, as the radio messages became more frequent, over and back, like invisible fireworks over our heads. The Nimrod started to talk to us.

'Rescue 115. This is Rescue 11. You have 60 miles to go. We

are on scene. There are multiple targets out here. We are trying to identify your target. We have an interpreter talking to the captain on HF, standing by to give him instructions. The weather is misty with low cloud at about 400 feet. Winds from the north, light and variable. Visibility one mile. QNH pressure setting 984 millibars. Looks like a heavy swell. Unable to identify a suitable winching area.'

'Rescue 11. This is Rescue 115. Roger. Copied. Thanks for your help. Hope you can get that vessel onto a suitable course for us by the time we arrive.'

There was a fleet of them. We had to identify the correct vessel quickly. In pitch darkness, not that straightforward. We could use direction finding, homing to the radio transmissions as we got closer but that would be time consuming, fuel consuming.

We listened as the Nimrod finally got the vessel's position, course and speed. I put it in the navigation computer. John McD put it in his hand-held nav computer, while Pete plotted it quickly. We all groaned together: having planned to meet him inside our maximum range, the vessel was marginally outside it.

We had completed our preparation, our brief, our checks. We continued, as the top cover crew tried to get the vessel to take up an into-wind course. It got closer on the radar. We opted to transdown straight into the light wind, positioning ourselves, dog-legging, away and back again. Our bank and speed, visible only on the instruments, an oily film of night, making it pointless to look outside. Our 'Transdown Gate' arrived, the point where we would start down, sliding towards the vessel and the sea.

Complete cloud cover above us, complete black below us: a 'Black Hole' approach. Mark flew totally focused on the instruments. I monitored, so that I would not get fixated by the detail, waiting to have enough to see outside, to take over control. My sixth sense started to scream at me. Something was wrong. We were not anywhere near the hover, and yet the torque was too high. There was no wind. We may even have had the wind behind us.

As we reached our decision height, John was at the open door, looking at what was coming into view. The swell below us was very very big, 10 metres plus. The vessel wallowed and rolled, as we saw that it was dead in the water, drifting. We couldn't hover. There was so little wind, and our power was so high. We must have ended up downwind. The wind was so changeable and variable. We quickly agreed to fly away and try again. We had no choice.

We continued to sink, our airspeed increased slowly. We were using all the power available. I could see the vessel, peripherally. We were at about the same height as the masts, then climbed up and away.

Not knowing whether to laugh or cry, we made two more attempts to get down to it searching for wind that was not there, unable to get to the vessel. No one had known it was without power. Then we realised that not only was it drifting, it was under tow. No one had known that either. In the darkness, the tow line stretched nearly 500 metres to another vessel. We only realised it, when we saw the bow being pulled down suddenly into the swell by a tow line that emerged, dripping from the water in our searchlight's beam. It was impossible to get any meaningful instructions to the two vessels, in the conditions, and in the time we had available.

So we made another three attempts to reach it, trying to wallow beside it as it wallowed, trying to stay at a safe height, where we could have some sort of fighting chance of seeing a space on the deck. As the clock wound down, the four of us knew that it was not going to happen. It was not just dangerous for us: it was dangerous for the winchman and the casualty on the vessel.

We climbed up from the pitching wallowing deck. Our fuel tanks said, 'Go home'. Chicken fuel. Bingo fuel. Leave Dodge. *Now*. On the intercom, one last conference call: 'Home lads?'

Three voices, in unison, saying 'yes'. We announced our departure, the Nimrod acknowledging it in a matter-of-fact way. As we left the scene, the skipper of the vessel called us on the marine radio, pleading: 'My crewman is dying. My crewman is dying.'

On the way back from that job, I had plenty of time to think it over. I felt crushed by my failure to complete the job. I had let myself down. Let Shannon down. A man might die now because of it, I thought to myself. The others in the crew rallied around me. 'It was not your fault,' they said. 'The conditions were awful. It happens. No point in risking everything. That was a big swell. How the hell were we to know the vessel was being towed? If we'd known that, we would have waited until they were at a closer range.'

They tried to buoy me up, to stop me from being hard on myself. 'Your not as good as your last job,' they reminded me. 'Only as good as your next one. Put it behind you.' I found that hard to do.

The man lived, by the way. A few hours later, a royal navy Sea King from Prestwick in Scotland, reached it, and managed to complete the winching transfer. I do not know whether the conditions were much different, whether they had been helped by some extra wind that had picked up. An extra 10 knots might have made all the difference. I did not know whether the vessel was closer to shore when they got to them. But I could not help wonder how they had managed, when we had not.

The swell would have been the same. It would not have changed in a few hours. Maybe the confusion with the tow had been sorted out. But they did it. When I heard later that they had succeeded, I smiled privately at my reaction. The bastards, I thought, envying their skill. Fair play to them, I thought, admiring their success. Thank God, I thought, that someone had saved the crewman's life after all.

22

DOOLIN DEEDS

To a brave man, good and bad luck are like his
left and right hand: he uses them both.

Anon.

Irish Helicopters had held the contract for five years. As the government had not sanctioned the purchase of new bigger helicopters for the air corps, another contract was awarded. It was a body-blow to Irish Helicopters when Bond Helicopters, another Aberdeen based company, was chosen, starting January 1997. We waited anxiously, wondering what that would mean for us. Would we lose our jobs?

We did not. The new contract consisted of changing the name on the door, learning new company-speak, and welcoming a few new faces to the crew to replace the ones who had left and returned to the UK when the contract changed. Simon Cotterell returned from Bristow Helicopters and the Falklands. Ian Dunn joined from Irish Helicopters. He who had sat patiently with me in Cork airport, chatting over cups of coffee, explaining how civil flying worked. Words from the wise. Steering me clear of pitfalls. Knew all there was to know about helicopter flying around Ireland: rigs, lighthouses, ESB pylon inspections, cargo slinging and then rescue. The Irish Aviation Authority was lucky to recruit him in later years

Having settled in with the new staff, I disappeared home,

waiting for our second baby to arrive. When baby Niamh came, (how effortless it is for a man to say that), it started raining pink fluffy rabbits again, just as it had done for Alyson. Changing company, and night callouts, were the last things on my mind. Changing nappies and trying to get a night's sleep, were. For a while anyway. Two sisters, one promoted now, and getting used to the new arrival. Our exhaustion from looking after a two year old, a new baby and each other. Grannies and Grand-dads, cradling the new arrival in their arms. The Offaly OY, and Monaghan MN registered cars, taking it in turns to park out-side the house. Mary Black singing 'Wonder Child' again in our kitchen as she would for each baby that arrived in our family:

> This child will build a violin, One will follow the travellers love,
> Another will the bow apply, To reach the one above.
> I see her in a golden room, with the moon and stars above her ...

When I came back to work, I caught up on the news and the gossip. The crew had been called out at night to the cliffs of Moher, after a boy had fallen. They had not been able to get to him, which was understandable, given the 600 feet height of the cliffs. The boy had survived, not just his fall but also the ordeal of being hauled up the cliff by stretcher. The helicopter did return later to take him to hospital from the cliff top but our reputation had been damaged, especially in Doolin.

The Doolin coast guard unit is made up of volunteers living locally who come to the aid of anyone in distress along the cliffs, in the Burren, along the coast from Kinvara all the way to Lahinch Bay. Scaling the cliffs to reach people who have slipped onto ledges. Recovering the dead from the sea below the cliffs, either from the RIB, or by swimming right in to the breaker line, where the wave energy is thrown up on the rocks and boulders. Searching for the injured or the missing.

There isn't much they can't do alone. It is rare enough that they would ask for helicopter assistance but the life of a young man called Peter Fitzpatrick, a local lad, hung in the balance that night. When the helicopter arrived from Shannon, it flew over high, could not get to the position of the casualty, and departed – not straight away but it departed. When the contract was awarded to a different company, teams like Doolin wondered privately whether the Shannon SAR service would be adversely affected. They feared that there would be new pilots and crew unfamiliar with the Irish coast and that some rescues would not be done. That night they felt their fears had been justified.

We decided to take the bull by the horns. We had not really been in the habit of training with cliff rescue teams up until then, although there had been the odd exercise. We rang Doolin, and spoke to the team's boss, their area officer, Mattie Shannon. We suggested they visit us and have a training and briefing day. Mattie politely pretended not to see any need for a visit but he agreed all the same, to come along with some of the team.

It was obvious when they trooped into the hangar that something was wrong. There was tension and the body language was defensive as we lined up to meet each other but, as we talked it over, the crackle in the air disappeared. We walked in and out of the helicopter, around it, sat in it, showed them everything there was to see. After a while, we were drinking cups of tea, trying to remember each other's first names. What a brilliant day it turned out to be. We answered their questions:

Well, why couldn't ye get to the cliff?

I thought ye had an infra-red camera. Could ye not use that?

Could ye not use your lights to get in to where the casualty was?

Could you not just hover over the cliff and lower yourselves down?

I thought that computer could tell you the wind direction. Could you not use that to get in?

But I thought ye could fly at night?

We went through it all. How we could fly at night but needed to be able to see the ground to hover. How the wind that night had been easterly, spilling over the cliff, creating dangerous downdrafts where the casualty had been positioned. How dangerous that was for the helicopter in terms of performance. How the weather that night, had seemed clear when looking up vertically at the stars but horizontally it had been quite misty with drizzle at times making the FLIR camera less effective in the dark. How it was great to be familiar with the area but not essential. How the procedures allowed us to go anywhere. Sure weren't we called out to Wales and Scotland now and again, and we didn't know those areas very well?

Then we took them flying in daylight to the cliffs of Moher. We flew at an altitude lower than the cliff top, straight at the cliffs, coming from the sea. As the cliffs got closer, we slowed, getting closer and closer until they towered above us. The helicopter shuddered as we hit turbulence. We tried different approach angles, different approach heights and asked them to imagine each one in the dark, pitch dark.

We told them what we could do, what the conditions and wind would need to be, in order for us to make approaches to this or that area on the cliffs. We learned a lot that day about each other and got to know some of the names: Thomas Doherty, climber, coxswain and diver, Ray Murphy and Conor McGrath, both paramedics and cave rescue specialists too, Pat Hartigan, the radio and navigation man, Brian McMahon, coxswain, and Mattie Shannon, smiling and running the whole show.

That afternoon was the foundation stone of future co-operation between the Doolin team and us. It paved the way for frequent exercises, and successful joint SARs. But not just in Clare: it had a ripple effect around the coast. The coast guard started to send us to different units, doing the same thing in Killala, Dingle, Kinsale, Toe Head, and also to mountain rescue teams. We were not to know that at the time. At the time, we finished off by asking them about what had happened that night, when the helicopter turned away, returning to Shannon airport. This is their story.

On top of the Cliffs of Moher is a stone tower called O'Brien's Tower, popular with visitors. It looks over a steep and narrow path, which winds its way down from the top of the 550 foot cliff. A local boy, Peter Fitzpatrick, slipped as he got close to the bottom. He was seriously injured. His friend, who was walking with him, ran back up the track to raise the alarm. It was late afternoon.

The Doolin team were alerted as it got dark. They assembled at the cliff top, and quickly set up a climbing tripod anchored into the ground, a safety line and a rope. A paramedic abseiled down to check on young Peter, wrapping him in heat blankets. It was obvious that he had extensive injuries and fractures. He radioed to the cliff top about what he had found.

By this stage, the generator was running, the bright light stands were secured into position, illuminating the area at the top of the cliff, and just below it. Radios crackled as the team paced at the cliff top waiting to do something, keeping the villagers back from the edge.

Four other members of the team prepared themselves: Thomas Doherty, Conor McGrath, Ray Murphy, Ian Lambe. Climbing harnesses checked. Helmets on, headlamps fitted. A radio between each pair. Whistles. One by one they stepped to the edge, gave the signal, smiled at the familiar faces who were watching for the first time, and disappeared from view. The rope creaked on the tripod, the tackle straining as they descended 550 feet. Then the stretcher was sent down.

The helicopter crew had been called. The welcome sound of its approach soon filled everyone with hope but doubt crept in when it did not descend. People strained to hear what they were saying on the radio, as they called in. The helicopter could not approach the cliff.

Relatives looked up into the sky with disbelief as the flashing lights of the helicopter faded away. Mattie Shannon played the cards he had been dealt. Better to light a candle than to curse the darkness. He spoke to the lads at the bottom of the cliff by radio. They would have to do a stretcher lift up the cliff. They had trained for it but they had never done one this big. No one hesitated. Peter was already stabilised in the stretcher. At the top of the cliff, safety lines, extra ropes and a hauling line were prepared, and then thrown over into the darkness.

Their head torches illuminating the cliff just above them, the four stretcher-men looked up at the distant bright lights at the cliff top. The sea was breaking on the boulders 50 feet from where they stood. The whistle and whip sound, announced the arrival of the ropes and safety lines.

They took a safety line, one for each pair, connected themselves, checked each other. They attached the other safety line and the hauling line to the stretcher. One man with a radio. One with a whistle. Radio calls to say ready. Head torches dazzling each others eyes as they nodded to each other. Sweat trickling down their faces.

Up above, the same checking and double checking. The villagers were ready. They could not remember if they had ever had a tug-of-war team, but they were going to pull Peter Fitzpatrick up this cliff in double quick time. Fucking right they were. An-

other of the team paced back and forth along the cliff edge. The
Cliff-Top-Man or Breast-Man, to use his correct title, he was
the communicator. He himself was secured and belayed to a
spike in the ground in case he slipped. When the radio signal
came from below that they were ready, he told the rest of them
at the cliff top.

The hum of chatter stopped. The hauling team, made up of
the Doolin Cliff team, Peter's relatives and local villagers, took
the slack and got ready. Two others manned the luff tackle, the
clutch-like mechanism on the tripod. At least five others paced
around, checking they were doing the right thing.

'Don't look at me Joe. Look at the man at the head of the
rope. Good man.'

'Turn off that phone please, missus. You'll have time later
on.'

'Sorry lads, you'll have to move back behind that line.'

'Paddy, just check that line there.'

'Sorry there lads. A bit of *ciúnas* (quiet) please. Keep the
noise down.'

From below, three clear whistle blasts were heard. The cliff-
top-man, leaning over the cliff edge, signalled to Mattie to
pull. Quietly, Mattie passed on that command to the hauling
team, nodding and moving one hand from a vertical position,
in a chopping motion downwards, pointing away from the cliff
edge. They started to pull.

Four men and a stretcher. Well over a thousand pounds
weight. Inching up the cliffs at night. Three whistle blasts to go
up. Keep the stretcher off the cliff. Don't let it bump or make
contact. Four men trying to keep balanced. Their head-torch
beams trained on the area above them. Gradually inching upwards towards the sound of the generator. The glow of light
at the cliff top grew with each pull of the rope. Knowing that

if they made one slip, one false move, they would be all right.
The years of practice, the trust, the teamwork, the cohesion of
the team would hold them if they lost their footing. The team
members above, Brian McMahon, Paddy Connaghan, Patrick
O'Brien, Andy Basher; carrying out their assigned tasks, watching each other and the villagers too. Eye contact now and again.
Concentration. Silent prayers, knowing the danger better than
the others. Myles Duffy, Kevin Griffin, Ritchie Jones and Pearse
Shannon; no joking now.

Checking Peter. Pause. One whistle blast to stop the pull.
The rope stops. Immediately. The silence while they check Peter,
broken only by the heavy breathing of the four of them. Ready
again. Three whistle blasts. The rope pulls in and up they go
again. Rock gives way to grass. The gradient reduces. They know
each and every inch of this place. They have another rocky section after this.

The signal for going down, to descend, is two whistle blasts.
They whistled to stop to check Peter. One whistle blast. They
whistled to go up again. Three whistle blasts. But never two.
Not that night.

It took several hours. The hauling team was replaced by
willing volunteers switching in when instructed, out when instructed. Another of the Doolin team walking along the hauling team, making eye contact in the reflected light of the light
stand: Are you OK?

Do you want a break?

Eyes only, no words. A nod in reply.

I'll take a break.

A tap on the shoulder. A waiting volunteer takes his place,
takes the strain. The man he replaced lights a cigarette as he
walks away. The flare of the match in his cupped hands, singeing
his eyebrows as his hands shake. As the stretcher team got close

to the top, Mattie called for the helicopter again. Could they take Peter from the cliff top?

The stretcher team appeared over the cliff edge at about ten o'clock. Out of the darkness they came, dripping sweat, concentrating on the last few feet without allowing themselves a smile. The villagers did not know whether to be shocked or happy. Peter's life was not saved yet. They had also been warned, reminded: 'Stay in your position when they come up. Don't try to help. You are helping. When they come up, it's not over. Not yet. We have to get them all secured. We have a cliff top stretcher team ready. They will replace the team that comes up. Once we have Peter and the stretcher taken away, we'll get you all moved away too. Let's have no more fallers tonight, lads.'

The helicopter returned. It carefully made a successful approach to the cliff top, landed and took Peter to Galway Hospital. They watched as it left, steam rising off them. Then Peter's mother started into a prayer. Those that were starting to walk away, and could not hear, were tugged by their sleeves, and stopped, seeing the heads nodding towards where she stood with her head down, eyes closed. The 'Our Father' in Irish was said:

In ainm an Athair, agus an Mhic agus an Spiorad Naoimh, Amen.
Ár nAthair atá ar Neamh,
Go naofar dAinm,
Go dtaga do Ríocht,
Go ndéantar do thoil or an dtalamh,
Mar a dhéantar ar Neamh …

Peter made a full recovery. I listened to that story on more than one occasion: in the hangar that day, hill walking in the Burren and the Twelve Bens with some of the team who are still my friends, in O'Connor's pub in Fisherstreet, the local name for Doolin, as music played.

Over the next few years, the Shannon helicopter got to

know the rescue teams around the coast, and they got to know us. There were numerous calls which involved not just Doolin, but many of the teams around the coast. Thanks to those exercises, briefings and familiarisation flights, we operated more effectively on real searches and rescues.

There is a cliff near Black Head called the Mirror Wall. It is popular with climbers because it is a technical climb, and is as smooth as glass, about 100 feet high. We exercised with Doolin there one year, taking new members flying, winching them in and out of their RIB, which was on the water nearby. We winched them on and off the cliff too. It was a spectacular sight: the breakers below the Mirror Wall, the cliffs of Moher in the distance behind, seabirds wheeling around us as the orange-high-visibility-clad Doolin team swarmed about the place. Volunteers every one. Unpaid. Farmers and carpenters. Plasterers and plumbers. Musicians and artists. Husbands, wives, sons and daughters. Dreamers. Heroes.

23

ROARINGWATER BAY AT NIGHT

We carry within us, the wonders of the world without us.

Anon.

Middle of the night, 3 a.m. to be precise. Just about to start our descent into a bay to search for a missing man. Couldn't see a thing. Didn't expect to be able to see much during the search either. Cloud cover stole away any starlight. Below me was familiar territory. Beautiful familiar territory. I pictured it in my mind on a sunny day as we got ready to descend. I pushed the swings in the playground in Schull, as I had done not long before. Pushing a giggling Alyson, as I looked south towards Cape Clear, across Roaringwater Bay.

Great name for a place, Roaringwater Bay. The name alone tells its own story. South-west corner of Ireland. The first place the Atlantic swell meets the shore. The first place the south-west winds arrive. The first place in Europe the Gulf Stream warms. A terrible beauty in a storm: true. But at its majestic best, when the sea and the wind are peaceful, when the storms pass and the water no longer roars, Roaringwater Bay sighs and blinks in the sun.

It took Him six days to do it all. The major construction work was done on day one: the Heavens and the Earth. Busy Man. Day two must have been when He set everything spinning and toppling, because that was when He created day and night. He came up with the 23 degree inclination on day two as well, giving us the seasons. The stars in the sky were next. That is what it says in *The Book* anyway.

Day three was the one. That's when He did it. He created the earth and the seas on day three. He put four or five peninsulas on the south-west corner of Ireland. He found it hard to get them all the same size, although He almost got them all parallel. Just as He was going to continue with His work, on some other place on the orb that He had started to spin, He added some decoration. Like an artist standing back from his easel, then coming forward to make one more flourish in the search for perfection, He delved out the bay (to about 30 fathoms), and placed the clay back carefully within. He created one hundred islands, three large ones in a row in the middle, three more slim ones in a line, different lengths, on the north side, another two bigger ones at the mouth, and to one side of the bay, a pointed rock at the entrance. The leftover earth, He scattered here and there.

He hardly had to do any work there on day four. The plants needed no urging, grass and hedgerows bursting forth in forty shades of green. By day five and six, Roaringwater Bay, its water and its islands, teemed with life. When He rested on the seventh day, Roaringwater Bay smiled back at Him. Hare Island, The Calf Islands, Long Island, Skean East and West, Horse Island, Cape Clear and Sherkin, blushed in His admiring gaze. I'm losing it, I thought, as we slipped into the cloud.

'Cork Radio, this is Rescue 115. We'll be commencing search in five minutes. Endurance three hours.'
'Rescue 115, Cork Radio. Roger. Listening out.'

The SAR crew numbered six people. Two of them were often overlooked, often forgotten. The two engineers who maintained the helicopter were the ones who kept it airworthy, fuelled, greased and inspected. There are three sub-divisions within aircraft engineering: engines, airframe and avionics. Each is a discipline in its own right. Complexity in every one.

The two jet engines deliver no thrust, unlike an aeroplane. They turn the rotor head to which is attached the five enormous rotor blades, each weighing over 200 lbs, and just under 30 feet in length.

There was an electronics bay under her nose. Opening it up like you would your car bonnet, revealed what made her electronically up-to-date: gyros, accelerometers, communications and navigation boxes, GPS navigation, the FLIR camera. Complex and more sophisticated than her old airframe suggested, there was plenty to keep our engineers busy. They knew her inside out though. Listening to vague descriptions of vibrations or poor radio reception, or erratic auto-hover height holding, they would pinpoint the solution almost instantly. It is no exaggeration to say that their knowledge and ability to solve complicated engineering problems saved lives. They were under a different type of pressure to aircrew, but pressure it was nevertheless.

They say that a helicopter, particularly one like the Sikorsky S-61, has more moving parts than a Boeing 747. Whether that is true or not, it gets the point across. With a weight of 10 tonnes, those moving parts had to be finely tuned, balanced and monitored. This was demanding work, particularly given the often harsh environment where the helicopter flew. The added pressure on engineering in Shannon was the time constraint of remaining on fifteen minute readiness by day and forty-five minutes by night.

Despite what sceptics outside civil SAR might have thought, the engineers were well able to do their work and give us the machine immediately. They could do the maintenance and still close up panels and give us the machine within fifteen minutes by day. If they needed longer, they would do the work at night, using the longer response time to do deeper work. If they had to pull the helicopter apart, they would swap around and use the standby machine.

The helicopter change was laborious. They would come into the crewroom, and gleefully announce that we had an aircraft change. Groans all round. 'Why does this always happen when I'm on shift?' someone would say, because we had to strip all the equipment out of the helicopter, and put it in the standby machine: stretchers, sea tray, hoist fitted, FLIR console and camera, maps, charts; every damn thing. Then they would go to work and we would continue with our duty, but in a less equipped helicopter.

The standby helicopter was identical in every respect, except that it had no auto-pilot or auto-hover and flew like a pig. Or maybe we flew it like a pig. Either way, we were not as keen on night callouts when we had the replacement machine under our backsides.

Our procedures were second nature to us. One pilot flew, the other monitored. Without the automatic systems, our safety net was gone. We were confident we operated to the same standard as the fully equipped machine, but we were well aware that a loss of concentration could have catastrophic results. One of the biggest threats was the danger of ditching into the water while operating low level due to disorientation. We had radio altimeter 'bugs', which we set below the height we required. These chimed and illuminated if we went too low but recovery was still manual.

The night we went to Roaringwater Bay, we had the standby helicopter. Dave Duthie, a likeable no-nonsense Scot who had joined since Bond had taken over, was co-pilot. Al Clapp and Graham Goosey were the winchcrew. We were to search for a man who had not returned from being out in his boat. The bay is big, but confined. We made ready for the search, starting by descending south of the Fastnet Rock lighthouse. Fastnet ahead of us, Mizen further west, both flashing. We checked them again.

Our plan was to create a chain of waypoints in our navigation computer which would lead us into the bay. Then we would search using the radar to keep clear of the shores, the FLIR camera to look for the missing man and the radio altimeter to stay at our agreed search height.

In flying, there is a very simple rule regarding flying near mountains, especially where SAR is concerned. If you cannot see the terrain, fly at least 1,000 feet above it. For searches like that night's, the first step was to get down low enough to see the sea. Then we could begin the navigation into the bay.

Below the cloud again, in the clear, but with nothing to see except the Fastnet itself, we headed north at 500 feet above the sea. 'What height do you want again Graham?' I asked as we made our way in. Graham checked a graph again, that recommended search heights for different targets in different conditions: man in the water, multiple targets in the water, ship in the water, etc. The physical size of who or what we were looking for also dictated the search patterns and their dimensions. We constructed our search pattern so that we would overlap each time we turned, so the missing man would not be in between the lines we flew. We had already constructed our search pattern while flying over the Kerry mountains, forty-five minutes previously.

Once we were at the radio altimeter height, we set the pressure altimeter so that both would read the same. If we became disorientated or flew into cloud, this would be crucial in helping us know when we were 1,000 feet above the sea and local terrain.

Duthie watched his instruments like a hawk. The final proof that our search pattern was accurate was when we turned and faced into the bay. With the radar tilted down, mapping what lay ahead, we could see that the latitude and longitude of each search way point was good, each one clear of the shore. Where the pattern expanded, it went over the shore, over terrain. We would worry about that later. Small adjustments would sort that out.

He watched, I watched. The sadistic low level flying training exercises that we often flew proved their worth on nights like that. We spent the next hour and a half, scouring the bay, looking for the missing man. After a few minutes of flying, intensely concentrating, the flying pilot would get the feeling that it was easy, trimming and balancing the controls, turning the heading, tightening and loosening the friction on the collective, following the radar picture clear of the many islands on each side. But the moment you felt that it was easy was the time to hand over control.

We flew for fifteen minutes at a time, then switched over. Al and Graham did the same in the cabin as the FLIR monitor tired their eyes. It was a nice night, dark under the cloud cover, but not too windy. The lights of Schull, Baltimore, Crookhaven and the village on Cape Clear slid across the top of the instrument panel as we searched.

We could hear the radio calls of the others on the shore and on the water: Coast guard units from Goleen, Baltimore, Toe Head and the RNLI lifeboat from Baltimore. Now and again as we passed the shore, we would see their flickering torches, hear their radio chat back and forth. Below us on the water, we saw the lifeboat's position lights and their sweeping searchlights. My mind turned to home to Alyson and Niamh, asleep in their cots. Had I woken them as I left? Were they asleep, or drifting in dreams? These search teams, these nameless people that I would probably never meet, were out in the early hours, away from their families too.

We could find nothing. Having spent two hours searching, our low fuel level made us break off and head to Cork airport. We spent as little time as possible there, returning quickly. We arrived again, the majesty of Roaringwater Bay laid out before us just after sunrise, the low light behind us showing every fold in the landscape, the water calm and quiet, hiding its secret. We could see by the light of the early sun, and found the man after less than half an hour. He was lying in shallow water, submerged and muddy, beside one of the many islands.

He could have been there when we were searching, his body giving off either no heat at all, or else the water acting as a barrier, between the FLIR camera and his cooling body. We recovered him. We took him in a stretcher to Cork University Hospital. He was flesh and bone, but soulless, as confirmed by the doctor who met us on arrival. We were back in Shannon by half-past eight in the morning. I don't remember anything after that.

We didn't discuss how we felt. That crew or any crew. We briefed and de-briefed, but it was never the done thing to talk about how we felt. Our frequent meetings with the dead and the injured appeared to leave no mark on us, morbid humour at times our balm. There was one night when I saw a side to one of my colleagues, one of the winchcrew, that surprised me. Pleasantly. A few pints, good music, catching up, the conversation drifted back to work. I had just done the callout to Roaringwater Bay.

John listened, and said that he had been on a similar callout the previous year, a man missing found dead. In some ways it had haunted him and left its mark on him. We traded secrets

as the pints flowed, as the barriers disappeared. I confessed that
hugging and kissing my children was now a part of my daily
ritual, that I would look in on them in the dark in the middle of
the night, whenever I was called out, that I found himself saying small prayers, sometimes for their safety, sometimes for my
own. This colleague of mine nodded in agreement. There was no
suggestion that I was going soft or insane.

His story was almost identical, although in a different place
and by day. After about twenty minutes searching, he had
thought he saw something on the shore. He guided the pilot
to the position. Across the bay they flew, slowing and getting
lower as they reached the shore again. He described majestic
mountains, sweeping down to a white crested blue sea. In the
pub, the chatter was gone: we couldn't hear it. As he talked,
my mind conjured up images in response to his words. I pictured shafts of morning sunlight, breaking through white puffy
clouds. He described the normality of it all. The green fields
with cattle grazing and sea gulls screaming above them. Reeds
waving in the fresh wind along the shore.

As the helicopter came to the hover over the marshy shore,
the reeds parted to reveal their secret. Here was the reward for
their hours of searching. Invisible to all but them and the birds,
wheeling and soaring overhead. The man lay still on his side, the
downdraft from the helicopter whipping at his coat. John was
lowered beside him and sank to his knees in the mud. When his
footing was sure, he disconnected himself from the winch cable
and waved the helicopter away. The thud of the helicopter was
replaced by silence, broken only by the sound of birds singing.

John began to examine the man as he was trained to do.
There was comfort in the routine. It allowed him to work
quickly while deflecting the shock of death from himself. He
could not allow himself to be distracted by wondering about

the manner or pain of the man's death. Kneeling in the water, insulated from the cold wetness of the mud, he looked for the first time into the dead man's eyes. It was a sight he had seen before many times but it still made him uncomfortable. It was irresistible, magnetic and chilling.

Thoughts flashed through John's mind as he checked for vital signs of life. Mud was caked all over the man's face and hair. He knew immediately that he had to clean it away. The shore and cliff teams had been searching before they had arrived and would see the helicopter as it stopped and lowered one of its crew. No doubt relatives would have been with them, exhausted, tired and hollow with fear for their loved one. It did not take him long to clean the man's face and hair, but when it was done John felt better. There was a semblance of dignity, a peace then, as the evidence of the man's fear, pain and dying moments was washed away. The struggle between man, wind and sea, the yielding up of the force of life, was replaced by the serenity of everlasting life. The cleansing and anointing of water, taking away some of the pain. He had realised he was saying a prayer, listened to his own voice, as if it was not his own. He had looked into the man's lifeless eyes, closed the eyelids with his gloved fingers and radioed to the approaching searchers that he had found the missing man.

24

YIN AND YANG

A winner never whines. A whiner never wins.

Anon.

With five miles to go we could see the trawler on our radar. We descended to 200 feet. Clearing the cloud, we saw the ocean for the first time since leaving Shannon. Myself, Dara Fitzpatrick, the co-pilot, and Pete Leonard, the winch operator, were lost momentarily in private thoughts, as we saw the power and fury of the ocean below us. Noel Donnelly, winchman that night, was surely apprehensive going out on the line on such a night.

The sea was white, angry, boiling. The wind was whipping the tops off the wave crests. The swell lived up to the forecast. It was raining. At two miles to go, we peered out to see where the trawler was. The radar showed it straight ahead, but still it was out of sight. The windscreen wipers smeared the rain left and right but the trawler lurked just outside the searchlight's beam.

I knew we would soon see it. I moved the intercom microphone away from my mouth. I repeatedly inhaled deeply and exhaled forcefully. I did not want the others to hear my heavy breathing, either to laugh at it or worse, be unnerved by mistaking it for fear. This was my final preparation, like an athlete preparing himself for one last big effort, one last jump into the long jump pit, or a rugby player setting himself for the last scrum of a match. Oxygenating myself and preparing for the struggle and effort of what lay ahead.

I loved and hated this moment. Arm-wrestling with the elements, we descended and slowed down as we approached the position where the trawler should be. Through the rain I saw the dark shape come into view, wallowing on a wall of water. As the helicopter slowed at a height of 80 feet above the ocean, each of us took in the spectacle. The auto-pilot took us forward at its pre-programmed hover height, my hands covering the controls in case we got out of synch with the swell. I began to coax the helicopter closer and closer until the rotor blades were within twenty feet of the back of the deck. We watched the deck's movements.

The trawler's efforts to move in a straight line were made more difficult by the swell that hit it broadside. Its movements were like a wounded beast, as its tail slewed sideways across the crests. It slowed, rose up the next swell and suddenly dropped, sending a huge wave crashing over itself, disappearing momentarily from view.

As it fell, the back of the ship slowly raised itself out of the sea, the dripping propeller churning the air, searching for water. We could almost hear it groan. The aerials on the wheelhouse scythed this way and that, wickedly whipping at the rain. The erratic movement slowed and stopped. The trawler lay across the swell like an exhausted wounded animal, panting and getting its breath back. This period of relative calm was short-lived but we watched, hoping to see a pattern. Knowing that a man's life depended on us finding some order in this chaos. I thought to myself, 'How in God's name are we going to do this?'

I remember my thoughts. I remember so many thoughts going through my mind, none of them positive. I remember the realisation that this was bloody difficult. My outward optimism was a charade. I knew that we might not complete this rescue and that someone might die as a result. A cold sweat. Fear of not being able to do the rescue and afraid of the fear itself. I struggled to fly in harmony with the trawler and the ocean. I was either off my game, or the sea was chaotic, or luck was against me, or was it all three? Each time I was close to getting my hover stable, the trawler moved, lurching away from me, or dropped or rose as if to swipe the helicopter with its aerials. The stopwatch running all the time. The fuel being gobbled up by the thirsty engines. Less time. We played a waiting game. High stakes: a man's life.

The four of us were sweating. Pete tried to coax me to that magic hover position. Dara watched the fuel, and made sure I was flying the hover accurately, looking down past our feet, glimpsing the spray washing over the deck in our searchlights, turning her gaze back to the instruments, to watch them and them alone as their indications rose and fell. Not liking what she saw outside I'm sure, and finding little comfort in what she saw inside. One of the search lights, mounted under us in the nose of the helicopter, could swivel. It was controlled by a switch on the collective lever, in my left hand. As I tried to make sense of the hover, of the sea and of the deck movement, the thumb of my left hand controlled that search light. When I felt I almost had a good hover, and when the deck would slip away, forward or sideways, my left thumb made the searchlight follow it. Like having a lead on an over-eager and enthusiastic dog, my left thumb would keep the deck in sight and within reach. Slowly moving the helicopter back over the deck, placing the beam back where I wanted it. Keeping the beam on the mast over the wheelhouse, or on the rise and fall of the ships bow.

I remember that I got angry: silently, privately, stubbornly. I remember thinking 'If it's a fight you want, I'll give you a fight.'

I coaxed myself, shouted at myself silently, urged myself on. I almost fought the trawler. As it bucked and weaved, I slid and adjusted. When it rested, so did I. It had a life of its own.

I was angry but I became peaceful, trying to struggle through, but somewhere in me, the knowledge that the possibility of success was not in my hands. The Man Above would decide. That realisation came to me as it had on other occasions. It brought me peace. It brought me calm. As the struggle and effort to complete the rescue continued, I watched us from afar, the opposite of a bird of prey, trying to pluck someone to safety. Over the horizon. Out of sight or earshot of land. The Atlantic Ocean. Darkness.

From the time we arrived we had enough fuel for thirty minutes in which to complete the rescue, not a lot of time. We struggled and cursed, sweated and held on. And on. And like a match-winning score in injury time, we managed to winch the casualty off the deck. Pete used every trick in his experienced book. Encouraging me as we ran in. Being more insistent, his patter urgent and more punchy, as we got closer.

'Deck crew taking in the hi-line. You're descending, up three. Winchman has the hook in hand, attaching to the stretcher. Forward and right two. Steady. Steady. Winching in slack cable. Up gently. Winchman and casualty clear of the deck. Back and left one. Steady.'

Winching in in pace with the deck and my hover. The trawler released us from its grasp. We made off with our prize, honey from the bees' nest.

That was not the end of it though. The weather was lousy back on the coast. We had eaten into our reserves, the winching transfer taking longer than planned. Instead of returning to Shannon, we used Plan B, and made for Kerry Airport. Approaching from the west, up Dingle Bay, using the radar to paint first Inch Strand, and then the eastern end of the bay, hoping that the cloud would be high enough to crawl in to the airport at Farranfore. The cloud was low and we could not climb because of icing conditions. We did not have enough fuel for the full procedural instrument approach either. We broke off and headed for Tralee hospital, running low on fuel as the cloud forced us lower and lower; the darkness pinpricked by farmhouse lights, as we strained to see the ground.

With about twenty minutes' fuel left, a familiar glow appeared ahead, behind the shadow of the Dingle peninsula ridge: Tralee. Instead of having to stop in the middle of nowhere, with a critically injured patient, we got to the hospital. We shut down. The patient was taken to A & E, rushed into surgery, and lived. While we waited with cups of tea in the waiting-room for the refueller from Shannon to arrive, one of the doctors came out and said that we had saved his life. It was only when we got back that I remembered that he had been speaking to us, as we dozed in that waiting-room.

Yin and yang. Those sorts of missions thankfully accounted for a lesser proportion of our callouts. Jim Kirwan came from the air corps around that time, and we enjoyed something that we had not done for years: flying together. We got a call to a vessel that was way outside our range one day. Summer months, pleasant weather, lots of daylight and time to think it over. It was over 300 miles offshore with a crewman who needed to get to hospital, but this one was different.

Oil and gas exploration takes place at different positions around the Irish coast. Each exploration rig has a helicopter deck, and helicopters fly out regularly to them with supplies and duty crew changes. Once they are in Irish waters, they become what is called an SAR asset. That week, a rig, the *JW*

McClean, had arrived in the area, positioned about 100 miles offshore, so with a little bit of number crunching, we confirmed that we could accept the tasking straight away by refuelling on the *JW McClean,* rather than wait hours for the vessel with the sick crewman to come closer to shore.

My flight with Jim was uneventful, other than it was about 280 miles off shore and we refuelled on the rig. I do remember enjoying that flight, the good weather, the security of the off-shore fuel, the rig radio talking to us as we approached, asking us what meals we would like.

What meals we would like? Oh yes, what meals would you like: beef or salmon, Jim? Red or white? Would sir like me to bring the dessert trolley? We took off from the rig after a short stop, heading further west for the vessel, full of fuel again. Thank you very much, over the radio. You are very welcome, safe flight, in reply. Taking it in turns to eat a hot meal from the silver foil tray provided, then having coffee and a bun, from the selection in another tray. 'I could get used to this,' said Jim. 'Oh, it's like this all the time, Jim. This is standard.'

Another callout, refuelling at Blacksod, before the familiar hike out west. Another windless night. Stung by my memory of the swell on a previous callout, and listening to Vincent's caution: *'Bígí cúramach,* lads. There's a heavy swell out west of the Inishkees. I was onto a Dutch vessel that's on the way in.'

We took a little less than full fuel. It was not a maximum range job. When it was time to go, there was no wind at all. We lifted off into the hover, looked at the torque and then each other. We were damn close to maximum already. How were we going to get over the granite wall around the lighthouse? If we were in a field or at an airport, we could skim along the ground, gradually accele-rating and climbing away, swapping the ground effect cushion of air, for forward speed, but we had no room to do that.

The other option was to climb up as high as we could, using the power available, and then nudge forward over the wall. That could mean dropping off the cushion of air and hitting the wall. However, by repeatedly climbing on the spot, and descending again, the cushion of air beneath the helicopter would get bigger. It would get trapped within the confines of the surrounding wall, and climbing up and down again a few times, would effectively inflate it. I am sure that theory could be disproved, but it had worked before, so we gave it a try.

I cannot remember how many times we climbed and descended but then we went for it, nudging forward towards the wall, slipping off the ground cushion of air. The wall got closer, and then we were away, an extra little pitch down with the nose, clearing the wall with the trailing tail wheel, just like a high jumper clears the bar with the trailing leg. We Fosbury Flopped it, delighted with ourselves.

The Atlantic throws extreme swell and wind at SAR crews, but this is not always a problem. The swell can be significant, but if it is a long swell, it can be managed. A long swell can be smooth and gradual. The automatic hover may be able to hold the height, leaving lateral positioning with cyclic control to the pilot. It may be night time, but sometimes the moon will be out. Hovering by the light of the moon is not quite daytime but it's not quite night time either.

And not every mission is to maximum range. Difficult rescues at shorter range give the crew more time, less distance offshore, more fuel. Then there are the special moments. The little snippets of rescues that remain when dates and locations are gone. Hovering by day over a fishing vessel, as an RAF Nimrod watches overhead: 'Rescue 115. This is Rescue 11. Nice hover chaps. Mind if we drop down to take a photo?'

'Rescue 11 from Rescue 115. No problem.'

'Roger Rescue 115. Descending low level. Approaching from the south-west.'

Concentrating on our task, we would pause if we could to see the bright landing lights of the former Comet airliner, turning to face us, its exhaust plume behind, as it streaked towards us. And then as it went pass, some one on the Nimrod crew transmitted: 'Cheese'.

And when we were finished with the winching, casualty on board, heading back to the coast, the Nimrod would stay with us, silently, faithful, like a sheepdog getting us home. There were not any hard or fast rules about when they would disappear and head back to Scotland, but they normally stayed until we were within about 40 miles range of the shore, so that the RNLI and coast guard lifeboats could reach us if something happened and we ditched.

'Rescue 11, this is Rescue 115. Thank you very much for the service today. We are happy to release you. Safe flight home.'

'Rescue 115, this is Rescue 11. Our pleasure. Well done. We have passed on your ETA to the coast guard. They tell us that Galway hospital is awaiting you. We have also passed on the medical history of the casualty. I believe you have the up-to-date weather information. Is there anything else we can do for you before we go?'

'Negative Rescue 11. Safe home and thanks again.'

I associated the name Nimrod with the music of Edward Elgar, and the Tullamore Gramophone Society. A piece from the Enigma Variations, a favourite of my parents, played in our sitting-room at home in Tullamore. And again at their recitals. Each of the fourteen variations representing one of Elgar's close friends. My father introducing the piece, and explaining about each of the fourteen variations, to his neighbours and friends. The Nimrod was my favourite. Because it had been my parents' favourite. And although my knowledge of classical music was limited, whenever Top Cover flew overhead, and whenever the pressure was off and we were homeward bound, the conductor, Herbert von Karajan, would tap his baton, and it would begin.

Trundling along at our modest 120 knots, 2,000 or so feet above the sea, we almost felt a roar and a vibration, as the Nimrod bounced us from behind. Its shadow darkening our cockpit for a second as it passed above. Gracefully climbing straight ahead, up steeply, wagging its wings as it went. The strings sweeping them to heaven. The melody carrying us home.

25

THE INVISIBLE ARMY

A helping hand is worth a thousand words of advice.

Anon.

Gene O'Sullivan was a busy man. He was in charge of the Valentia coast guard radio station, perched near the cliff on the north side of Valentia Island. He also acted as the area controller for the marine rescue co-ordination centre in Dublin. Over the years, titles change and so do responsibilities, but Gene had the onerous task of managing the cliff and coast rescue teams (CCRS), around one of the most hostile coasts you could find.

I can't remember when I first met Gene but after a few years in Shannon, it was as if we had always known him. Cheerful and helpful, but with an unforgiving responsibility, he would ring or call in, ask questions and start making plans.

'And lads, on the evening of the twenty-fifth last month do you remember there was some confusion on the radio, about the position of that incident? What happened there lads? Just so I know for again.'

'They want to train up some of the coastal units. Some of them have never seen the helicopter, not to mind, been in one. Maybe we could arrange to go around the coast, exercise by exercise, and do some briefing exercises? What do you think?'

Going around the coast was arranged, now and again, not too often. We tried to strike a balance, not much point in spending

five or six hours flying, briefing and exercising, only to get a six
hour long-range mission when you returned to Shannon. We
used to arrange the training days for the mornings. If we had
been called out the night before, we could postpone easily. No
hassle. There were over sixty rescue units in our area. Mind you,
the Shannon area started in Rosslare, Co. Wexford, extending
to Killala Co. Mayo in those days: CCRS units, RNLI lifeboat
crews, civil defence units, MRTs as well as one or two community rescue teams. We made a schedule and flew to meet maybe
six teams at a time.

And that is how we came to know people like Eddie Butler,
the area officer of the Old Head of Kinsale coast guard cliff unit.
He waited in a football pitch in Ballinspittle with teams from
Crosshaven, Oysterhaven, Summercove, Kinsale, Seven Heads,
all the names of places you associate with sunshine and seafood,
weekends away and pints of Murphy's, the task they perform
not so well known. Searching for the missing, the fallen or the
dead. Grim work done without hesitation. We touched down
and after introductions, the training began.

We did the same all around the coast, nibbling away at the
enormous task: Glandore, Toe Head, Baltimore, and Goleen.
One afternoon we did winch training with the Baltimore RNLI
lifeboat. There were over a hundred coast guard volunteers, some
marshalling the landing site, others controlling the exercise search
area we had chosen, others just smiling and laughing up at us, as
the downdraft blew fresh cut grass in their faces.

One night we got stuck in Tralee hospital without fuel, and
the Lakes of Killarney civil defence sprang up out of the long
grass: 'Do ye need anything lads? Say the word now lads, we're
here to help. Electrical power, fuel, telephone, food? I'll drive ye
to McDonalds if you want.'

Michael Forrest, Paudy McKenna and Steve McSweeney,

busied themselves helping us while we snoozed on plastic chairs, blinking under the fluorescent lights in A&E, our immersion suits stripped to the waist. They rigged up electrical power for the helicopter. Then we got chatting and before you know it, we made a plan to fly with them on a display at the Lakes of Killarney. Weeks later, we did a winching display on the lakes, with Muckross Castle as a backdrop, for a large gathering of Tralee Roses. It was the start of many such exercises. Waterville, Co. Kerry, another beauty spot, this time a cliff exercise followed by training flights around the area, taking the opportunity to take in Derrynane, Puffin Island and the Skelligs on the way back around the coast.

These days out were not popular with everyone. Potentially tiring us out unnecessarily, when we should be concentrating on rescue, some said. But most of us enjoyed them.

We were getting to know the controllers in Dublin better too. People like Norman Fullam and Eamonn Torpey, became our link between the coast guard units and hierarchy. Sometimes coming with us, changing from suits and ties, to our immersion suits. Leaving their laptop computers in their cars, and putting on life-jackets and helmets instead. Thanks to them and Gene, and countless others whose names memory does not record, we got to know the teams in our area very well. Becoming on first name terms with quite a few of them. That ultimately strengthened the whole network, ground, sea and air. We were to find out just how extensive that network was very soon.

An October evening 1997. The 'Bat Phone' rang in Shannon. Automatic increase of the pulse rate.

'Missing boat north Mayo. Air corps Dauphin from Finner on scene. Tasking you to take over the search when he has to leave due fuel.'

Gerry Tompkins was the co-pilot, an experienced S-61

captain himself; John Manning the winch operator and Noel Donnelly the winchman. The weather was fine, just some mist across the country. No need to go around the coast, there was no cloud, even though it was dark, winter and cold, straight across the Burren we went, then Galway Bay and up towards the position they had given us. Still bright at 4,000 feet, maps rustled in the cabin, latitudes and longitudes being noted, plotted and entered in the computer as we flew north. Gerry flew, while the three of us got an idea of what was ahead.

Daylight fading, the radio was alive with chatter as we got closer. We had discussed all the questions and options we had. Where would we start the search? What search pattern would we use? Where was the nearest fuel? What was the weather forecast for the area? Where was the nearest hospital? Who else was searching? We announced our ETA, our endurance (how long we could stay), then kept quiet, staying high and waiting. As we got closer, we could see the flashing position lights of the Dauphin below us probing the cliffs with its searchlights. We recognised the voice and got him to switch to the aero band, so that we would not clutter the marine band with chat.

'Hi Dónal. How's it going?'

'Hiya Dave. We've been here an hour and we are going to head for fuel now. There's three people missing in a small boat, you probably know that by now. There's very little wind here and it's a bit misty but it's OK. We've been up and down the coast about ten miles. If you're ready we'll give you the co-ordinates of the box we've searched. They seem to be concentrating on a sea cave here now.'

We said our hellos and goodbyes. We knew each other so well, almost the entire crew. I had spent many SAR duties with Dónal Scanlan and he had taught me so much. It felt unusual to be speaking to him from a different search helicopter. As they departed, we were asked to position beside the cliff that Dónal had mentioned. As we descended, the glow of the sun's last light gradually ebbed away, stolen once more by the curvature of the earth. Checking our GPS position, we descended down to low level, crossing the 600-foot cliffs near Belderrig. Once we got down low and well north of the Mayo coastline, we turned back for the cliffs.

The cliffs, we had flown along so many times on our way to Blacksod, were now straight ahead and getting closer. In the dark, the radar picture was very clear. We counted down the distance and made ready. As we came closer the stars began to disappear, blotted out by the cliffs. Shades of darkness could be made out as our eyes got used to the low light. We could see the shadow of the cliff-top line, we slowed and turned our search-lights on, the beam picking up the white water at the base of the cliff. We could make out other lights on the water, and realised that there were several fishing boats and the Ballyglass RNLI Lifeboat, bobbing about close to an inlet.

Beside the inlet was a long, deep sea cave. While the vessels continued to search along the inlet, shining their lights into the cave entrance, we were given co-ordinates to search. In case the boat was overturned. In case they were clinging to it somewhere. In case … In case they were somewhere, alive, and that our FLIR would find them and we could all go home and celebrate.

We searched for an hour and a half. Back and forth, the heli-copter flying on auto-pilot, following the programmed search pattern along the cliffs. Then back to the cave entrance when we overheard someone on Channel 16 say that they thought they had seen light inside the cave. We hovered close to Horse Island, a rock that stood at the east side of the inlet, trying to shine our lights and help. Hovering at about 150 feet, we could see and hear the search around us.

In a search, particularly a complex one, one of the most

difficult tasks is management. The on-scene management in particular. The manager of a search or search and rescue is the on-scene-commander (OSC). When you are trying to carry out your own duties as a searcher or rescuer, it is a significant task to be told you are OSC as well. The best comparison I can come up with, is a team sport like rugby. The captain of the team has not only to do his own duty on the pitch, he also has to watch the game, use everyone according to their strengths and weaknesses, plan tactically and make it work.

The OSC that night was Superintendent Anthony McNamara of Belmullet gardaí. He had a huge task and did it magnificently. He would say modestly that he had a great team, and that was true too. As we hovered, we could see the lights of the Killala CCRS cliff teams above us, walking the cliff line. We listened as they were considering setting up an abseil and climbing rope, just as Doolin had done at the Cliff of Moher. Rather you than me pal. Local trawlers, *Bláth Bán*, *Sinead* and *Pamela Ann* were ready at the cave entrance to help any way they could, co-ordinated by the Ballyglass lifeboat.

There was some hope that the missing people were at the mouth of the cave. The lights of the searchers reflected back off the breaking waves at times, giving us false hope. The helicopter was too close, too noisy and not helping, so we broke off and let them listen. We waited north of the area while they listened and shouted, but they heard nothing. We said we had to go for fuel. We left them to it.

We landed in Blacksod once again. Silent handshakes. No smiles. 'Bad business,' said Vincent, 'It's all over the news.' We kept the rotors running, so that we could return immediately having refuelled. I managed to get through to the coxswain of the lifeboat by radio phone patch. 'Get your fuel and a cup of tea. Take a break. We'll see ye then, it's going to be a long night.'

We shut down and waited.

Sweeney's Lighthouse Restaurant was in full swing: Doreen making sandwiches, Vincent collecting them and making tea, the fire lit, the place warm and homely, the smell of turf. We devoured the sandwiches and smoked a few cigarettes, and then got ready to return. Before we departed, Dublin MRCC rang us: 'How long can you stay?' they asked, referring to our flying and duty time limit. 'As long as it takes,' we replied. I rang home and told my wife I would not be home that night. 'It's on the news,' she said. 'Mind yourself.'

Over the next few hours, countless people from the local community converged to try to find the missing people. We came and went from the area, trying to help. Local divers went into the cave, hoping to find and rescue the missing people. Michael Heffernan and Josie Barrett, members of the local Gráinne Uaile Diving Club, both swam in, but only Josie came out again. He described wild conditions in the cave. He was lucky to come out alive. We all hoped that Michael had survived and was in the cave, but we feared the worst.

After midnight we were sent to Dublin to collect members of the garda underwater unit. Arriving at about 2 a.m., near runway 29, Dave Mulhall, Joe Finnegan, Kieran Flynn, Ciaran Doyle and Seán O'Connell were waiting for us with all their gear. Without shutting down, we loaded up and headed back to Belderrig. As we flew, we told each other all we knew.

We made our way to a nearby village where a landing site had been prepared. We were not sure what we were going to find. The weight of the divers and their diving equipment had not allowed us to carry much fuel. We had enough for one approach and then we would have to go to Blacksod. We got closer to the coast, the radar picture clear once more, but our lights reflecting back at us from the mist.

We were greeted by an amazing sight. A glow of light from where the village should be. Radios crackled that they could see us now. The landing site was illuminated with huge standing floodlights, positioned at each corner of a large field by Ballina, Crossmolina and Ballina Fire Brigades. A big field. Not completely level, but a pretty good choice all the same.

We could see firemen with extinguishers, ambulances, coast guard members and gardaí. And in the shadows beyond we could see the others: the locals, the community, unknown people just trying to help. We had been on the go a long time. We had just been to Dublin and back. We were tired. But seeing this, seeing the way they were organised and how this collective effort was fighting for the lives of the missing, was humbling. The divers trooped away, too busy and intent on their task to say farewell. We would meet again. We departed for Blacksod and waited once more.

By daylight, which was not long away, the garda divers had made their assault on the cave. They had managed to enter with the assistance of Seán McHale and Martin Kavanagh of the Killala CCRS unit, on their second attempt. Conditions were appalling. They got into the cave and found the missing party. The only way they could get them out was for Ciaran Doyle to swim back out with a line. It took him twenty-five minutes in life-threatening conditions. The people were hauled by the safety line out of the cave, and with them came their account of the terrible tragedy.

Earlier that day, Mr and Mrs Murphy and their daughter, had gone on a boat trip with Mr von Below. He knew the coast well, the conditions were calm and clear, and he took them to show them an enormous sea cave. As they entered the cave entrance, the swell surged, their boat was rushed into the cave, von Below suffered a fatal head injury from rocks, and the Murphys were stranded at the back of the cave on rocks. The cave is almost a kilometre in length. When the garda divers eventually got to them, they found them dangerously hypothermic. Beside them was not only Mr von Below, but also Michael Heffernan, both dead.

We arrived back at the cave entrance as the Murphys reappeared. Everyone waited with bated breath to see if there were any fatalities, hoping there would be none. Seeing the Murphys heading rapidly to the pier in a RIB gave us encouragement. We landed again and took them to Sligo hospital, listening on the way for news. We found out that Mr von Below and Michael had died. We took the casualties to Sligo A&E. They had been through a harrowing ordeal and were in shock, hypothermic and lucky to be alive. They made a full recovery physically, but emotionally, it took years for them to get over it. Survivor's guilt is a terrible thing. And not just for them, but for Michael's diving buddy who went into the cave that night too, Josie Barrett. The guilt of survival, pervading his life for years to come.

We headed north to Finner for fuel. I loved flying in Finner. I loved Donegal. It was a beautiful morning. I had never been there with the Sikorsky. I was pleased to see Dónal Scanlan and his crew again. But we were banjaxed. We felt hollow. A fellow rescuer had died. It felt like one of us had died. We refuelled in a perfunctory way and flew back to Shannon. We could have declined the flight on grounds of fatigue but we flew back because it would be easier all round, both for us and the new crew, and also for the SAR service in general. We got back to Shannon at about 10.30 that morning after about twelve hours flying and not much sleep.

When I arrived home, I found that they had heard it all on the news. My wife, her sister Shirley who was visiting, their children. 'Tell us all about it. Who was the man who died? Was he one of your crew? And he had a young family?' They said on the news that his wife is expecting a baby, oh God, the poor woman. You must be tired. You look tired. Are you all right?' I told them what I could. I was shattered. I put some ice in a tall glass, filled it with whiskey and went to bed.

Kevin Myers of the *Irish Times* highlighted the heroism of the night. He suggested that Michael be commemorated by having a national bravery award named after him. This was taken up by his friends and fellow divers in the Grainne Uaile Diving Club. Meeting again at Michael's funeral in Ballina, the various rescue teams whispered at the back of the cathedral, 'It could have been you. It could have been me.' Rescuers around the country took up the gauntlet, starting with those involved on the night, raising awareness of Michael's heroism.

How could we help the family? How terrible it was for Annamarie. Maybe raise public awareness of what had happened? How about attempting to break the around Ireland RIB speed record? Involve all the units? Show the media all the teams? That is what was done the following summer, August 1998. A team drawn from north, south, east and west, succeeded, taking the new record down to just over twenty-one hours which still stands. Money was raised for Michael's family too, but more importantly, the media became increasingly aware of the 'invisible army' of volunteer rescuers all around the coast.

The record run and the fund-raising that went with it involved agencies from Northern Ireland and the Republic: the Irish Coast Guard and Northern Ireland Coastguard, inland and coast units. Everyone. From car boot sales on Ballyheige beach, to church collections in Northern Ireland. From Tullamore Harriers and Rugby Club to officers and NCOs' messes around the army, the length and breadth of Ireland. Shops in Ennis, businesses in Shannon, to almost every yacht and sailing club around the coast. And the island communities. And the lifeboat crews themselves.

Michael Heffernan was survived by his wife Annamarie, who was expecting their second child, and daughter Leighanne. Annamarie declined the money raised, using it instead to fund a bronze statue of Michael at Lacken Pier, near Belderrig, one of Michael's favourite places from which to embark on diving trips.

The collective effort that night, was one of the biggest, if not the biggest, concerted search and rescue efforts in history. Units involved were:

Killala Coast Guard (CCRS at the time)
Ballyglass RNLI
Ballina Fire Brigade
Crossmolina Fire Brigade
Western Health Board
Fishing vessel *Sinead*
Fishing vessel *Bláth Bán*
Fishing vessel *Pamela Ann*
Grainne Uaile Diving Club
Garda Diving Unit
Air Corps Finner SAR Helicopter
Coast Guard Shannon Helicopter
Malin Head radio
North Western Fisheries
Blacksod Lighthouse
Sligo General Hospital
Achill Coast Guard

The Gallantry Award for the garda síochána is the Scott Medal. For military personnel in the defence forces, the award is The Distinguished Service Medal. The gallantry award for the volunteer members of the Irish coast guard now bears Michael

Heffernan's name. Forever in Ireland, when the state wishes to honour someone or some team or organisation for gallantry, the yardstick by which they will forever be compared will be Michael Heffernan's act of supreme sacrifice.

26

THE SHADOW OF MORDOR

Greater love hath no man than this, that a man lay down his life for his friends.

John 15:13

Michael Byrne cycled to our house. A basket on the front of his black bicycle. The tyres crunching the gravel as he arrived. The three volumes of the book *The Lord of The Rings* in the basket. I think he was a law student at the time. Knew my parents because my mother helped to collect historical information about Tullamore and helped him record it and file it. He subsequently wrote lavish and comprehensive histories of the town and surrounding area. But the reason why he called that day, was to deliver his own copies of that book to me. Three separate books. Hardcovers. With dust jackets. And maps and appendices with explanations of how to speak elvish, the pronunciations of invented verbs. Given to me, with formality, like the Third Secret of Fatima.

He knew I was reading *The Hobbit*. The book my brother Philip had started me on. A paperback that sent me on my way, away from Enid Blyton and the famous five, leaving the shire in my imagination, until I found the Ring. Then Michael arrived with the books that told me the terrible truth. That the Ring had to be destroyed. Cycling in and out of town, to nervously debate, against Rahan or Mountmellick, in Irish or English, whether or not we lived in a pluralist society ('What does pluralist mean dad?' 'Look it up in the dictionary'). Or to football training, where I discovered that I could not field a ball, shamed by Aidan Scally or John Dowling or Pat Spollen, who rose to the ball, plucking it out of the sky. While I watched in my leaden boots. No wonder they later wore the green, white and gold of Uibh Fhailí [Offaly].

Content instead to console myself when I came almost last in the cross-country races, mud spattered and red raw from the wind, that I had bigger fish to fry. The Dark Riders, the Uruk-Hai, the All Seeing Eye of Mordor, of Sauron. Searching for me as I stumbled through the pages. Stopping to get my bearings with the maps provided. Reading and re-reading, until I knew that trolls could not stay out in daylight, as they would turn immediately to stone. Trying to solve Gollum's riddles, covering the next lines that held the answer, to see if I was close. Imagining what elves would look like, and whether Lothlorien looked anything like the wooded valleys up past Clonaslee.

The Shadow of Mordor. The constant weight of dread. The constant leaden feeling that we were being watched. In later years, finding that Tolkien had been traumatised by the first world war. The trenches, the carnage, the evil of war, the suffering, the misery. So much so, that he fought evil in his books. One chapter of fear and the pursuit by the Black Riders, the next the magic of elves. Another, where I almost had to cover my ears because of the scream of the Nazgul, and then the encounter with the talking trees, the walking Ents.

Like the hobbit Bilbo, and later Frodo, I lived in the shire of Offaly. Unaware as I grew up, of the Shadow of Mordor, the power, the fury and the malice of the sea and of the elements. But in much the same way as that story goes, eventually the shadow was cast across my path. In 1981, as I got closer to my dream of flight, the *Penlee* Lifeboat disaster happened.

In Storm Force 12, *The Union Star* drifted onto the coast of Cornwall. A royal navy helicopter from Culdrose went to the scene but the conditions were impossible. The *Penlee* lifeboat launched, managing to take four people off. Just after that, they made their last radio call. Eight lifeboat crew died. Their names were:

William Trevelyn Richards, Coxswain
James Stephen Madrow, Second Coxswain
Nigel Brockman, Assistant Mechanic
John Blewett, Emergency Mechanic
Kevin Smith, Crew
Barrie Torrie, Crew
Charles Greenhaugh, Crew
Gary Wallis, Crew

In Tullamore, right in the middle of Ireland, the only sign of coastal storms is sea gulls, chasing off the blackbirds and crows from the fields. Raucous, aggressive and strong, as they need to be on the coast, the inland birds are no match for them. They stay until the storms blow over, then return to the sea. But I remember that disaster. Coming home from the Curragh. On the news headlines. My parents: 'Isn't that terrible. Those poor men. What must their families be going through.'

Canon 'Kerry' Waterstone, from the pulpit, translated their deaths into something his congregation could comprehend. The laying down of life for a friend. The holiness of the fishermen, the followers of Christ. The lifeboat crews who went to save them. Looking at the sea on the news the next day, in disbelief. Collecting for the RNLI. Plastic blue boats and stickers. The dark shadow cast wide.

The shadow reaching out again, just over eight years later. Claiming the life of Able Seaman Michael Quinn, in Castletownbere. The night the vessel ran aground on Roancarrigmore

Rock. And then again in Belderrig. Not a storm. Not a windy night. But a swell and a conspiracy of events, that claimed Michael Heffernan. And almost Josie Barrett too. The shadow darkening. The shadow deepening. The turning of the earth, the queue of storms, the tides, all aligning for another strike.

Soon after Belderrig, in November 1997, another good man died. A man I never knew. I was long gone from Tullamore then, long gone from the shire. I was well aware of the Shadow of Mordor, I respected the ocean. I lived near it and flew over it. I tried to keep at a safe distance, if you can call a 40-foot hover a safe distance. But keeping your distance is not enough. In a cage with a lion, it is the lion that chooses to walk past the lion-tamer, ignoring the pathetic whip if he so chooses. In the rescue of ten crew from the vessel *Green Lily*, aground on the southern Shetland Islands, winchman Bill Deacon was killed.

The vessel ran aground at the sea cliffs at Bressay. A huge cargo vessel, it made its Mayday call too late, the local currents and the storm force winds driving it aground. The Sumburgh coastguard Sikorsky S-61 responded to the call. Bill Deacon was winched onto the deck in mountainous seas and a 70 knot wind. Read that again: mountainous seas and a 70-knot wind. The swell was over ten metres. Suddenly meeting a cliff. Unstoppable force and immovable object. Seventy knot wind. That is so strong, you would have great difficulty standing up straight, never mind connecting the crew of a sinking ship to a hoist cable. And guess who was stuck in the middle?

He sent the crew members up in twos and threes on the winch cable. Having disconnected, he stood waiting on the deck, which was being pounded by the waves. Before Bill Deacon could connect and go home, the dark shadow of Mordor, the lidless unblinking eye, looked at him. Bill's comrades witnessed from above. The lifeboat crew from Lerwick saw it too. Their first hand accounts, show clearly that Bill Deacon sent those men to safety in the full knowledge that he was probably going to die himself. He stared back into the all-seeing eye. Here is what Colin Scott Mackenzie, sheriff of Grampian and Islands said: 'The bravest are surely those, who have the clearest vision of what is before them, and yet notwithstanding, go out to meet it.'

Some of the Shannon crew knew Bill; in passing, not that well, but he was one of us. The same incident could have been at Loop Head, or Sybil Head, or Toe Head. And it could have been our helicopter, our crew and anyone one of us. We spoke about it. We wondered about it, but some things cannot be resolved through discussion. Sometimes there is no point in talking it out. We shifted uneasily, then changed the subject, not wanting to ever know if we could return the stare of the lidless unblinking Eye of Mordor.

27

SILVER

It is better to begin in the evening, than not at all.

Anon.

The base had about four crews: about ten winching crew and ten pilots, slightly fewer engineers. We rotated through the roster, sometimes working with the same people day after day, week after week, sometimes not. Captains worked as co-pilots and winch operators worked as winchmen too. Commercial civil helicopter SAR did not allow us the luxury of separate roles.

This meant that captains did not get rusty with co-pilot's duties. It also meant that the physical work and the medical traumas that faced the winchcrew were shared out equally. The callouts kept coming in, sometimes after a pause, sometimes one after the other, seemingly endlessly.

The phone rang all right. But not for me. My logbook records a quiet winter after Christmas 1997. Lots of training as usual. Night deck winching with the ever obliging RNLI crew from Fenit with new crews whenever we needed. With Andy Mottram, the Australian SAR swimmer/diver, who became part of our crew for far too short a time, before returning home. Steve Duffy, who went from oil rigs to SAR, to senior management in rapid succession. We had many enjoyable flights together. Some tricky, some not so tricky but all a pleasure.

One night while we were training we saw red flares off the

Clare coast. They were fired by a small vessel off Seafield pier near Miltown Malbay. The flares were still hissing in the water, we arrived so quickly, hovering nearby, illuminating their deck while they baled the water. They limped to the pier and we departed only to have some sort of instrumentation failure ourselves. Flying home at night at low level, with no instruments, watching the shore lights for orientation on the way home. The runway lights at Shannon were a welcome sight. Thanks be to God it did not happen in cloud.

On another exercise, the spine of the Dingle peninsula was beside us, as we chased the Fenit lifeboat towards Castlegregory, looking ahead as the shore got closer. 'He's going to run out of sea room.' Getting the winchman off the deck as the lifeboat crew announced their imminent turn, then turning away from us, taking away our visual references as we sped away, climbing while taking the winchman in again. 'He does that on purpose you know', we said on intercom, half cursing, half laughing.

Ahead of us, Brandon Point, its shape silhouetted against the setting sun in the west. The Magharee Islands over to our right, almost floating on our horizon. The Little Samphire Island Lighthouse, guarding the rock beside Fenit, flashing out its warning.

We tested ourselves flying in the mountains: the Twelve Bens. Cloud covering the jagged tops as we arrived at Maam Cross, then to Recess, where my parents used to stop to buy Connemara marble ornaments, north into the Inagh Valley. We picked out ridges and corrie lakes, to see if we could approach the top of Benbaun. We flew around the valley beside it, like a dog sniffing at a bone, talking it over, different opinions. 'Well, we could make an approach to the saddle, that's clear of cloud. If we have a problem on the way in, we can break away to the valley floor on the right. If there was a casualty up higher, we would at least be able to get the MRT team to the saddle and save them time.'

That was how we trained. What-if scenarios. What do you think? I don't agree. We probed and tested ourselves but for training, no risks. It is funny the things that stick in your mind. That day we got to the saddle. Hovering there, we could see that the wind that was blowing across and above us, was blowing a clear area to the top of Benbaun. As we waited, the cloud cleared slightly, giving us a view of the other valley to the west.

Slowly we climbed up the mountain, sideways and to the right. The up-draughting air was lifting us smoothly. Our power was low and before we knew it, we were hovering over the top at 2,400 feet. We did not hang around. The clouds forming were fickle. We climbed up and away. All good training, done in ever-changing light, and cloud and shadows and mood.

While the others were called out in winter storms, my domestic life was all that was on my mind. A two-year old to tame, a baby to feed, books to read, Barney to watch, dinners to cook for the sisters, sisters-in-law and brother and grandparents that visited. Loads of nieces and nephews, looking in at the baby, admiring her every move and sleepy sigh. Moving house and all that goes with it. Busy times.

'She's just like you. No, I can see her granny, clear as day. It's the eyes. Look at the eyes. She has the same toes as you. Look at this picture of your mother when she was that age. It's unbelievable, it could be the same baby.' The black-and-whites compared, held up to the sleeping Niamh, or the pouting Alyson. The drawing gene, obviously strong in the male side of both families, both granddads sitting with Alyson on their knees, drawing cars, cows and flowers. Wide eyed wonder as the flowers appeared on the white paper before her, then trees beside them, sprouting green leaves.

'What does the cow say?' 'Moooooooooo'.

'What does the cat say?' 'Mioooowww'.

'See you all later. I have to go to work now. Bye. Kiss daddy. I love you.'

We got an unusual, even funny, call in May I remember. There was a medevac required from a vessel about 210 miles south-west of Shannon, which was a long way, but not at maximum range, given that it was closer to Cork on the return. The information about the casualty is gone from my memory, although probably not from his.

Weather: I cannot remember details, other than it was a nice day, with light winds. We got the call in the evening, and set off, planning to winch the man off before darkness. Carmel again, Graham and Eamonn as winching crew, settling in for a straightforward flight. Flying diagonally past the Kerry and Cork coast. Looking east along each peninsula and bay as we passed. The familiar landmarks along the way.

We found the vessel heading away south-west. As we approached, they said that they could not turn into wind or onto any heading. They were stuck on their course because they were laying a cable. Cable layer? That was the first we had heard that. He kept that quiet. Bit of a cheek getting us to come all that way and forget to say he could not, or would not change course. We positioned beside the vessel which was a substantial one. The course it was on was not suitable for us to hover to, in the conventional sense. What were we going to do?

We looked at the bow, but hovering there would place the helicopter right in front of the ship. That would mean hovering downwind, and if we were to have an engine failure, not only would we ditch, but then we would be run over by the ship itself. No thank you pal. Move the fucking casualty. Quick.

We found ourselves laughing on the intercom as we probed the dilemma. He wants us to what? As we hovered in front of the ship to assess our power, we could see it was pointless and dangerous. We found a place to winch to, on the starboard side, and readied ourselves for a parallel deck. Hovering beside the ship, moving backwards, as it continued to lay cable, we could see some of the crew on the bridge, leaning at the railings, smoking cigarettes, watching the show. 'Ah come on,' we said on the intercom, using the now popular catch phrase: 'You're 'avin a laugh !'

'Check safe single engine,' said Graham. So that he would know what to do if an engine failed. Safe single meant, we would be able to hover and fly away if an engine failed. If we were not safe single, an engine failure would mean ditching. Part of the brief was to know which situation you were in so you could anticipate. As per that ditching drill, in emergency underwater escape training.

'Negative safe single engine.'

We put Eamonn on the deck quickly and he started to prepare the casualty. It had taken a few minutes to get all these options weighed up, to decide what to do and then to do it. We were eating into our fuel and time. This was getting a bit tight. By now darkness had arrived. Sitting in the hover, we had been busy getting ready, so the fading light came almost as a surprise. The deck lights below us gradually got brighter. Our own lights started to become more noticeable.

But we did not have a problem. We did not have an engine failure. The winching position we chose was a good one: it worked. It exposed us to potential ditching for a while, but what can you do? And while we waited for Eamonn to do his medical magic on the casualty, getting him into the stretcher, and securing him, we waited and enjoyed the view.

The ship rose and fell beside us, gently. It was not a big sea. The sea taking shape in front of us, as the sun dropped below the horizon. The waves, the light pattern of a small swell, advanced towards us, like a ribbon blows in a breeze, undulating and graceful. By the time Eamonn was ready, it was dark. We must have arrived and got into position right at the last light. We could no longer see much beyond our lights as we hovered.

Graham eased the casualty and Eamonn off the deck. We moved slightly away from the ship and started to take them in to the helicopter. Descending slightly, as we always did when we could, keeping them at a safe height. A safe height being one from which they could survive if they fell.

To Cork hospital after that. Moonlight on the way home. Flying home with our moonlight shadow behind us. The sea in every inlet, every bay, shining like silver, reflecting the moonlight. The darkness of land in between. The clusters of sparkling lights of each town and village as we returned. And then Shannon. And then home.

Getting home after midnight. Finding the house lights still on. My wife and parents at the table still. An empty bottle of wine beside the sink. Another one on the table, half full. Laughter and my mother saying, 'Ssh; you'll wake the baby.' Putting the kettle on for a cup of tea. A squeeze of the hand from Lynda as I sat down at the table.

'How was your day?' I asked.

'We had a great day. I got up to make a cup of tea and found Niamh up already. She even let me give her some bottle. She didn't make strange with me at all. And then Alyson woke up and I read her some stories ...'

I listened as my parents told me about being with their grandchildren, our children. Getting out to Lahinch and Liscannor, the glass of beer at O'Looney's seafront bar. The chowder at Vaughan's. The fresh air, the surfers. Memories of their own visits in years gone by. Day trips in the old Ford Cortina. Making tea on a primus stove, fishing off Black Head.

'And how was your day?' they asked.

'It was perfect. A perfect day,' I said, and told them about it over a cup of tea before going to bed. Hoping the phone would not ring again.

28

CIRCADIAN RHYTHM

People who say they sleep like a baby, usually don't have one.

Anon.

Nature synchronises our sleep and wake cycle with the twenty-four hour day. Almost. Studies show that the body naturally cycles between sleep and being awake with the help of external cues such as light and dark, meal times and social habits. These are called zeitgebers or time givers. However, the body naturally cycles through twenty-five hour periods. We impose a slightly shorter cycle time so that we conveniently match the twenty-four hour day.

A measurable indicator of the low point in the cycle is body temperature. It reaches it lowest point in the early hours of the morning, whether in a twenty-four or twenty-five hour cycle. At about 5 a.m. the body temperature rhythm and the sleep/wake cycle are in unison. This is the time when it is reckoned that staying awake is most difficult. In SAR, that coincides with the time of the day when the most demanding missions take place. Give or take a few hours.

There are many techniques, both personal and scientific, that can be used to combat our low performance in the early hours. Coming to work completely rested would be possible if SAR crews had no families, no domestic chores and responsibilities. Resting all the time would be ideal, except that SAR demands that crews are prepared and constantly training. Like anything, it is a matter of balance. But a difficult balance to achieve none-theless.

Adrenaline is a great thing. It blows the cobwebs away, no mat-ter the hour. The language, the SAR lexicon, forcing us awake.

'Crew of ten. Vessel taking water. Life-rafts deployed.'

'We are tasking you with a life-or-death mission. The crew-man is unconscious. When can you be airborne?'

'Man overboard from a fishing vessel, at a position 140 miles west of Castletownbere. *LE Deirdre* routing to the scene. Six vessels have started searching. Tasking you with a FLIR search.'

The calm routine. Straight to the helicopter with zero brief when we knew the weather from the previous evening. Know-ing from the drive into Shannon in the car, that weather was not a problem to take off or return. Or if there were weather issues, the captain and winch operator sussing them out, while the co-pilot started the helicopter, and the winchman prepped the cabin. Can we do it? What's the return weather going to be like in five hours time? Can we delay until this fog clears? Just how bad is that crewman?

You are not long waking up, with those questions being thrown at you, listening to the sound of the rotors starting to beat outside. What are you going to do, John? Are we going, Jim? Make a fucking decision, Dave!

So getting up and running would not have been a problem. Too much adrenaline. Too much short term reward for get-ting under way. The adrenaline junkies taking to the air again, listening to the information, making the plan, sorting out the navigation and the medical side of things. The whole nine yards. But four hours later. That was a different story.

Four hours later we would be almost home. We would be within 50 miles of home, wherever we were coming from. The adrenaline would be long gone, replaced by God knows what:

exhaustion, apathy, complacency. Hard to shake the feeling that the hard work was already done. Particularly if it had been hard work out there, like a search that had gone on for hours. Back and forth, continuously plotting. Continuously adjusting the navigation system's search patterns. Continuously looking at the area in the searchlight's beam or in the FLIR camera monitor. Time to go home lads. Zzzzzzzzzzzzzzzz.

The getting home, the final phase of the flight, statistically, was fine. No problem. Low level approach into Blacksod or Castletownbere. An instrument approach into one or other airport. But every now and again, the shutters would close on us. How much adrenaline does the body have?

In the summer of 1998, our crew was called to a Russian ship. I think it was a merchant vessel. A very big ship called *Akademic Shatsky* with an injured crewman requesting a medevac. Robert Goodbody from Galway, who had joined that year, was the co-pilot. Graham and Eamonn were winchcrew. A spectacularly forgettable day from the weather point of view, because it was summertime. The vessel was due west at a distance of 190 miles.

We had time to sit quietly on the way there and on the way back. The vessel was enormous. Our only difficulty was trying to understand from the heavily accented English, where exactly they wanted us to hover. The vessel was moving vertically a fair bit. The winching position was amidships by the bridge wing. Hovering beside it was like hovering beside a block of flats, except moving up and down slowly.

So sitting there quietly on the way out, I rummaged about in my subconscious mental store, trying to find something Russian to contemplate. All I could come up with was The Red Army Choir. But they were damn good. I could remember the melodies of quite a few of the tunes. The reason: my father in the Second World War and The Tullamore Gramophone Society.

We did not need the radar as we got closer to the ship. It grew on the horizon as I advanced towards it, 'Russia, My Fatherland', resounding in my head, picturing the smiling Red army from the grainy propaganda films, marching into Berlin, as we identified where to winch. The deep baritone, the balalaikas, the accordions. The proud folk music of the country and the cossack, that had been adapted to sell Russia after the Cold War, stirring me. 'Kakinka', the famous Russian folk song, that builds up slowly, gradually and powerfully to a crescendo. The stylus needle on our old record player at home in Tullamore. I could hear it again. The scratchy music, my father telling me about Berlin in the war. Berlin. Tullamore. One hundred and ninety miles west of Shannon. Music from my youth and from my father's stories, providing a backing track, as Graham said, 'Winchman has the strop, placing it on the survivor. Steady. Winching in the slack. Prepare to lift; up gently. Winchman and survivor clear of the deck.'

The tracks changed a couple of times on the way back to the coast, lifting the needle in response to questions or chit chat. Miltown Malbay and Doonbeg came into view. The west coast of Clare always a welcome sight. We coasted in near Quilty, passing over Mutton Island and Seafield pier, over the low hills that screen that part of Clare from the east. The hills that were once a hindrance to contact with the outside world, now a protection against it. Secret interwoven roads with grass growing down the middle. Sheepdogs that are rarely disturbed from their roadside sleep. Fairy forts and writers.

My Russian music was put away at that stage. Carefully lifted from the turntable, not touching the grooves, just the sharp edges. Slipped into the paper inner sleeve and then the cardboard outer sleeve. Setting it down and seeing the leaping soldier on the cover again.

You could not fly over Doonbeg or Miltown Malbay with

that class of music playing in your head. Not at all. Pictures of the Willie Clancy festival week in my head. Children lining up outside classrooms to register for fiddle and banjo lessons. The boisterous pubs, automatically falling silent, heads bowed in respect, as the first bars of an air commenced. The travelling musicians arrive. Out comes the concertina. Sharon Shannon warming up as we got closer to the coast. Belting out a few tunes. Smiling at us like a bold girl that stole money out of her mother's purse. The Willie Keane Memorial weekend. The session at the end. Gussie McMahon singing *sean nós* style, stepping up with a bit of encouragement again, and tipping across the stage, dancing *sean nós* style as well. Martin Connolly on the accordion.

Shannon ATC interrupts, the approach checks. The call on the marine radio to Shannon Radio: 'Rescue 115 landing at Coonagh airfield in five minutes. Can you confirm that the ambulance from Limerick will meet us there?'

Coonagh airfield, just outside Limerick, the home of a busy flying club. A modest clubhouse, heated when needed, by a Calor gas heater, the walls papered with charts and flying information, the shelves sagging with books on how to fly, how to understand weather and all the subjects that start a fledgling pilot on his or her way. Years of patient instruction feeding pilots into the airlines and helicopter industry, not just in Ireland, but worldwide. We were welcomed by one of them, whose name we did not have time to register. A 'hello' on their club frequency. A welcome wave. A goodbye and good luck.

We started that mission at one o'clock in the afternoon, right after we arrived on duty. We finished it after five o'clock. We were all tired. We settled in for the evening. We went home at nine o'clock. Remaining there on forty-five minutes standby. I would have been home at about quarter past nine. I would have looked in at Alyson or helped with Niamh if she was awake. I would have asked my wife about her day. She would have asked me about mine. I probably put the kettle on for a cup of tea. But I didn't get a chance to drink it that night. The phone rang. It was MRCC Dublin.

'Got a job for you', the voice said.

'OK … You're joking … Again? … Further out? … Medical urgent? … I'll be there in twenty minutes.'

No time to talk. Had to go immediately. Quick hug and a kiss goodbye. Reassurance that the weather was OK. Telling her that we had to go back to the same damn vessel again for another medevac.

Déjà vu. Shaking our heads in disbelief, as we got dressed and ready. The adrenaline well gone as we lifted off at eleven o'clock at night. A fine summer's evening, but no one was enjoying this sunset. What a coincidence that the same vessel needed us twice in succession.

Two hours later we could see it from miles away. Its lights looking more like a lighthouse on a rock, than an ocean going vessel. It was at a distance of 220 miles from Shannon this time, having resumed its original course, whatever that was, after our first medevac. As we got closer, Graham joked that we could take the deck brief as read, done, completed from the previous visit. And so it was.

Darkness concentrating the mind. The winch transfer went smoothly. We arrived. We saw. We did not brief this time. Casualty taken off the bridge wing again, this time on a stretcher. Home, James. *Dasvidaniya.*

Further out this time compared to the last mission. Another two hours to get back to the coast. Once more, my mind playing games as we made for the Blaskets and Tearaght Lighthouse. The Russian music again, but this time female voices. I could even see the dance. Where had I seen it before? A semi-circle of balalaika playing male musicians wearing red coats, black boots and caps, strummed gently, as pretty girls in folk costume sang quietly behind them. The song building, as the girls moved forward between the musicians in unison. Their song growing in strength, the dance around each balalaika player, wooing them and then looking away. One hand outstretched, fingers pointing to the heavens. Looking up to that outstretched hand as they sang. The other hand on the hip. Gliding across the stage, the movement of their legs hidden in petticoats. The song finishing, as they walked to the edge of the stage, each couple side by side. Balalaika players and singers, reaching a haunting and stirring finale. The finale for our Russian crewman had arrived. At Tralee hospital, in the dark, many miles from his home, he was wheeled in blinking under fluorescent light.

We got back at about 5 a.m. It was just brightening. It was August after all. We were shattered. A few hours later, we were replaced by the next day's crew, or rather that day's crew, who came in early to let us off home. I drove home on the back roads, going through Quin. It was sunny and quiet. Ten o'clock. The abbey looked beautiful. I stopped the car just to have a look. Right outside the Abbey Tavern. The owner, Brendan O'Sullivan, may he rest in peace, walked by and said 'hello'. He recognised me because I was a customer of his and because I was in uniform. He had visited the base too. He asked me what I was at, where we had been, and when I told him, he said to come on in. I didn't refuse.

'I'm working out the back,' he said. 'I'm opening up in about twenty minutes: be my guest, help yourself.'

There are many ways to overcome the effects of fatigue.

Many methods of adapting your circadian rhythm, to the disturbances of being called out at night on rescues. But I can not think of a better way of realigning your body clock, telling it to put the adrenaline away before you go to sleep. To counter the zeitgeber of daylight, than drinking a pint that you have just pulled yourself. In an empty pub. Looking out at a fifteenth century Franciscan Abbey on a sunny morning.

29

HOWLING RIDGE

When you are sorrowful, look again in your heart, and you will see
that in truth, you are weeping for that which has been your delight.
                                                            Kahlil Gibran

March 1999. A Sunday afternoon. It was one of those spring days when you hope that the weekend will be quiet and that the pleasant weather would mean a restful day for us. We checked the weather in detail, as well as the tides, sea state, sundown and sunup times, while sipping cups of tea, and then settled into our own routines. Either watching sport on TV, or dozing in a comfortable chair. Almost a full ex-RAF crew with Derek Nequest as co-pilot, Al Clapp as winch operator and Graham Goosey as winchman. Me the odd one out. We were strictly speaking, poised for action, but happily reading the Sunday papers in peace.

The engineers told us that we had a different hoist hook fitted, because of maintenance. Graham, Al and I went to the hangar to have a look. The hook was an old fashioned design, and did not incorporate the safety locking pin that the other had. Temporary measure. Just for a few days. Perfectly legal and approved. Graham was winchman. He was not happy. I could not blame him. We agreed that we would not train that day, and would take it up with management the following day. 'Well, let's hope we don't get a mountain callout,' said Graham.

At home, my parents settled into their usual lunch of a sandwich and some soup, as they too read the papers and discussed the headlines. Now that they were older, the cooked Sunday dinner was only reserved for the days when children visited with their grandchildren. Cups of tea took them into mid-afternoon when their body clocks signalled the time for their own rest. For years my father had told my mother to go and lie down, that he would watch the football match on TV. She kissed him on the forehead before she left the room and soon she was asleep in bed. She knew he too would soon be asleep in his chair, his increasing deafness shutting out the match commentary.

In Shannon, the 'Bat Phone' rang an hour after we arrived, just after the match had started that my father was watching at home. The television was turned down and we silently waited as the details were written down. Someone was on Carrauntuohill with head injuries. Not much planning was required, as the weather was so clear. All that was needed was to get the local map of the Magillycuddys Reeks and decide on the fuel load to get us to and from the scene via the nearest hospital. We were instinctively suspicious of the fair weather and knew that rescue missions which can appear straightforward at first glance, are the ones that can get complicated and dangerous. Better to be pessimistic and proven wrong. Even though we had a fifteen minute allowance to get into the air, we were gone in half that time. No mention of the hook. No hesitation from Graham. A callout is a callout.

At home my father was sound asleep, slumped into the cushions that supported him. My mother woke as she always did, never really sleeping for long, and reached for her book, her glasses, her cigarettes and her ashtray. Her cigarette after waking up in the afternoon, especially at the weekend, was a quiet moment that she savoured. While she relaxed and enjoyed her cigarette, we were on our way.

Leaving the airport behind us, we crossed the Shannon and

climbed higher over the patchwork quilt of south Limerick farmland, making best speed in the clear afternoon air. Once level at 1,500 feet, we could see the Reeks, their jagged tops softened by the 60-mile distance that separated us from them. The flight to the mountains was only twenty-five minutes but there was plenty to do on the way. We communicated with the coast guard radio station at Valentia and plotted the exact position on the local map. On the other radio, we were cleared direct through first Shannon and then Kerry air-traffic zone.

Talking with none other than Declan Smith, a Drogheda man who had been in Baldonnel, and who had been second row in our victorious rugby team.

'Hi Decky. Rescue 115 here again. Heading for the Hags Glen. Any traffic?'

'Hi Dave. No, it's all quiet. QNH 1015. Mind yourselves up their lads. I'll be listening out if you need anything.'

'Thanks Decky. See you later.'

We passed the Lakes of Killarney and established radio contact with the local mountain rescue team who were already on the scene. Passing near the Gap of Dunloe and Kate Kearney's cottage, and the hills and fields where my great grandfather grew up. Carrauntuohill loomed above us as we entered the Hag's Glen, climbing up along the western ridge of Beenreeragh to check the local wind and turbulence as we approached. Our radio homer was switched to the emergency channel, so that we could use the mountain rescue team's own transmissions to point to them and find them rapidly. We knew the area well. I had walked with Paudy McKenna from Tralee civil defence there frequently.

Throwing aside the maps and following the local placenames up to the Hag's Glen, towards the Devil's Ladder, the Heavenly Gates and the Howling Ridge, beside the Eagle's

Nest. Circling near the Howling Ridge, we slowed the helicopter and could see the teams in place at about 2,300 feet. Above them, amongst jagged rocks on a 70 degree slope, we saw the two casualties. They were about 2,800 feet up the 3,414 feet mountain.

In Tullamore, my mother finished her cigarette, dressed, walked quietly into the kitchen and put on the kettle for a cup of tea. The match commentary was still on so she made my father a cup too, not bothering to ask him. She saw that as usual, he had slumped to one side and was fast asleep. Her poor eyesight didn't register the saliva dripping from the side of his mouth, the flicking of his eyes or the twitching of his left side.

The climbers were in a precarious position. One looked unconscious on the ground and the other was kneeling, braced against the mountain watching us. Below them was an almost sheer drop. They were in a jagged boulder field and we could see that if indeed they had fallen, they were lucky to be alive. The wind was light for a change but that would be a mixed blessing. We were going to run the risk of not having enough engine power and of blowing the casualties from their already dangerous position.

We flew along the mountainside low over the ground, contouring around the corrie bowl and short hanging valley, feeling the wind and turbulence to see just what the wind effects were, all the time watching the casualties and re-assessing them. Moving into a position once we knew we had power, I hovered while we all discussed the next move.

As Al talked through a brief, and Graham got ready, I watched the terrain above the casualties, wondering how much blade clearance I would have, while Derek watched the power. Normally in the mountains, especially in the Magillycuddys Reeks, turbulence and down draughts are the problem. It can often be impossible or utterly dangerous to try to hover. On that day, instead of too much wind there was hardly any. The helicopter was hanging onto the air, by its proverbial finger tips. Just as the climbers were.

When we had settled on how we were going to do the job, we got ready to put Graham on the wire. The preferred technique is to winch a man out to a height described as safe. As the helicopter moves into position, the winch operator lets out or in winch cable, keeping the winchman at the same safe height. He also patters the pilot to climb or descend over the terrain as they get close. It is a three dimensional ballet. The theory being, that if the engine fails, the helicopter breaks away, dropping vertically if necessary to gain speed, to the valley floor and a safe, or relatively safe landing.

After the engine fails, the hoist cable is sheared by one of the crew. An explosive bolt cuts the cable, allowing the winchman to fall to the ground, the mountain slope, or into the sea, wherever the mission takes place. The shear bolt is sheared by either the captain, who has his or her left thumb over a guarded button on the collective lever, or by the winch operator, who has a similar switch at his door. Forget to press the button if an engine fails; the winchman trails to the valley floor under the helicopter on the winch, trying not to swing into the tail rotor. If that doesn't kill him, the single engine landing will. But if the button is pressed, being at a 'safe' height of 20 or 30 feet, he will survive with broken limbs, and will retire with full medals and a disability pension. It is not always possible to keep a winchman at a safe height though. Graham had to do a space walk suspended high above the boulders, with no hope of survival if he fell.

So when Al asked, 'cleared to winch?' I could visualise Graham, the hook without safety catch, the Howling Ridge beside us, the valley floor far below between my feet, flashing through my mind, knowing that it was flashing through Graham's mind too. And Al's. They were good friends.

'Cleared to winch,' I replied.

'Winchman attached to the cable. Winching out'.

In such moments, men risk their lives. In that instant, Graham Goosey, an Englishman, in an Irish coast guard helicopter, put his life in God's hands, for the sake of two French climbers that he did not know, and would never know. On countless occasions, I had seen winchmen sliding on oily, wet, dark, pitching decks and then as they carried a stretcher and their medical gear down into the unknown, reeking, rocking bowels of a fishing trawler, to a man that might die without their aid. That is bravery.

I held my position as the helicopter's centre of gravity changed slightly, adjusting as it tried to nudge towards the rocks. I waited until Graham was well below, plumb below me and out of sight, and level with the casualties. On Al's instruction, I squeezed the cyclic sideways and the mountain started to move. We inched painstakingly slowly towards the casualties, making sure our downwash did not disturb them. Our engine power was high because of the lack of wind. Easing forward and sideways at a walking pace so that Graham would not start to swing. Listening to the numbers in the patter, so that my deceleration would be gradual and ease Graham into position.

My head turned slightly, so that my scan was both outside onto the mountain, and inside onto the instruments to check power.

The scan outside showing me the arcing curved line of the blade tips, as they got closer and closer to the rock. Then buzzing a few feet from it, the blade tips tracing a neat line, a few feet from the rock. Each movement of the light wind, each change in the helicopter's centre of gravity as the winch reeled out and as Graham touched onto the mountain, I could see as the blade tip path wobbled and careered towards the rocky slope beside us. Straightening it with the help of Al's patter. A squeeze of cyclic control holding it back from smacking into the mountain. The mountain would mock us if the blades struck rock. Smithereens of blade would be followed by smithereens of helicopter. With us inside.

Graham disappeared behind a boulder, out of sight now of the winch operator too. He fell to his knees, immediately assessing the casualties' medical condition and their safety. When the cable went slack, the winch operator knew the winchman was in position. Seconds ticked by. Then the winchman in one movement unclipped from the hoist hook and swung it away from himself, while attaching himself to the climber's belay.

'Winchman with the casualties. Winchman off the cable. Winching in.'

I did not hesitate to fly away. Graham was no longer attached to the cable, or to us. We flew away and waited for Graham to call us back. He was in a precarious position at that point, belayed to the mountain, while medically assessing the injured climbers. One was in a bad way, with head and leg injuries, but conscious.

In Tullamore, my mother brought in a cup of tea and said she was going for a walk. My father said nothing. She repeated what she had said and he slurred some sort of response. She thought he was just playing some sort of sleepy joke. Then she realised that he was not playing any joke. She froze. She said his name. Many thoughts went through her mind, but she did not panic. She put down her cup of tea and asked him if he was all right, now sitting beside him rubbing his forehead. His eyes were closed and he sagged heavily to one side, breathing noisily.

We circled safely away from the winchman and waited for him to call us back on the radio. He worked quickly, having readied the more seriously-injured casualty for the stretcher. The other casualty was walking wounded, uninjured, probably shocked but otherwise fine. The priority was to evacuate the more serious casualty and make sure the second was securely belayed to the mountain at all times.

Working in the confines between the boulders, Graham unfolded the stretcher that he had brought on his back, belayed it to the mountain and then placed its two component parts on each side of the casualty. Working with the other climber, he assembled the stretcher under the injured man and then tightly secured him in position. When he was ready, he called us back on his hand held radio. He resisted the temptation to reach for the hoist hook as we hovered overhead, our blades beating the warm air noisily. Instead he remained fixed in position with the stretcher, his eyes on the other casualty. He watched in case the other climber tried to grab the hook, as it swung lazily over their heads towards them, potentially putting him off balance. The hook reached the winchman and in one movement he had it in his hand. He attached himself and the stretcher to it while unclipping from the mountain belay. Sleight of hand. Steely nerve. Concentration. Technique. Experience.

Above him I waited for the weight to come on the winch, for the power to increase and for the instruction to fly away. He tugged on the winch cable, signalling that he was ready, it went taut and then he could feel the mountain fall away under his feet as we pulled him clear of the ground. His eyes remained fixed on the hoist hook and its unguarded mouth. He ignored the dropping sensation as the helicopter dropped away from the mountain, picking up speed as the winch cable drew him to safety above. Cradling the stretcher in his arms, never once taking his eyes from the hook, he came to the door, entered carefully under the winch operator's watchful eye and then lowered the stretcher gently to the floor, dropping with an inaudible sigh to his knees. He clapped Al on the back.

She rang a neighbour, Trevor Rainsberry, my bee whisperer. With another neighbour, Mickey Kileevy, he arrived in a flash. They sat him upright and then called 999. My father was breathing and alive but seemingly only just. A calmness came over my mother and although she was upset, she was facing her husband's fate, whatever that would be. Instinctively she knew he had had a stroke. A great tiredness came over her, even though she fought the desire to carry him to the car herself, and bring him to hospital immediately. The ambulance arrived. They reassured her but not enough. Poor eyesight did not stop her seeing and registering their reactions. One of them said that it had been a stroke, possibly a major one and that my father might not survive. She got my father's washbag, a towel and a change of clothes.

The stretcher casualty safely in the helicopter, we positioned to pick up the other climber. We radioed our plans to the mountain rescue team. I found out later on that Ben Heron was on the ground with the Kerry MR team. The senior winch operator and paramedic in the air corps, we had flown together many times. One of many who had tutored me in the mountains. Looking up wondering was it anyone he knew.

It was going to be dark quite soon, so Kerry MRT were glad we could help. The terrain would have made for a time-consuming and technically-demanding stretcher carry and evacuation on the ground, especially by night.

Picking up the second climber was a much quicker job this time round. Once we had him on board, we banked away and followed the valley out towards Tralee hospital. The sun started to cast long shadows beneath us. We completed our checks, radioed our intended arrival time at the hospital to marine rescue, and said goodbye to the teams on the ground.

In the hospital my mother sat holding my father's hand as he slept. He was quite different. The stroke had changed him. In the space of a few hours he had been transformed. How unfair. He was stable and they were doing all they could to prevent another stroke, stabilise the blood count; time would tell. She stopped taking in what they were saying to her. They spoke to her in a way she recognised, using the hushed reassuring voices she knew were reserved for relatives of the sick and dying. She refused their advice to go home and rest. She sat and held his hand.

The helicopter settled lightly on to the pad at Tralee hospital as the emergency staff approached. The casualties were quickly taken away and disappeared into the relative calm of the emergency ward. The sun was low over the Magharee Islands in Tralee Bay as we climbed into the evening sky towards Shannon. There was a quiet satisfaction amongst the four of us knowing that we had been successful. Having landed back at base, the kettle was filled, the dinners heated and each settled back into the waiting game again.

My mother held my father's hand and thought nothing and everything. My father moved and groaned from time to time, his life hanging in the balance. She struggled with these thoughts and the helplessness she felt. The nurses were busy but even though she screamed inside, the inevitability of whatever lay ahead brought to her a sort of tranquillity. She stayed where she was and thought how best to break the news to me and the rest of the family.

At 9 p.m. we went home from the base but remained on night call. I put the kettle on and kissed Alyson goodnight, tucking her in to bed before checking the baby. My wife and I talked about the day's events and then we went to bed with cups of tea and books to read. Just as I was about to go to sleep, the telephone rang. I groaned. I wondered if it was another rescue callout. I answered the phone and was pleased to hear my mother's voice.

'How are you?' she asked. Without noticing, I became a boy again. I told my proud mother of my day, just as I would have done as a child or as a teenager, if I had scored a try or won a match. I told her about the mountains that I loved and about the rescue. Just as she had always listened and encouraged, so she did again. She listened as I said the children were well but now asleep. Then she told me that she had had a difficult day. She told me that Dad had had a major stroke. I listened in disbelief. It was 11 p.m. and my wife noticed the change in the tone of the conversation. I hung up the phone and told her the news with tears in my eyes.

30

THE CHAIN

Go Mairidis Beo – That Others May Live.

Air corps helicopter rescue motto

Whenever good weather returned in spring, lunchtimes in Baldonnel were a hive of activity. Taking the opportunity to exercise, snatching quick sandwiches before returning to whatever duty or office to which we were assigned. Whenever there were enough of us around, we used to play soccer at lunchtime at the officers' mess. Pilots, engineers, air traffic controllers, army officers; anybody and everybody, providing you had boots and forty-five minutes to spare.

Very few of us were qualified to play 'the beautiful game'. When we played, it was more like 'the ugly game', as hurlers, Gaelic footballers and rugby players, squared up. The collisions were spectacular, as nobody hung back from fifty-fifty balls. Picking ourselves up, tangled together, tempers would flare and then subside, hands shaken, and the game would resume.

That's my memory of Mick Baker. A few years younger than me. A Wexford man, a sublime hurler, hard as nails. He punished me many times on sunny afternoons going for fifty-fifty balls. I did not fly with him, but I always remember his cheerfulness and smile. It is what came to mind when I heard he had died in Tramore.

My memory of Dave O'Flaherty was very similar, being from the same town, and the same school, but knowing him only slightly better. When I finished border flying, I gave him my detailed maps of the border counties, just as he was starting to fly the Alouette 3. Up and down to Tullamore on days off, we swapped gossip and news from home. Another man who would leave you battered and bruised after a game of lunchtime soccer. Not close friends, but invisibly supporting each other, proud of our town, and standing up in its defence, if there was ever any criticism or slagging going on. Another Tramore victim.

I knew Paddy Mooney best of all. Although that is probably not true either. Rank separated us. But duty united us. I worked many times with Paddy. As I was growing up and learning to fly and learning to fly rescue, so was he. We learned together. Made mistakes together. Celebrated success together. As a winch operator he was coolness personified. As a sportsman, especially as a Gaelic footballer, he would skin you alive, laugh at you and then shake your hand.

I did not know Niall Byrne but I may as well have known him. To try to imagine him, all I had to do was think of any of us when we started helicopter SAR. Whether as pilots or winchcrew. Brimming with enthusiasm. Positive, and with his whole career and life ahead of him.

That was the crew of the Irish air corps Dauphin that crashed on Tramore beach in July 1999. Returning from a sea search for missing people in a boat. At night in fog. So close to home. So close to life. I got a phone call the following morning from one of our own crew: 'Have you heard?'

When I heard, I thought, there but for the grace of God go I. Whispered conversations over cups of tea revealed that others felt the same. Helicopter SAR is dangerous by nature. There are so many events that lead to an accident. When one event follows another, a catastrophic sequence is set up. An accident chain, with many links, leading inexorably to disaster. Helicopter SAR is one type of flying, where it is possible to be on a mission with many of the accident links already in place. Being tired, flying at 4 a.m., going to maximum range, language difficulties, huge seas, lives at risk and depending on you – the list is endless. The other links, the final lethal ingredients to disaster, waiting to merge. Some final thing to tip the balance. Not necessarily a big thing. The crease of a folded map, hiding a rock, sticking 200 feet out of the sea. A danger area or hazard, printed in ink on a chart, that your red or green cockpit light doesn't illuminate.

Many people who work in SAR have near-disaster stories of their own. The procedures and the training, the hours and hours of practice, the accumulated wisdom, prepare you and equip you for the unknown. But we can only do so much. We control only what can be controlled. There are so many other forces at work.

I remembered hearing of a helicopter that was searching a coastline at night. Quite a clear night. The coastline featured cliffs about 200 feet high. The crew were looking for missing people in a boat. Up and down the coast they flew. Using their radar and their FLIR camera. As they turned to commence another search line, the co-pilot looked out and saw a sheep in the search light beam. The wind had picked up, and invisibly, had pushed them out of their pattern towards the cliff. He took over manual control with a shout, pulled collective power, and climbed to safety. God only knows how close they came to disaster. They diverted, landed, debriefed and went home. It later turned out that no one had been missing at all.

Another crew was returning to Blacksod after a long range medevac. Normally, the combination of positioning to Blacksod, refuelling, doing the rescue, returning to Blacksod, taking the casualty to Galway or Sligo hospital, and then returning to Shannon, can take nearly nine flying hours. Often all at night.

This particular crew was tired. Probably very tired. As they approached the coast again, looking forward to landing at Blacksod, they had their weather radar turned off, because the night was clear. Flying at a couple of hundred feet above the sea, they flew over one of the islands that lies west of the Mullet peninsula. They flew very low over it. Their radio altimeter registered that they had flown to within 50 feet of the ground. An audio warning and flashing light prompted the flying pilot to apply power. He climbed higher and they landed at Blacksod. They completed the mission, the casualty was taken to Galway hospital.

A Dauphin crew returning to Blacksod at night was met by dense fog. So dense, that even at the minimum hover height, they could not see and land. They had to divert, flying inland, only fumes left in the fuel tanks. Spotting a gap in the fog, they landed safely in a field. Beside a pub called The Happy Landing, would you believe.

That is just three stories. There are lots more. Those crews were saved. The accident chain was either broken or prevented from being put together. But what saved them? Skill? The radio altimeter in one case? The co-pilot's alertness in the other? A gap in the fog? The Man Above? Lady Luck? Whatever it was, the fact that the final accident link was not joined to the chain saved those crews' lives.

Tramore reminded us, reminded me, that you cannot control all the variables. Searching for missing people, fearful that you are their last hope, is a pressure that most people never experience. Crews do not want to land with loads of fuel after a search. Loads of fuel means they did not give their all to the search. They did not try to the nth degree to find the missing. At least subconsciously, that's what they may think.

In June 1999, a month before the Tramore crash, Anna

was born. While my father struggled to cope with his disability, Anna's arrival made him smile again. Made him cry, happy tears, to see new life in our family, a healthy baby, to reassure him, given that his body was irreparably damaged. But when the crash happened, it upset him. It worried him. He had known Dave O'Flaherty. Tried to help him prepare for interviews for the cadetship while I was away. As the town mourned, he started to suggest I find another way to make a living.

I went to Dave's funeral. I walked past the gate of the Christian Brothers' School where Dave and I had both attended. Past the top of the New Road, and then joined the stream of townspeople making their way to the cemetery. As I got to the bottom of the hill, someone called my name. I looked across and saw Tom Lawless, former publican, undertaker, family friend, a man who, like many of my parents' friends, had encouraged me as a young lad leaving school.

The road was quiet, except for the sound of whispered conversation, shuffling feet and rooks cawing. Even Tom's shout was whispered. I crossed to say hello. He was at the end of the cul-de-sac that led to his house. He was wearing a dressing-gown. He told me he had recently had serious surgery, but was on the mend. 'Poor Lily,' he said. Dave's mother was a widow for many years. That day she was burying her son. Beside her stood Dave's widow, Maria burying her husband, with their baby growing inside her.

I whispered goodbye and good luck and continued to the cemetery. Thinking of another man who had died long ago. Lawless' pub had been on High Street. Our neighbours, the Adamses, used to send young Terence down to the pub when he was a youth for a pint of draught stout. Tom would pull the pint, and while it was settling, he would give young Terence a fizzy drink, a Club orange or a red lemonade. When the pint was settled,

Tom put a brown paper bag over the top. Terence would walk up the street slowly, the creamy head staining the brown bag wet, making sure not to spill it. Up the steps to where his father sat, waiting patiently for his pint, too weak to go himself. The life draining out of him.

Around the corner I turned, facing the fifteen trees planted after Offaly won the All-Ireland Hurling championship for the first time in 1981. There was a huge crowd. Motionless. Silent. Waiting. Up ahead through the trees was the railway bridge. Cycled over it every day to school. Beyond it Deegan's farm and further out the road, and down the lane, our own house. As we peered through the trees, the funeral cortege appeared over the crest of the bridge.

As they drew closer, I started to recognise the faces. Under peaked caps and berets, my friends and colleagues came to lay Dave to rest. I felt a lump in my throat, as I saw my former working life, and my home town merge. Uniforms where I had never seen uniforms before. Marching and salutes, ceremony and crisp military order, where I had never seen it before. Out of context. The tragedy all the more keenly felt because of it.

In Stamullen, Ennniscorthy and Killiney, that week, heart-breaking funerals took place for Paddy, Mick and Niall. The army came to town. Uniforms, sombre funereal music, played by proud military bands. Clear sunny bright days. On any other occasion, the gathered crowds could have admired the pomp and ceremony, children would have watched with wide eyes and melting ice creams. Instead, the crowds watched the marching columns, paying tribute to the dead, to the flag they served. To the motto they lived and died by: '*Go Mairidis Beo* (That Others May Live).'

Just as the fatalities of war-ravaged places must return to their peaceful homes, so they laid the four young men to rest.

The sunshine of South Lebanon seems so far away to the grieving families of those who have died there on UN duty. A search and rescue helicopter crew, searching for life, seemed remote from the sunshine of those funeral days.

In June 2008, the crew of the Tramore Dauphin were posthumously awarded the Distinguished Service Medal, with honour.

31

A PATCH OF SKY

Sweater, noun: garment worn by child when its mother is feeling chilly.
Anon.

We used to go to Stavanger in Norway to do our simulator training. The parent company was Helikopter Services, a giant of the North Sea oil industry. Pilots do not enjoy simulator training much. It is a necessary evil. Sitting into a darkened cockpit, knowing that disaster awaits you, the simulator instructor sits behind, turning off engines, starting fires and failing hydraulic systems, pulling circuit breakers/fuses, while you follow procedures and try to stay flying. Returning to the nearest simulated airport or rig, perhaps to do a single engine instrument approach, and then finding yourself unable to land. Then doing a missed approach/go around to some other airport.

Knut Hegle and Paul Ringholm were the examiners who used to persecute us, devising more and more sadistic ways to test us. Judging us on how we faced the system failures, and how we chose our options and took action. What are you going to do? Tail rotor control failure, tail rotor failure, double engine failure and auto-rotation. The exercises you cannot practice in a real helicopter.

Looking back at the last decade of my father's life, I often compared what he went through to a simulator ride. God the Examiner, failing this or that system, and watching to see if my father could still fly.

Problem: Grinding noise in the hip, followed by constant pain; what are you going to do?

Solution: Hip replacement.

Problem: Dizziness, followed by nausea, followed by the occasional fall? What is the problem? What are you going to do?

Solution: That could be vertigo; go to doctor, get medication.

Problem: Unable to move left side of body, difficulty in breathing, mental faculties impaired.

Solution: Major stroke. Try to keep cheerful while my life collapses around me.

Before the stroke, the visits from Tullamore were regular. The white Lada Riva, arriving from home with gifts and smiling, doting grandparents. It may as well have been a limousine. Even after his hip replacement, he still came. Sunny weather, he would not let the pain keep him away. After a few days staying with us, we all went to Doolin, very early on a great day. From Ennistymon straight ahead, over the hills and the forest plantations.

Arriving at the top of the hill that looks out over the Aran Islands, it took the breath away. The ground falling away in front of us to Fisherstreet and Doolin, Crab Island. The rocky coast stretching away to Fanore and Black Head. The islands, one, two, three, lined up like a picture postcard. Sunlight shining on the white lighthouse on the southern side of Inis Oirr.

Down to the pier, and then I sprang my trap. 'Will we take the ferry to Inis Oirr? It's a lovely day, we'll enjoy it. It's a short walk to the hotel from the pier over there and …' They agreed, giving in to my sales pitch. Getting on the ferry was interesting, to say the least. With the tide out, we had to get into large currachs at the pier, chug out to the waiting ferry, then clamber up the side. My father laughing outwardly, as he looked fearfully at the ferry, rising and falling gently beside the currach. Hiding a grimace as he felt a twinge of pain. The ferry departed. The wall of the Cliffs of Moher rising behind us as we slipped across to the islands. The low shape growing as we got closer, the patterns of the island's stone walls emerging from a heat haze. The wreck of the *Plassey* on the southern shore, the lighthouse further along, sea gulls wheeling overhead. The channel marker buoy that we sometimes hovered over, swaying in our wake as we passed.

No need for currachs on the island pier, the deep berth allowed us to come alongside. Strolling up to the island hotel, past the beach with the upturned black currachs lined up on elevated stands, the tar undersides glistening in the sun. Days like this. An island wedding that day. The doors of the pub open. Music and revelry spilling out, laughter and spontaneous dancing. Up and down to the beach to play with the children. Alyson paddling in the water. Niamh making sand-castles. Granny and granddad looking around at the paradise that my sister Ruth had described all those years ago, when she went to the Gaeltacht to study Irish.

Sitting in the sun drinking a pint with my dad. 'Is your hip all right dad? Are you sore? Will I get you another chair to put your feet up on?' Days you want to go back to. Days that make you smile at the memory of fleeting paradise.

The Aran Island's number three, excluding the rocky Eeragh on the north of the biggest one. They lie in a row across Galway Bay, their western cliffs bearing the brunt of the Atlantic's constant battering. The Irish for island is Inis. The biggest island is called Inis Mór, the middle one is Inis Meáin and the smallest is Inis Oirr. Meaning biggest, middle and furthest island respectively or Inishmore, Inishmaan and Inisheer, for English language convenience. In Shannon, we got used to calling them Inish Big,

Inish Middle and Inish Little 'un, so that everyone, non-Irish speakers especially, would know where we were going.

Late in 1999, we got a call to go to Inish Little 'un again. Typical night. Typical weather. One of those days when the English among our crew, wondered aloud why we depended so much on bottled water. Sheeting down. Horizontal rain. We soared unseen over the cliffs again in the early hours of a winter morning. Dropping down again east of the islands, and then turning towards the airstrip.

The visibility was not too bad. The strong winds and heavy rain made it relatively clear. Our wipers revealed the light at the modest airport building. We could not line up on the runway, the wind was too strong, so we crossed the runway lights, only seeing them as our wheels passed above them, landed and waited. In the torrential rain, a stretcher glided across the grass towards us, carried by four glistening, bent-over men. They passed beside where I sat. Walking just outside the perspex and below my feet, as they made for the cargo door and our waiting winchcrew.

Pausing at the door, one of them looked up at me. It was the barman who had served us on that perfect day in the summer. He paused. I was wearing a helmet so he probably was not sure who I was. He looked away as they busied themselves, getting the stretcher in to the helicopter. Then paused again before he walked away. A wave and a smile in the rain. We communicated wordlessly.

A nod: "Tis yourself again.'

A smile: 'It is. Bad night to be carrying a stretcher.

Eyes thrown to heaven: 'Wicked night altogether.'

A solemn expression: 'Thanks for taking this fella to hospital. He is not well at all.'

A wave, another nod: 'You're welcome. We'll have him in Galway hospital before you take your coat off at home.'

Then head down, as they walked away from the rotating, flapping blades. We hauled the helicopter up unceremoniously into the darkness. There was so much wind, we had 60 knots on the clock as soon as the wheels left the ground. It was rainy, dark and turbulent, but in my mind I could see the sunshine. I clinked glasses with my mother and father. Crossing the patterned walls below me, the ruined castle on the hill, wild flowers growing in the gaps in the walls. The sound of music that afternoon. The beat of the bodhrán, like the rhythm of the rain and wind against our thin metal skin as we flew. The pause in the bar that day, when a *sean nós* singer sang. The sadness and beauty of the tune, drifting through the bar's open doors.

After his stroke, he recovered, he adapted, we adapted. Instead of the Lada driving down to us, I used to drive up and bring them down. He would sit in the front passenger seat, wordlessly looking out as the midlands became the west. The flashing light and rotating bridge at Portumna announcing that some significant step had been made. As river cruisers queued and slid under the bridge, waving and taking it in turns, it was as if a bridgehead had been gained. The villages with names he had grown to love. The names that led to the sea, to the memory of walking unaided on two good legs: Whitegate, Mountshannon, Scarriff, Tuamgraney and Bodyke.

No longer able to walk without a lot of help, he did not want to go to town any more. He missed the paper shop, where he was cheerfully greeted as he got the cigarettes and paper. Missed the bumping into friends, going this way and that about their business. The town he loved so well. Where he had forgotten the war. Where he had started again, all those years ago, when I was a baby. With friends who helped him laugh again. Live again. Love life again. There was a period after his stroke when he was very strong. Having recovered and fought it, and before it returned once more to weaken him, he used to enthusiastically go to town for a pint when I called and stayed. The Hole in the Wall was where we went.

There was a routine to our excursions. I used to park outside, as near as I could. Then a quick look into the pub, to see if there was room for the wheelchair. The barman, Fergus Shelley, would see me poke my head around the door and by the time I had helped my father out of the car, Fergus would be there with the double door held open, and with great ceremony, he would welcome us.

'How are you Mr Courtney. Come on in. I've got that, Dave. You're up for a few days? Two pints, is it? And how are all the Courtneys?'

You know that American TV comedy called *Cheers*? 'Where everyone knows your name.' Remember that line? The welcome that we used to get, no fuss, no big deal, just knowing my father's name. That made him smile. That made him happy.

Niamh began taking her first steps around the same time that my father was taking his last. Visiting home, trying to find out when the nurse would call, was the home-help coming, and listening to the children giggling as they pushed each other around the room in his wheelchair. Just about to stop them in case he would be upset or angry, then seeing that he was laughing at their antics. 'Push her again,' he would say. 'Good girl.'

The Great Simulator Examiner in the sky, had pulled many circuit breakers, failed many of my father's systems but he was still flying. We got him to Monks in Ballyvaughan. He waited patiently as I parked the car so that his side was not jammed against the wall. He mouthed a thank you to anyone who held open a door for him. He drank his pint of stout, ate the chowder and laughed in defiance at the sky.

I loved the perspective that flying gave me. The scale, the speed that we flew, the unrolling of the living canvas of greens and browns and blues and greys. But you can go the other direction too. You can go closer and closer and see infinity in a raindrop. I walked the Burren with Joe Queally from Fanore. A fund-raiser for the RNLI, we began to plot this or that way of increasing the coffers of that life-saving organisation. As we plotted and organised, I would show him the expanse of the west coast. And he would show me a fragile flower. Near the Caher Valley, the well spring of 'Anam Cara' and John O'Donoghue's home place. I would show him the cliffs. He would show me a tiny ruined chapel, where people received mass during the Famine. I showed him places that could only be seen from the air. He showed me places that were beside the footpaths, where most people stumbled, as they sent text messages.

We used to take famous people flying. Musicians especially, who were doing concerts for the RNLI. Phil Coulter and Ralph McTell, walking onto the stage in the West County Hotel. Rapturous applause and then quiet as they sang. We took them flying to show them the sea, take them to Valentia, to the lifeboat there. Show them why they were going to sing. Show them where the equipment that their fund-raising would buy would be used. To meet the men and women that used it. Depended on it. With their very lives. Phil would tell them of his brother taken by the sea. Many years before, the memory fresh. And then he sang 'The Town I Loved So Well'. And once more, I pictured myself sitting in the corner of Adamses' parlour, eating a bag of Tayto, drinking a Club orange through a straw, Rory and Fergus elbowing me and kicking each other as Tom Horkan sang the same song. The rise of the chorus as the room joined in. Children looking up as the room rang with song.

In the West County again, Ralph sang. Many songs. Shaking his head in amazement, when the whole room joined him in the chorus, thirty years after he first sang 'The Streets of London'.

Instant replay. Thirty years before in Tullamore. Christmas time. My parents, all the Adamses, aunts and uncles, Paddy Lloyd, Emer MacCann, the parish priest, and the older brothers and sisters, singing, 'I'll show you something, that'll make you change your mind.' Their uncle Fergus, nicknamed The Count, singing 'I will Remember Vienna', Patsy Cannon singing 'You are My Sunshine', Monica with 'The Curragh of Kildare'.

I knew where Joe's mother lived. Often walking in the Burren, we would call in and she would give us tea, try to make us stay for dinner. Sitting beside the range in her sitting-room, the islands framed outside against her curtains, I sat and answered her questions about myself.

'Three. Three girls. That's right, three girls. Aged four, two and two months now. You had a big family yourself.'

'I did. I did.' She replied. Laughing proudly, and then naming them, one by one, looking out of her window in thought as her left hand gripped the arm of the chair.

A few weeks after one of our visits, she had visitors. Family from America no less. The house tidied in readiness. Plenty of turf, dried and brought in from the haggard and stacked neatly beside the range. Three generations of her family. Back in the rocky place whence they came.

'What's that noise?' someone asked.

Michael looked out through the window, and then went to the front door. Returning with a smile.

'It's for you,' he said to their mother.

She went to the door, followed by the American entourage as the noise became louder and closer. Up in the helicopter, I slid back the panel window and waved at her. She waved back. We turned and raced away, and then flew past with lights a blaze, and blades a beating away to Shannon.

'Who was that?' she was asked.

'Oh that's just the lads from the rescue in Shannon. Sure I know them. Don't they drink tea with me? They always wave and make a racket when they're out this way.'

I no longer fly over her house. Or the Burren. Or the Caher Valley. Or the patch of sky framed by it. But I walk it often with her sons. Starting or stopping at an overgrown holy well or ruin. And when they pause, and when they find no words, standing beside me in their barren paradise, turning their heads, ever so slightly away from me so I will not see, the ghost of her in their tears. The love of her, the fierce fight of her, that gave them life, and never asked for thanks. Then, I suck in my breath. I close my eyes. And know that I am not alone.

32

THE UNIFYING THEORY OF EVERYTHING

None but a coward dares to boast that he has never known fear.

Anon.

A closed loop. A beginning and end to a problem. In between, the process of argument and debate, logic and reason. Finishing with an explanation. Science loves to close loops. To explain how it all works, where it all started, where it will finish. So many opposing forces at work. So many different opinions on the beginnings of life. Sceptics and scientists. Theologians and physicists. Searching for the common ground that makes everyone happy. Searching for The Unifying Theory of Everything.

Albert Einstein, Isaac Newton and Stephen Hawking, among others, sought the solution in the black holes of space, and in their calculations of time travel. Personally, I could not follow their mathematical logic, preferring the story from the *Hitchhiker's Guide to the Galaxy*, to illustrate that the search was in vain. The one where the scientists build a super computer and ask it 'What is the meaning of life?' After many days it comes out with the answer forty-two.

I used to work in the defence forces with some very clever people. Computer geeks, communications experts, explosives geniuses, aeronautical engineers. That was a popular story in those circles. The men and women who knew so much, laughing at how little they knew.

But my theory was taking shape. A baby imitates the sounds

it hears and then speaks. Then imitates the music of the wind and the sea, and all that resonates with those forces, and sings. 'Port na bPúcaí' is a famous traditional melody in Kerry. And where does it come from? A man from the Ó Dalaigh clan, on the remote Blasket Island of Inishvicillaune heard a tune rising up from the sea. He memorised it and learned it and it is now forever enshrined. 'The Jig of the Fairies', to give it its English name, was inspired by the sound of whales. And it is not the only tune to come from nature or from whales. 'Port Ceann Boirne' is another. Its history is similar. A woman walking the road to Fanore, over the Burren from Lisdoonvarna, stopped to rest, and heard the whales sing too.

Before we had sophisticated communications, fishermen were the ones who migrated and fished, taking out their fiddles and whistles, far from home, and swapping tunes: the music of Norway, with its uncannily Irish sounding Hardanger fiddle, and of the Shetland Islands and the Outer Hebrides, Donegal and Tory. The Atlantic coast of Ireland. Mixing and coalescing. The sounds of the wind and the sea, and all that resonates with their force, joining as one. It is a Unifying Theory of a sort.

Waves and swell. Smooth as glass, then rising, and growing and subsiding again. Driven by the wind and the earth's rotation and the moon as well. The moon, orbiting earth and drawing the earth's oceans towards it. Its gravitational pull causes the oceans to surge every twelve hours or so: high tide and low tide. And when the tides and the ocean swell combine, science scratches its head, and tries to predict how big the waves will be.

Probability. The forecast will be made. A prediction of the average significant wave size. The computers fed the data from bobbing buoys at sea, ships, weather balloons and satellites. And just as the people waited for the super-computer to answer the question: 'What is the meaning of life?' we wait to see how big the waves will be. For every wave predicted, a percentage will be double that size. A smaller percentage will be bigger again. These are not freak wave predictions. Simply wave predictions.

A distress signal on a ship is transmitted omni-directionally. It goes everywhere: all points of the compass. Rescue helicopters and aeroplanes carry homing equipment so that they can find direction and go straight to the source of the signal. Ordinary aircraft cannot do that. They fly around the globe, listening to the international distress frequency, 121.5, in case a beacon starts to transmit.

If they hear a transmission, they cannot tell where it is coming from. They can record when they heard it first and when they heard it last: the signal heard position and the signal fade position. They pass this information on to the nearest rescue agency, and continue on their way. Other aircraft in the area, listen and pass on their signal heard and signal fade positions, giving the rescue agency multiple plots on the ocean chart.

While the rescue controllers plot on charts, and while the helicopter crews and lifeboats are alerted, Russian and American satellites orbit the earth and watch and listen in low-earth, geo-stationary orbit, pass on the signals they receive to the COSPAS–SARSAT system, which in turn tracks and locates mariners, aviators and yachtsmen in distress almost anywhere in the world. As a SAR operation swings into action, the satellites continuously update, getting increasingly accurate information, narrowing the search.

In October 2000, an aircraft flying over Ireland heading out into the Atlantic picked up a distress signal and radioed the signal heard/signal fade information to Shannon ATC, who called MRCC Dublin, who in turn called us. It was about 10 a.m. Very strong westerly winds. The usual warning from the met office of a heavy swell on Atlantic coastlines. With Mike Shaw co-pilot, Pete Leonard winchman and Noel Donnelly winch operator, we took off immediately, heading to a position about 130 miles from Shannon, 90 miles west of Loop Head, not knowing if the call was verified, real or spurious.

It happens now and again, that you find out that the call was a mistake, a hoax or the result of a technical fault somewhere. As we headed west, slowed by strong winds, we wondered too. Listening on the radio as we flew. We sought updates on the distress signal but there were none. We discussed what to do as we got closer. We got ready. We decided on our Bingo fuel to return to the coast. We did our pre-SAR checks. We waited. We looked out at the ocean. The white tops. The swell. It was big. Wondering if there was anything out there at all. Then a radio call from Valentia: 'Rescue 115. Valentia. SARSAT hit at the same position. Continue to original position.'

Then our radio homer sprang to life. Pointing straight ahead. The audio transmission coming in faint at first, getting stronger all the time.

'This is real lads. We'll start at the datum, see what we can see and then put in a pattern. How about that?'

Following the needle, arriving at the datum, the original position, the waves were wind blown and white capped. There was nothing. Slowing to a hover as we approached it, looking out in expectation. Nothing. Past the position and back around again. We repeated the run-in line once more, before starting the patterned automatic search.

'Debris in the water, twelve o'clock, one hundred metres,' said one of us. We had slowed at that point, come to a hover about 200 feet above the sea. The debris below us and ahead of us. Door open. Pete on the wire, attached and ready. Poised and looking. Mike and I up front scanning ahead. A movement. In the white water in between the windscreen wipers, in between the spume blown from the wave crests, we could see an arm waving.

'Target in sight. One o'clock. One fifty metres. Running in. Forward and right twenty, forward and right fifteen, forward ten and right …'

'In sight,' said Noel, taking over the patter. 'Pete's equipment checked, attached to the cable; forward and right five. Height good. Confirm clear winch.'

Noel put Pete out the door. Pete hit the first wave at the same time as the helicopter stopped its forward motion. No ceremony. No more chat. Pete shocked by the freezing wind, the freezing water. Concentrating on the men in the water. They rose and fell on the swell, up and down and holding onto a life-ring.

The helicopter held a hover, obeying Noel's patter, climbing as the swell rose in front of us. Rain and sea spray being cleared by the wipers. Noel was giving Pete enough slack cable to do his work. Getting each man into a strop, and then lifting them, one by one. Not too much slack in case it tangled them, and dragged them under. My job was relatively easy. The wind was strong, giving us loads of lift through the rotor disc, making it easier to rise and fall with the swell. Noel was looking straight down, concentrating on not drowning Pete or the three men in the water. Every now and then, I would warn him that I had to climb, so that he could winch out to compensate.

The men in the water were so relieved that it could have killed them. Our arrival sent their last reserves of adrenaline pumping through them so that it was depleted as we arrived. They were on the verge of letting go and sinking to their deaths. Pete had to work fast.

But he was a professional. He instinctively knew that he had to do a hypothermic lift. Had to keep them level, horizontal. Lifting them vertically, could be fatal. Royal navy experience. Three times he went down to them. Three times he winched them up and into the cabin. On the second last winch, he was in pain. He had wrenched his back dead lifting and manoeuvring one of them into the strops in an eight metre sea, 130 miles from Shannon in October in a 50 knot (60 mile an hour) wind. Noel quickly offered to switch places. Off intercom, Mike and I could hear them loudly discuss whether to switch. Pete insisted he continue.

When we had the three survivors in the helicopter, we started a search pattern, using up the last bit of fuel, to see if there was anyone else. But the men were hypothermic, and when Noel asked if there was anyone else, they shook their heads. We took them to Galway. They subsequently made a full recovery.

The afternoon crew in Shannon, refuelled when we returned, and went straight back out to search. Along with many fishing vessels, and a naval vessel, combing the vast expanse of ocean, searching for the other crew members. The ocean had committed the perfect crime. Again. No more clues. No trace. Thomas Kelly was not found. He was one of eight that perished when their vessel was hit by a big wave. The cruel sea. The men we picked up had been in the water for several hours, wearing light shirts and trousers. They had no life-jackets, and managed to survive by holding on to a simple life-ring. Just before we arrived, a fourth man who was with them, slipped his grip and slid away beneath them.

This same vessel had obliged us just the month before in practising winching on and off their deck. Thomas had just joined the crew for a few weeks. He was a member of the Fenit RNLI.

The SAR system worked. The satellite, the international

guard frequency 121.5, the alerting of the helicopter, the coastal radio network at Valentia, the position confirmation while we were en route. And finally the successful recovery of three survivors. But we did not feel that it was successful. The waves out there had taken eight men's lives. Hovering and collecting three survivors was like being at a safe distance from a tethered lion, sated, having already devoured the other eight victims.

33

TIGER BALM

He who opens a school door, closes a prison door.

Anon.

The Anorient incident happened during the day. We finished a little later than normal, but found ourselves back in our routine soon afterwards. My parents watched the news at home, knowing that it was me in the helicopter, half proud, half afraid. I rang them to put their minds' at ease. My wife did not know, being busy with the children at home. I rang her to tell her I would be late. We had to do a couple of interviews. 'Have you not seen the news?' I asked.

While the afternoon crew was flying up and back over a hundred miles offshore, I was at home with my three children again. They searched patterns given to them by the coast guard, calculated with the wind drift and time and current taken into account. Creeping line ahead patterns. Expanding boxes. While I sat with a cup of tea and watched *The Bear in the Big Blue House*, sniffing the screen, saying: 'You smell nice: have you been drinking milk? Warm milk?'

Sitting in our house, thinking of the sea. Noel's calm Tyrone accented voice, keeping me rooted to the spot above those floating desperate men. His voice competing in my head with Bear. The baby waking from her early afternoon snooze. Anna, cradled in my arms, so weak and defenceless. I held her close, not wanting the wind in my head to chill her. I rang my parents again.

And then it was bedtime. The children put to bed, the tiredness catching up. Sitting in front of the fire, ready to relax and talk about something else. Without realising, we had RTÉ 1 on. The number one item was the sinking of the *Anorient*. I watched again, and listened to see if there had been any bodies recovered. It struck me that it was an awful thing to hope for.

Rested and ready for action again the following day, I drove Alyson to school at Knockanean. If I did not, I would not see her awake at all that day. Six years of age then. Handed over by us to a school. Entrusting our first baby to strangers. As everyone does. Parents releasing the grip of tiny growing hands, watching them walk away. Hoping all will be well. I walked into the class with her. Not for her reassurance, but my own. And in those early years before I went to work, to try to pluck someone from death's grip, or to try to find dead bodies in the sea, the music that wafted from those classrooms, warmed me. Soothed me.

We crossed the school yard, the children playing before the bell rang. A game of soccer, with a goal post at each end of the yard. A game of Gaelic football played around the corner. The two games, with thirty boys running and scampering, sharing half the yard. Quieter children walked through each frantic, panting game, shyly making their way to their desk, their pencil case, their mooring for the day. Mothers walked the new ones, the little ones, child and parent red-eyed and anxious. Dodging in and out of each other, like a flock of starlings. Never knocking into each other, synchronised like the very starlings that gave their name to the school, Knockanean, Cnoc an Ean (Hill of Birds). I did not register at first, the principal, Pat McNamara, when he greeted me. Nodding and talking, and not knowing at first what I was saying. Then answering, his voice releasing me from my home movie.

Walking past the flower-filled window boxes outside, along

the corridor and the classrooms, holding her hand as she led me to her desk. Sneaking a look inside each one, as older children tuned their fiddles, or whistled away on their tin whistles, or asked for the notes for this jig or that reel. The tap, tap, tap of a fiddle bow, as Joan or Amy called them to order.

Alyson's classroom warming as the children trickled in gathering at different desks, like pools of water, giggling and fidgeting. The walls straining to hold up the colour. Thirty-one St Brigid's crosses, thirty-one multi-coloured paper daffodils smiling out from the wall, thirty-one home-made, black-and-red ladybirds made out of egg boxes, with eyes and black legs made from pipe cleaners. Freeze framed as they crawled up the walls, scurrying to God knows where. I went to work, happy. Recharged.

At work, we rested. Mike Shaw and myself again. New winch-crew this time, Eamonn Burns and John Manning. There had been hours and hours of searching done. By the helicopter and then by the navy and by fishing vessels. It is a harsh rule, but when a life is lost, the rescue helicopter has to reserve its energy for the next incident. You never know when the next one will come. At nine o'clock at night, we went home, on forty-five minutes standby again. I looked in at our sleeping baby, Anna, and then Niamh. Perhaps I read a story for Alyson. And then to bed myself.

4 a.m. Wake up call. Woof, woof. Pavlov's dog. No stumbling. No, I-wonder-who-that-is-at-this-time-of-the-night. Instantly awake. Instant calculation. Instant decisions.

'OK. Where? When? A couple of minutes ago. On my way. Ring the winch operator: that's John Manning.'

It was another foul night. Windows rattling and wind howling. Rain splattering against the bedroom window. The phone call woke my wife. The sound of the weather and the half conversation alarmed her. Talking as I staggered around the room, trying to get dressed.

'Fishing vessel aground near Galway. Bad night. We have to rush. We'll be fine. I won't be back.'

What I meant by that was that I would stay on the base after the mission was completed, but when I uttered those words they fell like spanners, clanging on the bedroom floor between us.

'Don't say that,' she said.

'Sorry,' I said, giving her a hug and kiss before I left. 'You know what I mean.'

The fishing vessel *Arosa* had set out from Scotland. Repaired, having been damaged, it set course for the fishing grounds off Ireland then sought shelter when a storm approached, force seven. Never making it to safety, fatigue and navigation errors led it to the Skerd Rocks, west of Galway Bay. There were thirteen in the crew. It hit the rocks just before 4 a.m. The sea and wind worse than the previous day, with the visibility down to a couple of hundred metres in fog. A Mayday call was made.

As I cursed and ran out the door, the crew were fighting for their lives on a windswept rock in Connemara. As we had done before, so we did again. Zero briefing. Zero fucking around. Get in. Get going. JFDI. Dive bomb into Galway Bay. Race across to the northern side. Handbrake turn before we hit the hills near Carraroe. Turn to face the datum. Turn to face the last known latitude and longitude of the sinking vessel. Flying only twenty minutes since we left Shannon, because of the tailwinds. Visibility zero from start to finish. Radar picture showed us a return. The red blob of the Skerd Rocks.

Once more Eamonn the winchman was ready. This time it

was pitch black. Plugged into the intercom as we descend to the sea below.

'One fifty. One hundred. Eighty. Sixty. Fifty. Surface contact.'

We could make out the sea. We drifted forward to the radar return, and then it appeared. A rock, about 90 feet high, higher than we were hovering, straight ahead, the sea frothing at its base, and boiling over on the other side too.

Possibly the worst moment of my rescue career happened then. Just a moment. Fleeting, and gone. But imprinting itself on me, and mocking me. We hovered there, just beside the rocks at Skerd, Doonguddle it is called. We could see the ship on the other side of the rocks, white water foaming around it, glowing with a phosphorescent light. A minute later, we saw the man whose life we would save, standing on the top of the rock, waving. But before I saw him, I saw something else.

Many, many life-jackets floated in the water. In the darkness, each had a light, that flashed and winked at us as the swell made them dance. I remember thinking, just for one moment, that we had arrived there in time, that they were all alive, that we were going to save everyone. We were going to move around the sea near the rock and pick them up one by one. Like an amusement arcade game, with a grappling hook, some coins and patience. We could pick them all up. But before I could express that thought, that hope, that dream, as a shout, or a silent prayer of thanks, I realised that they were all empty.

Damn. Damn. Damn. Or words to that effect. Visibility a couple of hundred metres. Storm force winds, hovering over the boiling sea, with 50 or 60 knots indicated on the airspeed indicator clock. We moved forward to the rock in front of us. It was higher than our hover. We climbed. The unseen wind rose over the rock, giving us extra lift to stay in position. I lowered the collective lever, so that we would not be lifted upwards into the low cloud. The helicopter shuddering in the torrent of confused air. John lowered Eamonn to the slippery wind-blasted rock below. Eamonn put a rescue strop over the casualty, shouting instructions to him. The man nodding, without understanding, yet understanding, as he tried to focus on the insistent communication in Eamonn's eyes.

He had only just scrambled onto the rock before the helicopter arrived. In the darkness, he had heard it, faintly at first, above the howl of the wind and the deep crash of the sea. Standing on the rock, he could not see the sea in the mist and darkness. Then the helicopter's light had appeared. Now that Eamonn stood in front of him, the man found it hard to concentrate. For behind Eamonn, illuminated by the lights of the hovering helicopter above them, he could see the walls of advancing water for the first time.

Once we had the man on board, his name was Ricardo by the way, we searched for others, hoping that some of the life-jackets were not empty. Backwards off the rock. Backwards and down, the rock slipping behind a veil of rain again. We saw one more man. We hovered, this time over the sea itself. Ricardo sitting in the back, shivering, with a blanket over him, peering out of a window, wondering if we would pluck any more of his crew out of the water.

The same sort of challenge as the *Anorient* lay ahead. Taking someone out of a big swell, but darkness and fog, added to the difficulty. As we hovered, I listened to John's patter as Mike cautioned me when we descended too low. I imagined Eamonn in the water below me. In my mind, I visualised him at the mercy of the sea and the wind, tossed and defenceless. Trying to pry one more man from death's grip. Trading with his own life into the bargain. Come on Eamonn, I thought. Knowing he would be fighting it out, with gritted teeth, eyes stinging from the salty water, hitting his face with the force of a pressure hose. John gave him slack cable, so that he would have room to manoeuvre. The cable going tight as a wave swept over him.

When that man was taken into the helicopter, that completed the first phase of the mission. Eamonn and John concentrated all their energies on that man. He turned out to be the *patron de pesca*, or skipper. It was about then that we heard Paddy Mullin, the coxswain of the Aran Islands RNLI Lifeboat, on the radio. Announcing that they were on scene, commencing search, helicopter in sight.

Wayne Stuart Cole on his first callout. Aongus Dillane, Johnny Mulkerrin and Joe Gill too. The RNLI crew that came out to train on sunny afternoons. Or in the evenings, pushing back their chairs at home, and saying '*Slán leat, tá na* lads *as* Shannon *ag teacht ag cleachtadh*/the Shannon crew is coming to train.' Meeting us so we could be ready for nights like this. Martin Fitzpatrick, Martin Coyne, Vincent McCarron, Pádraig Dillane, Michael O'Flaherty, Ronan MacGiolla Pharaic, Steve Kilmartin and David Beatty (RIP). Others whose names I didn't know. From before the Shannon Helicopter Rescue was established: Bartley Mullin, Gerry O'Toole (RIP), Michael Gill, Sinead Nic Giolla Pharaic, Pádraig Eanna, Martin and Liam Dillane. And sometimes Dr Marion Broderick herself. In snatched conversations, in *Tig Joe Mac*'s pub in Kilronan, once a year we would meet, to say thanks.

Mike and I searched as much as we could, moving over and downwind and forward again. Nothing. No one. We left and took the casualties to Galway hospital. Our priority to stabilise these survivors. An unspoken re-categorisation of subsequent flights as body searches. Leaving the Aran lifeboat to search in hope for living survivors, navigating their way amongst the treacherous fog shrouded rocks, on that huge sea swell, with currents trying to trick them.

That second man did not make it. It was his time. We tried to save him. Eamonn did everything he could, pulling him back from the brink of death. Then John and Eamonn together desperately worked on him in the helicopter, as we raced towards the hospital. The hospital staff at Galway tried to save him too. We did not fail. Although we thought it at the time. It was his time. God pulled him out of our grasp, slipping to the light and the peace of oblivion.

The Dublin rescue helicopter arrived, my friend, my rugby-playing, beer-drinking, joke-telling friend, Jim Kirwan, the captain. No friendship on the radio this time. No quips. Just the weather report, the latitude and longitude of the vessel, a brief of what we had done and what the coast guard wanted done. Over the course of the morning, we took it in turns to search. The visibility was too bad for us both to be in there at low level.

We left after a while, grimly saying goodbye to Jim and his crew. The dawn had already arrived. The radio was silent as we left. As other vessels joined the search, we could not find any encouraging words to say to our comrades in the Dublin helicopter.

Arriving at Galway airport once more. Greeted by the ever helpful, ever familiar voice of Tony Gibson. Used to shepherd us home to Gormanstonn, from his perch in the tower there. Still shepherding me home to safety and fuel and a welcome.

'Rescue 115, you're cleared to land. Wind 270 at thirty-two knots. No traffic. Have you time for a cuppa?'

''Fraid not Tony. Thanks all the same.'

Interviews with journalists after we returned. Telephone calls.

'Eamonn: would you mind talking to the *Indo*?'

'No. Not now. I've got to clean the sea tray.'

One of the oncoming crew, hand on his shoulder, almost gently: 'Take the call Eamonn. We'll clean the aircraft.'

Exhaustion. The sweaty lines and marks on our heads and hair, from the insulation pads of our yellow helmets. Unzipping our immersion suits. The smell of sweat. Lighting up cigarettes.

'*Limerick Leader*, Jimmy Woulfe on the line.'

Nodding a silent thank you, as someone placed a hot cup of tea in front of me. Placing it on the perspex covered chart of Galway Bay.

'Lorna Siggins, marine correspondent from the *Irish Times*.'

I sat at home that night. Back to normality. I went to bed for a while in the afternoon, and then got up in time to kiss my children good night. A story each. A kiss. An 'I love you'. Someone from the coast guard rang, apologising for ringing me at home. After the rescue. Well done, by the way. *Sky News* want an interview. Would I do it? Ten minutes later, sitting on my kitchen floor, with a glass of red wine, the phone cable twisting out through the closed door, I took the call.

'Chris Skudder, *Sky News*. That story in Ireland. Two fishing vessels in two days. Twenty men feared dead. On the line we have the captain of the coast guard helicopter, Captain David Courtney. Good evening.'

'Good evening.'

'Twenty men feared dead. What were conditions like out there?'

I immediately regretted taking the call. I felt unable to put adequately into words what it had all been like. His focus on the dead, unnerved me for a moment, but he was just doing his job. So I did mine. I ignored his questions, giving him the answers that I wanted. Four men saved. Tremendous co-operation between the rescue services. And all that. But twenty dead was how they introduced the interview and concluded it.

Over the following days and weeks, a huge search operation was mounted. As big as the terrible *Carrickatine* disaster off the Donegal coast in 1999: shore teams, helicopters, naval vessels, lifeboats, aeroplanes. The search area divided into boxes of reducing probability. Cut up and doled out on a daily basis, each team given a specific area to search for bodies. Flying in our helicopter, we followed made-up, unnatural patterns, with straight lines and acute angles, calculated patterns that came from drift and wind, from tide and local current. Everything that was known about the local natural forces, written into computer code, logic gates and flip flops turning the curves straight.

Antonio Gaudi, the great Catalan architect, detested straight lines. His designs flowed. His buildings echoed the scales of fish and the curl of leaves. Nature was his master. He its servant. Those search patterns we flew, those straight lines and angles, were mocked by nature. As we turned, the acute angle became a curve in the sky. The shapes of leaves and fish, replaced boxes and grids.

The search area grew, pushed out by the wind, flowing along the coast with the currents and tides. The islands near the Skerd rocks again. Mason Island, St McDara's Island. Up to Croaghnakeela. Roundstone and Muvey, where my dad and I had fished. The search taking us along the shore, past the creek where we used to swim when the tide was out. Looking for bodies where I remembered my sisters Ruth and Hilary screaming as they dived into the icy waters. The Adamses with us, Monica, Dolores, Terence and their mum and dad, Kathleen and Terry senior.

Back over the sea to search, the home movie stopped. Returning to the shore. Near Roundstone where Joe Rafferty's shop used to be, just outside the village. The sound of the car tyres, crunching the gravel as we arrived. Walking into the shop, the ill-fitting door jammed against the concrete floor. A push to open it, to get into the Aladdin's cave. The bell that jangled, as the door released. The rustle of newspaper from the back room, the paper put down, as Joe emerged

The shop boarded up now, as I watched it pass beneath my rudder pedals. The shop where I would pick out an Airfix model aeroplane from the row of toys to take back and make if it was raining. It slid past as we turned, continuing along the shore, in and out meandering in the hope that we might see a limb protrude from seaweed. Then back at the village again. Nestled at the foot of Errisbeg. The famous picture postcard view of the harbour and the Twelve Bens in the distance, framed between the top of the instrument panel, and the line that marked the beating of the blades. The harbour wall outside O'Dowd's pub.

'Come on now. Look at the camera. Fergus; stand still will you. Where's Ruth ? Monica; will you tell your mammy to stop talking and come out. And tell her we want Vera in it too. Cheeeese.'

The search was not in vain. Bodies were found. Not all of them. But bodies were found. I think we found the last one. At Gorteen Bay. A T-shaped peninsula, sticking out into the Atlantic. On one side, Dog's Bay beach. On the other, Gorteen beach. Both beautiful. I had walked those peninsula's from rock to rock. Looking for places to fish with my dog Laddie barking at the sea gulls, running excitedly after them. In the evenings, I used to run across the rocks to a small natural harbour when the currachs returned. They used to throw me the crabs claws: they only wanted the lobsters. The sea was calm as we approached. One hundred metres from that perfect crescent shaped beach, in the middle of that bay, was a shape. The FLIR camera picked up the shape, but not the heat. It was the same temperature as the water. As we came closer, we could see that it was a body. Naked, white and bloated and face down. We approached so that our downdraft would not push it back down again. We got ready. One of the winchcrew leaned forward between myself and the other pilot. He offered us some Tiger Balm.

'Just take a little bit on your finger. Dab it under your nostrils. You won't be able to smell anything. Only Tiger Balm.'

34

MOONLIGHT AND UNDERWATER TORCHLIGHT

To the timid and hesitating, everything is impossible, because it seems so.
Anon.

Shannon Helicopter SAR was no longer alone. In Donegal the air corps had a Dauphin again. In Dublin airport, a coast guard Sikorsky and crew were available just as we were. We overlapped and helped each other out. Most notably when the Shannon crew went to assist a fishing vessel on fire one night. The crew had abandoned ship, and were already in life-rafts when the Shannon helicopter arrived. At extended range and in heavy swell, the task of winching them out of those life-rafts, proved extremely difficult. Having managed to lift three of them, they departed, leaving their winchman, Noel Donnelly, behind.

The Dublin crew arrived. By this time it was light and, another fishing vessel had come alongside, skilfully taking the whole lot of them on board. They all survived. Noel was rightly awarded a silver medal in recognition of his bravery. Calmly detaching himself from the winch cable as the helicopter departed, 170 miles from shore at night beside a burning trawler. The image that most of us could not shake, however, was of the expressions on the Spanish fishermen's faces, circled around in the raft, when Noel took a waterproof bag out of his ankle pocket, took out his cigarettes, and asked in his strong Tyrone accent if anyone had a light.

Each year, about 150 missions take place. Everyone averages

out with easy ones, pleasant ones, difficult ones, and every winter, a couple of bastards, thrown in for good measure. Every callout was different. The west coast was not the only place with difficult sea and swell conditions. The average wave may be statistically higher there but the east and the south-east have other variables. The Atlantic swell wraps and bends itself around Mizen, changing its behaviour, its clean swell lines, shaped by local tides and races, as it curls around Hook Head and then Carnsore Point.

The Point where my Irish teacher, Eoin Rossiter, grew up. Did he soak up the wind as a child? Did he look out and see the Saltee Islands sitting on a mirror glass sea? And wonder if they would sink when the sea got angry? My unifying theory of everything, that made me smile in private contemplation as we flew, could see the sounds of the wind and the sea once more. Beside each beautiful shore, the Irish language clung, nourished instead of eroded by the force of it.

A new phase of my life. Drifting into it, like a carefree fisherman, in a small boat with no anchor. My father on his final slow journey. My children starting on theirs. The music of Knockanean washing over and back each day, washing the sea or the wind into them, the beat of it, the softness of it, the love of it and the grief of it. The teachers, Joan McNamara and Amy McGennis, John Corbett and Tina Gavin, custodians of the ancient flame they nurtured and passed on.

The Mazurka, Danny Murphy's, The Kerry Cow, Port na bPúcaí, Port Ceann Boirne. Places and people alive in the fingers of their fiddle bows and tin whistles. Though our children were not dancing yet themselves, they watched the older ones, mimicking and stumbling, laughing and falling over. Then starting on the dance itself. Until it became as much a part of them as their thoughts. Until they step and turn and pirouette, standing and waiting impatiently for mammy and daddy to hurry up the conversation in the shopping centre, or outside the post office.

'And how is your dad?' (Cross over and back, skip one, two three ...)

'We must all go out for a drink some evening. It's so hard to find the time, isn't it?' (Down, hop up, hop up, down hop up, point, back two three ...)

'I'll collect after school if you do the swimming run on Thursday.' (Turn one, two, three, four, cross and one, two ...)

'There's a race in Kilmihil on Saturday. Are you driving?' (Jump out, in and point hop back ...)

The hours and hours of practice. Their dance teachers in later years, Ann and Sharon O'Connell and Niamh Slevin, giving them the steps that marry the music.

Flying through the landscape of R.L. Praeger's book, we followed the way that he went to Maam Cross, through the Inagh Valley, Benbaun on the left, and so on before arriving at Clew Bay, to find Achill RNLI lifeboat waiting to play. Up and back. Concentrating on the business at hand, admiring Clew Bay as we turned to start again. The chapel on the top of Croagh Patrick, the white-washed walls shining in the sun. Who carries the white-wash up to do that? How long does it take? Do they do it more than once a year? (John Cumming from Lecanvey does it. Each June he spends a week painting it in preparation for the pilgrimage in July. Taking the paint and equipment up by donkey mostly, helicopter the odd time. The old and the new. No bother to a man that climbs the Reek sixty times a year, either to look over the chapel itself, or just for the fresh air and the exercise, or just for the hell of it. His own pilgrimage. He is the man that makes the chapel glow in the sunshine.)

And then back around the coast, by High Island and Aughras Beg, south to Aran, past Gort na gCapaill, where the writer Liam

O'Flaherty lived as a child, recalling his stories of cows falling over cliffs and catching fish and huge waves crashing.

Search exercises with the south-eastern mountain rescue team (SEMRA). Perhaps the Comeraghs or the Galtees. Collecting them at their carefully prepared landing sites in the almost secret Nire Valley. Dropping them close to the top of Coumshingaun, that corrie lake that Seamas O'Dea in the Christian Brothers told me about. Or with the Dingle coast guard team: Frank Heidtke, Tom Kennedy and Mike O'Shea and the rest of them, plotting ambitious exercises near Feoghanagh or Brandon Creek. Winching to and from the RIB just outside Dingle harbour, where Funghi the dolphin leaped. Or dropping them off along the ridge of Masatiompan, near the deserted ruins of the famine village. Gazing down at the Three Sisters, and on to Tearaght in the distance.

And often in our travels back and forth, we would meet the Irish Helicopters Bolkow, circling the coast continuously, servicing the lighthouses that are the first step in saving lives at sea. In days gone by, Fergus O'Connor, Tom Browne, Gay Rogers and Joe Durrin, then Seán Oakes and briefly his son Cathal, who now flies the S-61 himself, Mick Hennessy and Mick Conneely, and later Colm Martin. Perhaps slinging thirty tons of building material onto Eagle Island after a storm. A bit at a time, lifted from the helicopter deck of the ship *Grainuaile*, and carefully placed within the compound walls. The electricians and carpenters, painters and computer men, standing waving from the Bull Rock or Tearaght or Straw Island as we passed by. These are the modern lighthouse keepers. These are the ones who keep the lights as faithfully as those who lived there in times gone by.

We received a call one evening to help out in the Burren. The information was sketchy. I rang Mattie in Doolin directly to see what was up. A rock fall in a cave near Lisdoonvarna, had trapped a caver under a boulder, in a fragile cave. Doolin as usual were called to figure it out. We were on standby to take the man to hospital, whenever they got him out. While we plotted the position on the map, they built a wooden frame over the trapped man, so that he would be protected from any more rock falls. When we forgot that it was still going on, and heated our dinners in the microwave, the paramedics set up an intravenous drip.

It was taking hours. The young man was alive but the longer it took to free him, the more desperate it became. Doolin has cave rescue expertise in the team. Conor McGrath, Ray Murphy and Pat Cronin are certified cave rescuers. Or maybe just certified. The intravenous drip was to fight potential toxic shock. The trapped leg would pool its blood and fluid, releasing it would send a rush of blood back into the limb, saving it from amputation. But releasing the leg would release those fluids back into the body where their effect could be toxic and lethal. As they prepared to lift the rock, inflating a bag, given to them by the fire brigade and normally used for car accidents, we were called to the Aran Islands.

We flew out to collect someone for Galway hospital. On our way, at dusk, we found the rocky hillside in the Burren. Hovering nearby, we saw many cars, the ambulance and the flashing garda car. Spotting a place where we could land later in the dark if needed, we departed.

It went on for hours. Stabilising the casualty. Making the cave safe. Lifting the huge rocks. The air corps in Finner brought cave rescuers and equipment from Northern Ireland. They went to work stabilising him, making the area safe for him and themselves, bringing heat to raise the cave temperature by a few degrees, making sure to keep it ventilated. Carefully removing the rocks and boulders. Preparing the route, yard by yard, from the casualty, through the cave and to the waiting ambulance. Clawing the man out of the earth, out of the grip of death again. Technique and training, care and patience, sweat and aching bodies and fatigue. The man was freed in the early hours. They decided to send him by road as he was stable. One of the biggest cave rescues ever done, and done in our back yard, but no news of it. No applause. Hundreds of hours. Blood sweat and tears. Danger and risk and bravery. Ordinary people doing extraordinary work.

Limerick river rescue are another team we worked with. Originally Trevor Sheehan, Tony Cusack, Jimmy Connors and a few more, now numbering over twenty-five volunteer divers. Searching for those who have fallen into the fast flowing dark Shannon waters. Laying down search lines, marker buoys and weighted lines. Getting their underwater cameras and torches ready. Their wet suits, their regulators, their weight belts, masks and fins. Ringing Ardnacrusha hydro-electric power station to drop from four to two turbines so that the river flow rate will halve. Waiting forty minutes for it to take effect. Then into the water, while people walk past on their way shopping. Into the river to look for the bodies of those who have fallen in or who seek peace in the reeds. The blessing of a Christian burial depending on Limerick river rescue and other dive teams like them.

At mass, the priest invites the congregation to turn to the person nearest, to exchange the sign of peace. With nods and smiles, the hands are shaken. Perfect strangers exchange the sign of peace, saying 'Peace be with you'. And often when I see that at mass, I think of the cave rescue, the lifeboat rescue, the mountain rescue, the diver, the winchman struggling to keep his footing on a deck that is awash. I wonder if those people in the congregation, strangers to each other, would die for each other? Would they look for someone's body in the muddy reeds so that they might live or so that his family could bury him?

Would they be willing to lay down their lives for a stranger? Because that is what they risked in the cave in Lisdoonvarna that night. No greater love hath a man, than to lay it down for another. Isn't that what the bible says? The men and women suiting up in mountain, cave, cliff or lifeboat crew do just that. The invisible army marches against an enemy they cannot defeat, only hold at bay.

The cliffs around our coast are so lethal. A slip and it's all over. A walk, a gasp at the beautiful view, a gust of wind, a stone catching the shoe. A walk becomes a slip, becomes a slide, becomes an end. One evening, a young man fell down the 100-foot cliff on the west side of the Old Head of Kinsale. His family alerted the local coast guard unit, and Eddie Butler in nearby Garretstown.

Eddie Butler, the local area officer, in charge of a motley crew of volunteers. Eddie is from a lighthouse family, his father a lighthouse keeper. A path Eddie followed. Between them, they kept each and every light around the coast, at different times in their careers. Eddie, along with a big family, was brought up at Galley Head.

I was part of the crew that night. When Eddie called, we responded. I spoke to him about that night many times over the coming years. His memory of what happened was intertwined with Jesus and the bible. His spirituality allowed him to tell the story of how a man's grip on life loosened in his arms. His convictions gave him strength, and the others gathered round, as they watched us take the man away, to live or to die.

He told me that they had gathered at the top, and could hear the sound of the sea washing against the shore and the cliffs getting louder as they drew nearer. The night was clear, crystal clear and very cold.

They began to set up their abseil ropes, the luff tackle, the safety lines, the generators and the light stands, at the cliff edge. Below them, the sea shimmered and two moons watched them impassively: one up high, the other its reflection on the clean flat sea below. A gentle north-westerly breeze came up bringing with it the familiar smell of seaweed and brine. On the horizon, not far off shore, the lights of silent trawlers winked.

Within minutes the climbing ropes were in position. Tripods, angled backwards in the field beside the cliff, hammered into the frosty grass, held them. The light stands probed the darkness of the gully below, as silence gave way to the sound of a diesel generator, and the team's instructions. The young man lay crumpled far below, the sea lapping at his feet, waiting to wash away his mortal coil.

Eddie was ready. Steady Eddie. He harnessed himself up, connected to the abseil rope and gave a thumbs-up. As he descended, the noises above faded until they were just echoes. Soon it was just Eddie, the rope, the cliff and the sea below. He went from his world of control, to another world where the sea governed. The only sounds now were his own breathing and the lapping of the waves. He stopped at regular intervals, looking down to see his way to the young man. He moved to the left and to the right until he reached the bottom of the cliff. He looked up and saw the rope snaking upwards to the searchlights and the one or two faces watching him. He gave a thumbs-up and turned his attention to the young man. He was alive.

He knelt beside him, held his hand, listened and assessed the man's injuries: fractured skull, broken legs, each folded sickeningly beneath his torso, multiple abrasions and flesh wounds. As he listened to the young man's jumbled words, he fought the retching reflex in his stomach as the head wound opened and leaked black blood with every word, every strained movement of the boy's mouth. Eddie hid his reactions and his fears. Other team members came down the rope out of the darkness. They froze momentarily as they heard the boy's slurred words before turning their attention to the injuries.

They had already asked for the helicopter as the young man's life depended on rapid movement to hospital. He was fading. The team began to pray with him, one holding his hand, another making the sign of the cross on his forehead after each Hail Mary:

Sé do bheatha, a Mhuire,
Atá lán de ghrásta,
Tá an Tiarna leat,
Is beannaithe thú idir mná …

Then the young man stopped talking and breathing. They began CPR, taking it in turns and timing each other. Eddie started to say an act of contrition, as he had heard it as a child in Irish, his first language until he was ten. The words of the prayer echoed off the cliff that rose above them, mingling with sea and breeze, becoming one.

Eddie peered upwards towards the stars as he heard the distant drone of the helicopter. He made out its flashing lights high up in the sky. His radio crackled to life and then like magic the helicopter put on its searchlights. Eddie could feel the adrenaline in his veins, as the helicopter descended and we began our slow unfaltering approach to the searchlights above him. A moth to a flame.

35

ACCOUNT SETTLED

I adore simple pleasures. They are the last refuge of the complex.
                                                    Oscar Wilde

In early 2001, a Spanish fishing vessel, registered in Germany, sank in the early hours of the morning, 200 miles north-west of Donegal and Mayo, about 230 miles west of the western isles of Scotland. The *Hansa* had a crew of sixteen. Clyde Coastguard in Scotland co-ordinated the rescue operation. Once again an EPIRB started the ball rolling, its transmissions initially picked up by orbiting satellite. The nearest rescue helicopter, the UK Coastguard Stornoway S-61, was scrambled. Arriving on scene just after 3 a.m., they had to contend with a difficult heavy swell and storm force winds. They managed superbly. In the dark, at their maximum range from Scotland, they winched nine of the crew from life-rafts. That left seven missing. Before they could attempt to locate them and rescue them, they had to return to land due to their low fuel levels.

While this was happening, and suspecting that they would need extra rescue assets, to use their terms, they asked the Irish coast guard for assistance. They called us at home just after 5 a.m. We were in the air half an hour later, heading once more for Blacksod. With me was Cliff Pile co-pilot, Eamonn Burns winchman and John Manning winch operator. Dawn was breaking as we reached Blacksod Bay. One detail that was nagging at us was that we could not retract our undercarriage. We had to fly with them down all the time due to a minor hydraulic problem. This small detail was going to affect our day. Wheels down meant extra drag, which meant higher fuel burn and so less range and less time for a rescue.

We waited there on standby. Calculating. Scratching our heads. For some reason, call it Murphy's Law, we had zero weather information for Scotland. We reckoned that to get to the reported position, we would have to continue on to Scotland afterwards. We waited trying to get weather data. And waited. It was unclear whether they were going to use us or not. A royal navy helicopter from Prestwick in Scotland was also en route, battling against very strong winds. An RAF Nimrod was on scene too searching and acting as OSC, co-ordinating with vessels nearby, and the approaching helicopter. Mid morning, Dublin MRCC told us we were being tasked. We received an updated position and queried it. It was right on maximum range.

We took off anyway, knowing that someone would get us a weather report while we were on our way out and that if the Stornoway helicopter had returned home, we would surely be able to follow them north-east later on. On and on we went, very strong winds pushing us away from Mayo and Donegal, onwards towards the search area. The same winds would slow us to a crawl on the return. Our wheels being locked down, we would burn more fuel than usual. We were reaching our point of no return (PNR). Decision time. Could we continue? What's the weather in Scotland? What's the updated search datum? What will we do, lads?

'Rescue 115. This is Rescue 22. We have been informed that the rescue helicopter from Prestwick has turned back. Due head winds. We have a weather report for Benbecula. Understand you are waiting for it. Advise when ready to copy.'

Jimmy Quinn. Lt Jimmy Quinn from Clarecastle. Joined the air corps a few years after me. Flying the air corps Casa on a fishery patrol. Diverted to help by the coast guard.

'Rescue 22. This is Rescue 115. Go ahead with the Benbecula weather.'

Clearance on the forecast. With the Prestwick helicopter unable to get out to the scene, we were the only ones that could. We reached the PNR and passed it hopefully. Next stop Scotland. Jimmy handed us over to the Nimrod a few minutes later. We wished each other luck. I thanked him. Words were not enough.

By the time we reached the scene, we had agreed that we would go all out to 'get our man'. We agreed to give it twenty minutes or so on the scene, even though that would leave us with less than normal fuel reserves. As we arrived, we were told a man had been located a few minutes before and been taken on board one of the searching trawlers. He was alive, hypothermic and awaiting us to evacuate him to hospital. There was a low cloud base, and the sea swell was pretty big.

We found the vessel, guided to it with no delay. No winching circuit. Stop. Start. Winch. It was an awkward deck to winch to. In a big swell, we had our work cut out in the short time we had. We broke two hi-lines doing it, but we did not care. We lifted the man off the deck in eight minutes. Knowing full well, that whatever challenges we were facing, they were nothing compared to what the Stornoway crew had faced at 3 a.m.

We made ready to depart, then the Nimrod passed on another report of men seen in the water. Fuel running low. The Nimrod gave us heading and position which we hastily entered into the computer, then told us to fly at 100 feet because they were down searching low level too. With thirty feet waves, it felt like we were going to wash the wheels as we flew. The Nimrod whistled past, ghosting low between us and the cloud base above. We felt like ducking our heads.

Bingo. Bingo fuel. Chicken fuel.

'Rescue 115 departing. Can you confirm a course to steer for Benbecula?'

The score at the end of the of the search operation was God 6, rescue agencies 10. One for us and nine for Stornoway. We flew through a NATO exercise on our way back to Benbecula. Our computer, and our whizz wheels, and our admiralty chart and dead reckoned pencil plot, and our handheld Psion computers, all said that we would arrive with ten minutes' fuel left. We reached Benbecula where the weather was clearing, the same place I had refuelled on my way to and from St Kilda a few years before.

An ambulance took our man away smiling and shaking our hands, John Manning in the cold clear day, said he had always wanted to come to Benbecula. A HM coastguard official in a high visibility jacket, shook my hand and welcomed me. I started to tell him we would be ready to go again in about ten minutes, expecting to go back out to search again for the missing men. His phone rang. He answered and then handed it to me.

'Dave. Geoff Livingstone here. I'm with Liam. Listen, we just want to say well done. It's all over the news. They finally seem to be getting the message that the Irish coast guard and the UK coastguard operate together on operations like this. The minister has asked me to pass on his congratulations too. We're very proud of you all. Please tell the rest of the crew for me. Will you make sure now? … And Dave, you're not coming back. OK. Stay up there. The search for the others is continuing. But not with your crew. OK. They have aircraft and vessels and you're to go to Stornoway. It's all arranged. We have a backup crew and helicopter in Shannon already. Go and have a beer. We're buying.'

That was the assistant director of the Irish coast guard on the phone, and the director, Liam Kirwan, with him. During my military career, the only reason someone in a position like that had ever wanted to speak to me was to kick my arse. It was a pleasant change. And we all appreciated it. Especially not having to fly all the way home again.

'So you're telling us, that we have been ordered to drink beer in Stornoway, stay the night, and fly back tomorrow?'

'Yep. That's the last order received.'

The following day we flew back all the way from Stornoway to Shannon. Take a look at a map. Take out an atlas and see the line that joins those places. Ardvourlie, North Uist, Balivanich, Daliburgh, Barra. Looking east to Skye and Tiree on the way. The names, the knife cuts made by wind and ocean. The villages that cling to the shores. Then Ireland rolled into view. As Ireland scrolled under our blades, our helicopter like a slow moving computer mouse on a living chart, I thought again of Dave. And Mick. And Paddy. And Niall and Michael Heffernan as we passed Mayo. And those they left behind.

I heard music as we flew, watching our shadow on the scattered clouds, looking at the rainbow that we made on the white cloud as we passed. Only those who fly or climb mountains know that the rainbow is a circle, only seen from above. A perfect multi-coloured circle of light that follows us along. Depending on the time of day, the direction you travel and whether you look and see. And notice. Didn't Jesus say, 'Follow me, I am the light'? But we are afraid, not being perfect like Him. With too many cuts, cracks and bruises. But didn't Leonard Cohen also say, 'Cracks are what let the light in'? In that circle of light, that fleeting ghost of colour, was our shadow. The rainbow has no end, but it does have a pot of gold: our very lives. We are the living breathing pot of gold.

In Stornoway the night before, we sat in our immersion suits, rolled down to our waists, as more and more HM Coastguard people came to say hello. We met some of the Stornoway helicopter crews and swapped stories. While we did, the search was still under way for those missing men. Fishing vessels, naval vessels, the Stornoway S-61 again, aircraft from the NATO exercise as well as Nimrods.

We were all exhausted. The sea once more had taken lives. We were not in celebratory mood but in the bar, away from the wind and the sea where we all had been, there was an unspoken agreement to celebrate life: our lives, our company, the rare meeting of people who might never meet again. The method of recording purchases at the bar that night was to write down 'sandwiches' on the bar chits instead of 'beer'. The queen of England bought a lot of sandwiches that night. She never let the Irish coast guard spend a cent.

Drifting in and out of the conversations, I thought of the time when we had been defeated by the ocean swell, when the royal navy Sea King had managed to do what we could not. It occurred to me that the elements had been against them this time. The head winds had barred their way to success but the same winds had pushed us on instead.

Not that anyone keeps an account of these things. Not that anyone records the successes and failures of rescue. But if they did, if somewhere there was a ledger, equivalent to the recording of income and expenditure, I reckoned that I could consider it balanced. Account settled.

36

DANCING AT DUNQUIN

Walk easy when your jug is full.

John B. Keane

Decisions. Decisions. How to make decisions. Four people in a crew. Each carefully selected and trained. Each programmed to be assertive and knowledgeable. Each having the 'A type' assertive positive personality that copes with difficulties and relishes challenges. Put them together and then turn up the heat, increase the pressure, stand back, and watch the sparks fly.

That can happen in helicopter rescue now and again but it rarely does. Aircrew are trained and in the habit of decision-making, especially group decision making. It's now standard in aviation. Let's talk it over. Group hug. What do you think? The problem in helicopter SAR is that there are so many options. The flexibility of the machine can become a liability. You can almost do anything.

The process of decision-making is tackled by using acronyms. There are many. A popular one is DODAR, DIAGNOSE the problem, choose OPTIONS, DECIDE on one of the options, ACTION: take the action you decided on, and REVIEW how it went. That process goes on continuously during a rescue. It involves not just the crew in the helicopter, but also the other units working with it, controlling it, or being controlled by it, in the case of the helicopter being told it is OSC.

Picture the actor Tommy Lee Jones pursuing Harrison Ford in *The Fugitive,* striding purposefully along a corridor, as the latest news breaks. Staccato analysis and decision-making on the hoof, Hollywood style. His breathless gumshoes, trying to keep up.

'Let's work the problem people.' – Get ready for the brief.

'We have a fugitive on the loose. Armed and dangerous.' – Diagnose the problem.

'We can wait for him to strike again, or we hunt him down.' – Options

'I say we hunt him down.' – Decisions

'I want the city shut down, people. No one moves without my say so. Road blocks on every highway. Call out the National Guard and stop all flights out of the city.' – Action

And then the film is a process of constant review. And constant DODAR. Now picture the helicopter SAR crew. Backed up by checklists and routines and constant doubting. Any member of the crew who feels uneasy must say so. There can be all sorts of problems and complications. The fishing vessel captain may not speak English. The vessel may not be able to change course. The vessel may be still fishing and going in the wrong direction. The wind may have changed over the previous ten minutes. The navigation computer says you do not have enough fuel to get home. You have just put the winchman on the deck. You are flying around the coast at low level. Your radar fails.

The casualty is on the deck and ready to be winched. He is positioned on the worst area surrounded by fishing gantries and aerials. The winch operator thinks you can manage, you do not. Twenty minutes fuel left. Same as above, except you think you can do it and the winch operator thinks not. Same fuel.

There are a lot more scenarios.

The crew talk it over if time permits. Each has an opinion.

All must be heard. The options must be outlined. And a decision must be made. And then acted upon and then reviewed to see if it's right. And on and on and on and on. Until the rotor brake is applied back at base. And you fall out of the helicopter, exhausted from flying and from DODARing. And you try to learn. To listen. To be positive and patient. But it is tiring.

But then along comes experience. The day arrives when problems are smoothed over with trust and familiarity with each other and with everything you do. It is a powerful feeling, when the helicopter is armoured with the steel of a team that can be honest with each other, to be able to say, 'Let's give it a lash' or 'I can't do this'.

One night that stretched my armour-plated crew sticks in my mind. A Spanish trawler, 200 miles offshore on the Atlantic Ocean. Winter time at night. What else! We climbed into cloud and spent two hours flying to the trawler without sight of land, sea or stars. We were outwardly cheerful as usual, but the vice tightened on us all the way out. We flew north of the Dingle Peninsula. The outline of the coast was clear on our radar, drifting past us on our left side, then fading to nothing as we faced out into the Atlantic. Alone.

I thought of my wife and family, asleep, safe and sound at home. Oblivious. Thinking of them always warmed me and gave me strength. Especially that night for some reason. A prayer for each of our children, for my parents. And my wife. A prayer that this would go OK.

It was very dark. Sometimes there is a faint glow from starlight, or if you are lucky there might be moonlight. The waves may come at you invisibly in the darkness, but the white tops are sometimes ever so slightly lit with phosphorescence. It helps you to gauge the rhythm of the sea and the size of the waves. It helps you to predict when and how the ship will move. It helps get the job done. It can mean the difference between life and death. We watched the movement, our winchman mentally noting the fishing gantries, the railings, the fish boxes and the nets, registering each detail in case he started to swing from side to side as we approached the deck. A soft landing on the heaped nets if it all worked out. Watching the fishermen below us as they staggered on the deck, clutching the railings beside the stretcher where their injured comrade lay.

A smooth crew. No pressure. Trusted me, trusted each other. We can do it. Encouraging when the deck misbehaved, and when the winchman swung beneath us. Whether I flew well or very well, or the winch operator pattered well. Who knows? It worked. We arrived. We hovered. We did not have much time. We briefed. We flew the dummy deck which went well and then we put our winchman on the deck. It was like holding a cow which struggles before the vet gives it an injection and then stops moving, resigned to the fact that this has to happen.

Back to the hover over the deck again, to pick them up, winchman and casualty. Off the deck like a cork out of a bottle of champagne. Into the helicopter as we climbed away. The casualty was safe and on his way to a hospital in Ireland, far from his home. He was stable and going to live. He had a broken arm and leg, head injuries, cuts and bruises. Lying on the stretcher, he sat up and smiled as we looked back at him. '*Hola, Buenos Dias,*' we shouted to him.

Flying toward the rising sun, I imagined myself at home. My mental DJ played Spanish music. Rodrigo and his music of the mountains, serenaded me as the Blaskets drew closer. I imagined myself pirouetting slowly in our kitchen with Anna, our baby, holding her face up to mine, humming the melody. My father's music. Music that he would sit and listen to, leaning back, with eyes closed, tasting it, savouring the sound, as if it was a good

wine on the tongue. At home in Tullamore, in our bungalow beside the bog, the warmth of that turf fire, the smell of it.

And so my mind wandered to him again. I held his hand as
he sat in his wheelchair. The same music playing in our kitchen
at home. My childhood, my past, my present and my day dreams,
one. He snoozed as I reminisced about the sea trout I had caught
at Murvey in Connemara. And though I thought he was asleep,
he lifted his head and smiled. As we flew, I smiled back at him.
I smiled back at him as a child at home, thirty years before in
Tullamore. I smiled back at him in his wheelchair, sitting in our
kitchen, closing his eyes as he relished the wine, the music and
family. I smiled as I flew, smiling at the memory of a smile.

And there was my mother in Kerry. I pictured her sitting on
the wall by Mulcahy's pottery, Potadóireacht na Caolóige. With
Sybil Head behind her, she sat smoking a cigarette in the sunshine, my father beside her smoking too. And like a photograph
that you have seen many times, but never registered the detail,
as we flew, I could see that they were holding hands.

We flew back to the coast and the weather improved. We
were heading east to Tralee hospital. Grey morning light greeted
us. As the lighthouse winked at us, we watched the sun rise over
Mount Brandon. The clouds cleared and the dawn light bright-
ened. The grey began to evaporate. Encouraging us. Rewarding
us. Welcoming us back to shore. To safety. Lifting our tiredness,
unknown to us. I remember feeling myself smile.

'He wants a cigarette.'

Silence.

'He can't have one, can he?'

'Why not? He has broken bones. But his pulse is fine. It
won't hurt him.'

'On the grounds that it could be of medicinal value: will we
let him?'

'Fair enough, tell him he can smoke.'

Silence.

'Well if he's having a smoke, I'm fucking having one too.'

'Sure, why don't we all have a smoke.'

We all smoked. The casualty cheered up as the dawn light lit up his face. I remember thinking I saw people on the islands as we flew by in the early light. Although I only imagined them, they were real to me. The adrenaline of the rescue had long since subsided but in its place I floated in ether. I was never sure why, but I was aware that my senses were heightened. That sixth sense. We descended slightly, passing close to the high rocky lighthouse on Tearaght. A strange scene played out before me. The lighthouse keeper stood on the upper balcony beside the light. With one hand on the railing, he waved to us, his wife and children beside him, marvelling at us appearing out of the west unexpectedly. Dressed in turn of the century clothes, neat and trim; two boys in knee length pants, a girl in a pretty pinafore, the lighthouse keeper in uniform with his cap worn smartly.

I wondered if the Spanish crewman, lying on the stretcher, propped up slightly, smoking his cigarette, could hear music too. He could be from northern Spain. La Coruna perhaps? Wasn't their climate and their landscape like ours? As I daydreamed in the waking light, what did he dream? Was he looking at some harbour far away, where he had raced as a child when his father's ship returned? Or was he walking through long grass, wild flowers swaying as he passed by, hand in hand with his woman, whom he would now see again after all?

The music faded, with occasional conversation. The uilleann pipes. The pipes, the pipes are calling. From glen to glen ... A melody played in my mind. Davy Spillane leaned over as he sat and played. Cradling the chanter across his lap, the leather bellows gripped between ribs and elbow. The elbow, the uilleann, that gives them their name. Marrying the opposing forces of the drones and regulators together, so that they live and breathe together. The seven reeds within, gently vibrating with the echoes of his memory. His dead father. His dead mother. Fleetingly alive in his fingertips. The sadness and the beauty that he knows too well. We all know. Sweat dripping from his brow. His forehead creased with concentration. The skin of his face moving like it was facing a wind. The wind of music wafting over him. The music he played. Gathered from the stone around his house, blown there by the wind. Or picked up like the scattered driftwood, that lay on the boulder beach below the cliffs nearby. At Aill na Searrach. Musician, poet, dreamer, and now a member of the Doolin coast guard unit himself. Like the others, a searcher, climber, coxswain, stretcher carrier too.

My soundtrack played, as I thought I saw four currachs between Tearaght and Inis na Bró pulling a net between each pair. The drone of the helicopter and the crackle of the radios gone, replaced by the creaking of the oars and the screaming of sea gulls. The fishermen stopped their work and waved to us. As we passed by, I saw their nets were full. Along the north side of the Great Blasket we flew and then the long deserted village came into view, smoke coming from the chimneys. Villagers waved to us: I could see children and dogs running, the white-washed cottages gleaming in the dawn light. Four more currachs were rowing south from the village towards the Iveragh Peninsula. The seals on An Trá Bháin scattered into the sea. Over the Blasket Sound we flew, towards Dunquin and then to the hospital at Tralee.

I often return to Dunquin. I look out at the Blaskets and see the ghosts of the departed islanders. The islands reveal more to the patient observer in subdued and gentle light. Years later, visiting with my family in November, something reminded me of that rescue. It might have been the angle of the sun in late afternoon. Ebbing light, seen from the shore, just like the dawning light seen from the helicopter all those years ago. Looking west, I imagined myself years previously, looking east to where I now stood – comforted by the sight of land.

My wife and our three girls had walked the beach at Coomeenoole. We stood around with friends, debating whether to go here or go there, whether to take another walk before it became dark, or to go onto Dingle. I became detached from the conversation. I could see the sharp point of Tearaght furthest away. Inis Tuaiscirt, the Sleeping Man – on one side – on the other the Great Blasket casting a shadow over the Sound as the sun set behind it. I looked around at my children, and at my wife, the silhouette and swell of new life within her.

The feelings from that rescue returned. For a moment I felt them again, my heart raced. From land looking out to sea, remembering the fear of being in danger. In the bosom of my family now again, remembering the strength they gave me back then. The prayer before the rescue. Part of my private pre-transdown checks. Remembering the cold sweat when the adrenaline had run out. Seeing the ocean that night and feeling its power. Calm now as I looked out.

My girls were bored waiting. They started to dance in the fading light. The Second Jig, the Blackbird, the Orange Rogue, the Third Slip Jig, the Easy Reel. As I daydreamed about the islands and remembered that rescue, as the others chatted, the girls' shadows flitted this way and that as they danced. The evening was silent except for their laughter and the sound of them singing the melody and counting out the rhythm for themselves.

EPILOGUE

David sits with his hands on his knees, his legs slightly apart, his back straight, his face looking up, ever so slightly, his eyes closed, listening. Jim adjusts his sitting position, folds and unfolds his arms, as noiselessly as he can, raising his eyebrows now and then when he sees the picture painted by the spoken word. Ciaran looks at the speaker, no matter where they are in the room, as if some clue, or some insight into the tale, depends on his attention. Razor sharp attention.

Frenchman Jean nods. Chewing the words. Now and then, looking up and around the room, catching people's eyes. As if saying, '*Magnifique!* This is a good one. I like this one.' Some look down at the carpet pattern, not wanting to be distracted. Others look around the room, exchanging smiles or looks of surprise or sadness, as the spoken words dictate. Kathleen holds the small brass bell in one hand, pressed against her right leg, the clapper trapped, so it will stay silent until the five minutes is over. In her other hand the watch that she holds up close to look at, every now and again.

Outside the window of this living-room, a boat goes by on Lough Derg sliding past, muted by the glass windows. The sound of the occasional car, of children walking past, laughing and talking, cannot break the spell of the words that each in turn will speak. One by one, we take our turn to read what we have written; what we have created; what we have dreamed. What we have yearned for. What we have feared. Or just what amuses us. Chapters or stories. Poetry or travel logs. Kathleen ɟives us five minutes. Then the bell. Then we stop. Then the jury speaks, one by one.

'That didn't work for me. I didn't like the bit about the dog.'

'Oh no; the image of the dog and the man in the wheelchair, really worked for me.'

'Who was Nancy? Was she the sister of the one who died?'

'You have an error there. Sorry to have to tell you. That was in 1940, not 1939.'

'I loved the image of the rocking horse. The second verse reminded me of when I was a child.'

This group of people whom I stumbled upon first with Gerry, who listened over pints in Brogan's in Ennis, then saying, 'You have to write it down. You have to.' He brought me along after my first efforts appeared on the screen in front of me. The Writers Group of the Killaloe Hedge School. David Rice the key-holder, the ring-bearer. Kathleen the accomplice. We are the children he never had. He listens and guides. He writes and he teaches us to write. Give a man a fish, and you feed him for a day. Teach a man to fish, and you feed him for his life.

Hilda and Stephanie, Martina, Fiona and Dympna, everyone bringing something to the party. A different colour, a new angle. Brian scratching his head, then pointing out the flaw the others are too polite to mention. Tom has seen it all before and heard it all before, but never tires of listening and encouraging. The room becomes alive with the sound of steel capped boots, as infantrymen from the civil war march down the country lanes of Ireland, not so long ago. The rustling of autumn leaves, the swirling of them as they fall to earth, in rhyming lines. The sound of the chip, chip, chip of a stone chisel, as a dry stone wall is repaired. The abbey in Quin, floating on morning fog, the red orb of the sun rising behind it. The steam of the breath of cattle on a frosty morning, as the farmer throws them hay. Doggerel

that throws us off the scent, making us inquisitive: '… and after he finishes dancing, if not enough people applaud, Gussie
McMahon takes his seat again, looks into the crowd, and claps
himself on the back. Good man Gussie.'

'… and as Robbie Hughes says, it's as good as a concert.'

'… up for your ball, says Maggie Pepper.'

'… as Joe says, a good friend is never there when you don't
need him.'

John and Jack, Patricia and Ben, the two Kathleens. Turning to face the next speaker. The pages rustle. The silence in-
timidates. The voice falters, then begins. The reader takes flight,
and shares the written word. Metaphorically, the ink not dry.
Gerry flies above cobalt lakes in Connemara and while he soars,
Jean cannot help but think of when he dived in tropical waters.
Where does the time go? He listens now instead of writing. He
has so many tales to tell, but prefers actions instead of words.
Kissing each woman in the room when he arrives, once on each
cheek as is his custom. Bestowing mistletoe on each and every
one at the Christmas gathering. *Felicitations, joyeux Noël*'. From
his travelling farmers' market stall, he sees the kaleidoscope of
Irish life, nudging, elbowing each other out of the way, inspecting what he brings to sell. Bringing them alive, and into our
group, as we sit comfortable in armchairs, or cross-legged on
the floor, squeezed up against the silent TV.

Lorraine and John, Orla and Marita, patiently wait their
turn. And then we take a break, half way through. Seeking each
other out, as we balance our sandwiches and our cups of tea. Or
glass of wine perhaps.

'I really liked that. Well done. You brought tears to my eyes.'

'That was really dark. You created a great atmosphere in that
last bit. The moon and the wispy clouds; I could see it.'

'That was hilarious. I've seen that happen too.'

In such company, the cat's nine lives were revealed. Exploring the corridors of memory together. Returning to rooms I had left behind, shuttered. Laughing at the sunlight that streamed in as I spoke aloud. Picking up the remembrance cards of the dead that lay in the shadows. Reading them again for me. With me. Or just listening. Sometimes that was enough. The logjam rearranged so the words could flow. Patient companionship. And then at the end of each evening that we meet, going away, to live our separate lives. Into the night with a handshake or a kiss on the cheek. Carrying each others' thoughts and dreams.

APPENDIX 1

HOW BIG ARE THE WAVES OFF THE IRISH ATLANTIC WEST COAST ?

Like fishermen and the fish they catch, SAR crews are sometimes accused of exaggeration. Only they know how big the ocean swell was when they were on a rescue. But if the rescue took place in darkness, do even they know?

To try to answer the question, how big are the waves off the Irish coast, I found the KNMI's (Royal Netherlands Meteorological Institute) forty year wave study. It is a comprehensive scientific study of all available data. It presents a very clear picture of global wave patterns, and in particular, the global locations of the world's biggest waves.

There have been volumes written about wave's and ocean waves. Rather than extract from their report, or attempt to give a synopsis, I recommend that you visit their website: http://www.knmi.nl/onderzk/oceano/waves/era40/license.cgi and in particular, look at the 90% global quantiles.

The answer you will find is that among the world's highest average waves occur off the Irish Atlantic west coast. In winter months, their highest average magnitude is in the order of eight to ten metres plus. And that is just the average ...

(The highest wave measured in recent years, anywhere in the

world, was off the Irish coast on 9 December 2007. It measured 17.2 metres. Have a look at the Irish Marine Institute website: http://www.marine.ie/home/aboutus/newsroom/news/Result-sofWeatherBuoyReadings.htm)

APPENDIX 2

POSITIONS OF RESCUES/INCIDENTS
BY CHAPTER NUMBER

APPENDIX 3

RESCUE UNITS AROUND IRELAND

Irish Coast Guard:

Greenore, Clogherhead, Drogheda, Skerries

Howth, Dun Laoghaire, Greystones, Wicklow

Arklow, Courtown, Curracloe, Rosslar-

Carnsore Point, Kilmore Quay, Fethard-on-Sea, Dunmore
   East

Tramore, Bonmahon, Helvick, Ardmore

Youghal, Ballycotton, Guileen, Crosshaven

Oysterhaven, Summercove, Old Head of Kinsale, Seven Heads

Castlefreke, Glandore, Toe Head, Baltimore

Goleen, Castletownbere, Waterville, Dingle

Glenderry, Ballybunion, Kilkee, Doolin

Inisheer, Inishmore, Costelloe Bay, Cleggan

Westport, Achill Island, Ballyglass, Killala

Killybegs, Bunbeg, Mulroy, Tory Island

Greencastle

RNLI:

Portrush, Red Bay, Larne, Bangor

Donaghadee, Portaferry, Newcastle, Kilkeel

Clogher Head, Skerries, Howth, Dun Laoghaire

Wicklow, Arklow, Courtown, Wexford

Rosslare Harbour, Kilmore Quay, Fethard-on-Sea, Dunmore
   East

Tramore, Helvick Head, Youghal, Ballycotton
Crosshaven, Kinsale, Courtmacsherry, Baltimore
Castletownbere, Valentia, Fenit, Kilrush
Aran Islands, Lough Derg / Killaloe, Galway, Clifden
Achill Island, Ballyglass, Sligo Bay, Bundoran,
Enniskillen / Lough Erne, Arranmore, Lough Swilly

Irish Mountain Rescue Association / IMRA:
Donegal, Dublin / Wicklow, Glen of Imaal, South West
    Wicklow
South Eastern / SEMRA, Galway, Mayo, Sligo / Leitrim
Tramore, North West, Mournes, Kerry
SARDA / SAR Dogs Assoc.

Civil Defence:
Clare, Wexford , Carlow, Cork North
Cork West, Tipperary South, Cork City, Cork South
Dublin, Laois, Mayo, Cavan
Donegal, Kildare, Kilkenny, Leitrim
Limerick City, Limerick County, Longford , Louth
Meath, Monaghan, Tipperary North, Westmeath
Kerry

Rescue Diving Teams:
Naval Service Diving Unit, Garda Underwater Unit, Limerick
River Rescue, Boyne River Rescue
Grainne Uaile Diving Club

Community Rescue Teams:

Lahinch Sea Rescue, Ballyheige Sea Rescue, Ballybunion Cliff & Sea Rescue

Coast Guard Radio Stations:

Malin Head, Valentia , Dublin

ACKNOWLEDGEMENTS

Search and Rescue is a team activity. Writing about it has also involved the assistance of a team, a network of friends, former colleagues and family. Without their assistance, this book would not have been possible. I owe you all a huge debt of thanks.

For supporting the idea of the book. For their encouragement. For their painstaking reading and editing: Jim Martin, David Rice, Mary Feehan, Greg Murray, Noel O'Grady. To everyone at Mercier, for their patience with this first timer. For their help and support.

For their advice on all things naval and maritime. For helping me to remember life at sea, Cmdr Mark Mellett and Lt Cdr Brian Fitzgerald of the Irish Naval Service and National Maritime College of Ireland in Cork. For meteorological and historical advice, as well as encouragement and assistance, Kevin O'Herlihy, formerly of the Met Office in Baldonnel. And John Howe of Shannon Met Office. For support during the writing of the book, as well as their friendship always, Vincent, Doreen, David, Simon and Erica Sweeney of Blacksod Lighthouse. *Ar dheis De go raibh anam Daibhdhe.* To the 'standby' Sweeney clan too, Gerry, Dermot and Fergus.

To the Irish Helicopter management and back room staff of Ann Fennell, Deirdre Collins, Andy O'Brian, Guy Perrem, John Kearney, Buzz Barr, Ernie Perrin, Ray Kenny and Mick Fitzgerald who made long/medium range civil rescue become a reality.

To the Irish Coast Guard and the UK Maritime and Coastguard Agency. For assistance in research and access to archives. To former Air Corps, Army and Coast Guard colleagues, for dusting off their memories for me, and helping with research.

To Doolin Coast Guard Unit, one and all, who allowed me into their company and their lives. My privilege entirely. To the Old Head of Kinsale Coast Guard Unit, and to Eddie Butler for showing us that God is good, especially when it is hard to believe. To Greencastle Coast Guard Unit, and to Charlie Cavanagh, for the successful round Ireland RIB record. For gathering us together, making it happen, and ensuring that Michael Heffernan would never be forgotten. To Dingle Coast Guard Unit, Mike O'Shea, Frank Heidtke and Tom Kennedy and all the unit, for the training and advice over the years, in the shadow of Brandon. To the many volunteer rescue units, coast guard, RNLI, civil defence, mountain rescue, rescue divers military, garda and civil, thank you.

To Capt. David Browne in the air corps, for the prompting to write that came with the retirement of the Alouette 3 in 2007. For the assistance in research and for his time and effort. To the air corps photographic section, for generously allowing me access to their files, and for allowing me to include some of their photographs.

To Capt. Mark Kelly and all in CHC Ireland, operating helicopter rescue for the Irish Coast Guard. For access to their files and support during the writing of this book.

To Annamarie, Leighanne and Michele Heffernan, for talking again about Belderrig. To Lily O'Flaherty and Maria O'Flaherty. To Monica Mooney. To Vincent and Anne Byrne. To Tony and Mary Baker. For allowing me to talk and write about David and Paddy and Niall and Mick once more.

To Comhdháil Oileáin na hÉireann, the islands co-operative,

for supporting rescue always. For their help in research and for their support. To Dr Marion Broderick, whose help was essential in this book. Advice, research, corrections and most of all, her invaluable time. She deserves a sainthood.

To Lorna Siggins, for her dedication to the marine and rescue in her lifetime of journalism, and in her 'Irishwoman's Diary'. For her encouragement, and for her book *Mayday, Mayday*, which I have used frequently for research.

To John Maughan and John Fitzpatrick of civil defence for their help with research.

To Kevin Myers, for his highlighting of Michael Heffernan in particular, and volunteer rescuers in general, in his 'Irishman's Diary'. For his dedication to those often overlooked. And for his encouragement.

To Liam Burke and all at 'Press 22' in Limerick. Thanks for all the coverage and support over the years. The same goes for John Kelly freelance, and of *The Clare Champion*, for his wonderful photography. To Eamonn Ward, freelance, and of *The Clare People* and John McDermott for the front cover photograph of Shannon S-61 winch training with the Aran Islands RNLI lifeboat. Between them all, blending rural life with modern life, aviation and news, in the Banner county and in the Shannon area, with style, humour, soul and art. It was always a pleasure to take you into the air. To share what is yours anyway. To Rex Features in Scotland, for the photo of the S-61 approaching to land on a platform in the North Sea. To Anna Heussaff, freelance and of RTÉ, for her help with research and for letting me use her photographs taken during the making of a *Léargas* programme on marine rescue.

To Shane Begley of the Bord Iascaigh Mhara Fishery Training School in Castletownbere, for advice and help over the years. To Colm Martin of the Commissioner of Irish Light's and Irish

Helicopters, for support and advice. To Joe Queally of the RNLI, for walking and talking, for listening, for agreeing and disagreeing. A good friend is never there when you don't need him.

To John Leech CEO, Irish Water Safety, for support in all things safety over the years, and for advice during the writing of this book.

To Dr Andreas Sterl, of the Climate Research and Seismology Department of the KNMI, (Royal Netherlands Meteorological Institute). For allowing me access to his organisations superb study of wave behaviour. This study, called the KNMI/ERA-40 Wave Atlas, is an analysis of 45 years of global ocean wave data (see appendix).

To the RAF and RN, in Culdrose, Prestwick and Kinloss, for the help and support, both over the years and during the writing of this book. And to Flt Lt Andy Cant for the photos of Sea King and Nimrod aircraft given previously on operational and training (and social !) visits to Shannon.

To the Killaloe Hedge School and the Killaloe Writers Group. This would never have happened without your praise and criticism and your generous listening ears. To the friends who visit the Second World War sites each year together. To witness the pain of the past, to better appreciate the present: John Madden, Brendan O'Connor, Ray Farrell, David Rice, Brian Mooney, Colm O'Dwyer, Victor Davis, Jim Watkins, Bill O'Connor, Bob Hanna, Joe Queally. Lest we forget.

To Terence Adams for his help with Tullamore stories and for letting me share the story of the pint in the brown paper bag.

To those not mentioned by name I offer an apology. Space did not allow me to record all names. You know which chapters you belong in.

To my brother Philip, and sisters Hilary and Ruth, for allowing me to include them and us in this story. For their love and support always. To my mother, for her support. I know you can hear me. To my children, Alyson, Niamh, Anna and Ella, for forgiving me for not reading them stories at night, when I was writing them instead. To my wife Lynda. Most of all.

INDEX